I0071641

STRATEGIC THINKING AND DECISION MAKING

STRATEGIC THINKING AND DECISION MAKING

Varied Selections from
My Column at Inc.com

PAUL J.H. SCHOEMAKER

ANTHEM PRESS

Anthem Press
An imprint of Wimbledon Publishing Company
www.anthempress.com

This edition first published in UK and USA 2025
by ANTHEM PRESS
75–76 Blackfriars Road, London SE1 8HA, UK
or PO Box 9779, London SW19 7ZG, UK
and
244 Madison Ave #116, New York, NY 10016, USA

© Paul J.H. Schoemaker 2025

The author asserts the moral right to be identified as the author of this work.

All rights reserved. Without limiting the rights under copyright reserved above,
no part of this publication may be reproduced, stored or introduced into
a retrieval system, or transmitted, in any form or by any means
(electronic, mechanical, photocopying, recording or otherwise),
without the prior written permission of both the copyright
owner and the above publisher of this book.

British Library Cataloguing-in-Publication Data
A catalogue record for this book is available from the British Library.

Library of Congress Cataloging-in-Publication Data
A catalog record for this book has been requested.
2024944548

ISBN-13: 978-1-83999-290-2 (Hbk) / 978-1-83999-291-9 (Pbk)
ISBN-10: 1-83999-290-5 (Hbk) / 1-83999-291-3 (Pbk)

Cover credit: Public Domain and MaleWitch/shutterstock.com

This title is also available as an e-book.

Personal Dedication

To Joyce, Kimberly, and Paul who are my inner circle of trust, advice, and love in life. I hope this book will help them and others when examining complex issues or making important decisions.

Professional Dedication

To the 29 coauthors who joined me in writing one or more of the columns presented in this book. Their academic as well as practical experiences provided further color, depth, and managerial relevance. I hope all coauthors will enjoy seeing their various contributions reflected in the book's thematic chapters.

FRONT COVER IMAGES

The two faces looking in opposite directions at the center of the book's cover, with their minds somewhat connected, symbolize that strategic decisions usually get better when multiple minds are involved.

The colorful outer ring, artistically depicting ten people holding arms, further emphasizes that it may take a circle of trust, or an entire village at times, to create winning solutions for challenging strategic problems.

CONTENTS

ACKNOWLEDGMENTS

Numerous individuals and organizations helped me develop the content of this book, starting with Inc.com for launching my "Strategic Decision" column. I gratefully acknowledge the editors of my Inc columns, and especially Eric Schurenberg as their leader then.

Second, I am grateful to the 29 colleagues and friends who accepted my invitation to co-author a column with me as listed in Appendix A and B. Their names and affiliations are also footnoted on the first page of each essay, plus their title or position at the time of our joint writing. George Day, Steve Krupp, Viraj Narayanan, Jay Russo, and Phil Tetlock, merit special mention for having co-authored multiple Inc articles with me.

Third, I thank the Decision Education Foundation, a charitable non-profit in the Palo Alto (CA) for their dedication to teaching critical and creative decision making to adolescents.[1] I served for several years on its board and learned a lot along the way about the limits and promises of evolving minds.

Fourth, I am grateful for my long and diverse association with the Wharton School of the University of Pennsylvania, first as a graduate student, then as a teacher, academic, research director, and faculty colleague

Fifth, I am indebted to my Decision Strategies International colleagues and friends many of whom contributed directly to this book, as well as indirectly to my thinking about the diverse topics covered.

Sixth, I thank my wife Joyce and our children Kimberly and Paul for proof-reading various sections and iterations as this book evolved, giving good feedback and their help when evaluating cartoon options.

Lastly, I acknowledge my editors at Anthem Press for their kind support and professionalism in converting my writings into a cohesive book for managers, academics, and more.

PREVIEW OF THE THREE BOOK PARTS

Although the 15 chapters of this book are not cumulative, they do present a process view of strategic planning, decision making, implementation, and learning in different kinds of organizations. Little good happens in companies without some sense of vision, directions, plans, budgets, organizational design, incentives, culture, and talent. While a top-down view of strategy was traditionally favored, over time a deeper appreciation developed for bottom-up perspectives, since even the best laid plans do not always succeed. This behavioral view proved relevant when trying to explain or predict what might happen in organizations. The book provides due attention to contextual influences, group dynamics, emergent properties of organizations, and real-world settings. When these are not appreciated sufficiently, many well-intended strategies and actions can derail or back fire unexpectedly.

PART I: STRATEGY, PLANNING, AND UNCERTAINTY

Chapter 1 starts with the cognitive side of strategy with an emphasis on outside-in thinking, as opposed to the inside-out approach typically practiced in most companies. The traditional planning agenda labeled SWOT (Strengths, Weaknesses, Opportunities and Threats analyses) is discussed in multiple chapters with caveats and warnings. In real life, both rational and behavioral perspectives are needed, with Chapters 1–5 capturing this ying and yang of strategic planning. My overall approach in this book is to blend the descriptive realities of organizations with normative principles developed by management theorists, in order to yield the kind of sensible, prescriptive advice found in best-practice companies. The leadership challenge is to coalesce competing intellectual views about strategy in dynamic market settings while also respecting the unique organizational contexts involved. Since this challenge is increasingly complicated by uncertainty, my chapter selections address the role of peripheral vision, looking ahead, understanding decision traps, and improving strategic thinking at many levels inside the organization. All of these require attracting, developing, retaining, and coordinating diverse pools of talent.

Part I of the book advocates a forward-looking leadership perspective in terms of attitudes, mindsets, rewards, and skill sets. Chapter 3 covers methods for cultivating foresight in organizations via scenario planning, stress testing strategies, developing scanning capabilities, fostering doubts at the right time, and appreciating people's bounded rationality. Few leaders or managers have 360 vision or 20/20 foresight, so they must rely on others to be effective. They need to welcome diverse views, remain open to challenge, counter status quo thinking and defuse futile turf battles that create more heat than light. Chapters 4 and 5 directly address how to assemble sufficient talent in your teams to jointly navigate uncertainty in flexible ways. Overconfidence remains a big enemy of strategic planning and is often fueled by myopic mental models. This frequently results in flawed decision frames that fail to surface all relevant problem features and a paucity of good options.

The main managerial problem is not just black swans which nobody sees coming, but also grey swans that we should be able to spot and get a better fix on by challenging our own mental lenses and viewpoints. There is enough material in Part I alone to cover an entire book on just the above topics, but the leadership task would not be complete without also tackling important issues raised in Parts II and III. Like Part I, they also treat key strategy and decision aspects in bite size essays that can be read in isolation or together. They serve as the building blocks of various larger themes highlighted in the Introduction and these chapter previews. The combination of essays that I selected for each chapter and book part are not set in stone, just as a fine meal might offer dishes and drinks in a variety of ways with a rhyme and seasoning unique to the occasion. There is value in sampling the essays of this book out of order to create a different flavor or intellectual experience. Since the permutations and combinations of my 75 essays are numerous, multitudes of connections are embedded in this book, well beyond the current layout. Taking a random walk through the book may be more inspiring at times than a sequential read. In this spirit, each chapter offers a stand-alone selection of offerings, the way a top sushi chef might in Japan, and these can be enjoyed alone or in combination.

PART II: INNOVATION, FAILURE, AND LEARNING

Once the strategy, planning, and talent challenges are in good shape, such topics as innovation, customer management and learning from mistakes naturally arise.

Most innovations are about providing customers better products or services but a high percentage of these efforts experience setbacks or outright failure. The centrality of customers is especially highlighted in Part II, following Peter Drucker's adage that you don't have a company if you do not have customers. But leaders must move beyond just meeting this important *necessary* condition and think deeply also about the *sufficient* conditions required to assure competitive success and value creation for shareholders and other stakeholders. This raises questions about what growth path to pursue, what adjacent opportunities to explore, and how much to rely on organic growth versus mergers or acquisitions. Parts of these balancing acts are also about how to create, manage and maintain partnerships and strategic alliances with other players within the firm's ecosystem. The latter would include suppliers, distributors, customers, media, regulators, and other essential players, including rivals who may attack your business model. Doing all this well requires experience, education, advisers, seasoned judgment, and accumulated wisdom.

Metaphors and mental imagery play a key role in how people tackle complex business problems deep down. Metaphors draw on analogies that can help simplify the problem but they may also distort reality. For example, how should managers balance the need to be competitive with the importance of collaborating as well? Business is very much about people and how we treat them matters greatly, even if they are your rivals. The biblical admonishment that those who fight with the sword will die by the sword is especially relevant for managers who mostly see business as a war in which you don't take prisoners. To illustrate this, two chapters address the pros and cons of using poker as an analogy for business, given its popularity in the press and the many people who enjoy playing this card game. A later essay further examines the importance of war gaming when developing competitive strategies, in order to better understand your main rivals and their possible responses to your own strategic moves. That chapter ends with an important caveat about the inherent limitations of viewing business conflicts, and negotiations more generally, as a zero-sum game. The bigger gains in business typically come from emphasizing integrative bargaining rather than distributive haggling over a fixed pie. Smart leaders try to make the pie bigger for other key stakeholders in their shared ecosystem, which in turn often makes their own slice larger as well.

The topic of failure also assumes a central role in Part II since uncertainties, as opposed to numerically analyzable risks, are central in many of the strategic decisions that leaders face. It must be clear inside the company what game is being played and what root metaphors need to be embraced versus rejected to succeed. Traditional examples include adopting a product life cycle view or approaching business from a warfare perspective. But more generative mindsets may be required as well in which customers, technologies, partnerships, and digital savvy are placed more centrally. The unpredictability of the future means that many surprises will occur, from weak signals to black swans. To acknowledge this, the final chapter of Part II offers a potpourri of challenges that leaders have encountered in the past to illustrate miscellaneous challenges and key lessons. The first case in Chapter 10 is about the wisdom or folly of CVS having banished all tobacco products and other unhealthy offerings from its shelves. This meant letting $2 billion of revenue each year go up in smoke. But in return, this bold strategic move buttressed CVS's image as a company genuinely dedicated to improving consumer health, in word and deed. Fittingly, a later case example in Part II examines how Nelson Mandela became a transformational leader for the ages and impacted the world far beyond South Africa. His ability to overcome past injustices, elevate himself above the fray, adopt the long view, build bridges, and forgive his enemies stands out as exceptional and exemplary for all leaders.

PART III: LEADERSHIP, DECIDING, AND BIASES

Building on the inspiring profile of Mandela, Part III of the book tackles the question of leadership head on by articulating the defining characteristics as well as their main challenges. The first chapter lays out six traits and capabilities that individual leaders need to hone themselves to succeed in the different positions they may hold. Also, since their decisions and actions often serve as role models for the rest of the organization, the symbolic and inspirational dimensions of leadership matter greatly. Apart from Mandela, who is further examined in the first chapter of Part III, we also profile Dr Martin Luther King for orchestrating a social movement that continued after his tragic assassination at just age 39. We also address the role of Boards in Part III since leaders need to work both upward and downward, as well as sideways, when dealing with partners, suppliers, customers regulators, the media, and more. Unless the governance structures for interacting with supervisory directors and executive teams are sound for the chosen business model, the organization will fall short of its potential.

Ethical issues, including how to foster an internal culture of integrity, have become increasingly central to CEOs and Boards, including the risks of being surprised by either internal ticking bombs or external shocks. Chapter 12 examines how to defuse ethical time bombs that tick slowly in some dark recesses of the enterprise and then suddenly explode. One example was Volkswagen's scandal of manipulating mandated exhaust tests of tailpipes in Germany.

Another was Wells-Fargo not catching that some employees were secretly buying insurance policies in some customer accounts just to meet internal sales targets. They hoped to cancel these purchases later to avoid detection but their unethical ploys back-fired big time when revealed, resulting in loss of corporate reputation, internal morale problems, monetary fines, job loss and derailment of careers.

Apart from improving CEO and Board relationships, another critical component in any organization is how well management teams in charge of business units, functions or a division function. Chapter 13 addresses how to rally a team around a new strategy and developing a positive learning culture in case setbacks or other problems occur. The keys to higher team performance include clear communication, managing outside stakeholders, rewarding those who take ownership, and the fine art of open dialog and true debate when needed. The aim is to develop high credibility within the team itself and also to shore up its credibility in the eyes of others in and outside the organization. The chapters thereafter focus on the all-important decision-making process itself and the various traps or biases that research in behavioral decision theory has uncovered. Chapter 14 examines the role of decision framing up front, including how to balance speed and rigor, and the importance of staying flexible when knowledge is limited and uncertainty is high. The chapter also emphasizes the power of thinking outside-in and being honest about what you know and more importantly what you don't know (either alone or as a team). Lastly, the complex issue of conflict resolution is addressed, especially when receiving opposite advice from advisers you trust and respect. President Obama faced this conundrum when giving the go ahead to capture or kill Bin Laden in Pakistan, which initially seemed a 50–50 gamble to him since his top advisers disagreed on the odds of success.

Lastly, Chapter 15 returns to the enduring theme of biases in judgment and choice, starting with the power of nudges in lieu of paternalistic top-down directives from on high. One essay examines seminal research by Nobel laureate Richard Thaler, and his famous colleagues Dan Kahneman (also a Nobel laurate) and Amos Tversky, about common biases. Another essay discusses an insidious bias that distorts new information in the direction of one's initial leanings about a complex issue, especially if that tentative preliminary view rests on scant evidence. Even when it is known that much more important information will arrive later, for example when evaluating job candidates or alliance partners, the mind's unconscious desire for internal consistency will slant that new information toward reducing cognitive dissonance. Finally, the last two sections of Chapter 15 address the importance of separating facts from values when debating policy options, including the power and limits of the wisdom of the crowd. Whether to trust experts, and when to challenge, remains a contentious subject in our age of alternative facts, conspiracy theories and mutual distrust between polarized political camps. Leaders can play important roles in bridging these divides in their own organizations and beyond. The closing section offers some advice on how to set the right example for yourself as a leader as well as for others.

END NOTE

1 https://www.decisioneducation.org/.

INTRODUCTION

For over a decade, I ran a column for Inc.com under the banner "The Strategic Decision." This column was launched in 2012 to offer fresh perspectives on strategic issues facing leaders of small- and medium-sized growing companies, often privately held. The mostly short articles in my column focused especially on strategy, leadership, uncertainty and improving decision-making in dynamic business settings. As such, my columns covered such recurring topics as framing, uncertainty, judgment, strategy, innovation, failure, group dynamics, boards, biases, vigilance, and more.

I was invited to launch a column by Inc.com and accepted the offer since it connected with my own research, interests and consulting in the fields of strategic planning, innovation, and decision-making. I realized that this managerial column could complement my academic role as research director at Wharton of the Mack Institute for Innovation Management. Its main agenda then was to study why many large established public firms struggled with how to integrate newly emerging technologies, especially if disruptive.[1] In contrast, my column for Inc focused more on innovations by smaller, private firms who often embraced new technologies and used disruptive business models. I had always felt that small and large firms could much learn from each other in the areas of innovation, agility, and talent management but seldom did so as fully as possible.[2]

When Inc.com got launched, it was an online sister organization of Inc Magazine which was founded in 1979.[3] At that time, this print magazine was the only major media brand dedicated to bringing advice to leaders of private companies. It received the *National Magazine Award for General Excellence* in 2012 and 2014. Its total monthly audience reach for the new brand grew significantly from 2 million in 2010 to over 25 million a decade later. In 1982, Inc.com introduced the "Inc. 500" company list to showcase the fastest-growing privately held companies in the United States. Twenty-five years later, this was expanded to the "Inc. 5000."

1

My own columns at Inc.com were often inspired by current events and business case studies that connected with my own academic background. At times, I would invite a colleague to join me as a co-author to better round out a topic I was addressing business-wise or just to ground it better academically (see Appendix A and B). The chapters in this book therefore cover a wide range of problem types, business functions, industry sectors, and cultures; in this way, they mirror the complex managerial lives most business leaders live. The key in leadership is to develop various meta-skills for thinking strategically and then use these to make better business judgments. Leaders usually confront opportunities and challenges in muddled fashions and their main task is to size them up properly and respond with creativity and wisdom. These leadership challenges require integrative thinking and creative problem solving of a kind that is nurtured through hard won experience in the trenches. The kaleidoscopic flavor of this collection of essays reflects this holistic and more realistic view of leadership at ground level.

The purpose of arranging some of my Inc articles in book form, in addition to making them readily available in one place, is to highlight deeper thematic links between essays and to overlay a coherent conceptual structure across the topics covered.[4] One virtue of a thematic arrangement is that broader underlying perspectives come to the fore more clearly in each chapter. In this vein, the chart below positions the various chapters along two conceptual dimensions. The X-axis scores each chapter from 1 to 10 based on its balance between descriptive versus prescriptive content. The Y-axis conveys whether the chapter is more oriented toward the organization as a whole or mostly to the individual manager/leader. A score of 5 along either axis suggests an even polar balance. Scores higher or lower than 5 denote a leaning toward one of the two polar ends that define each scale, based on the topics covered. A higher score does not mean the chapter is better.

In the 15 chapters, readers can randomly sample topics and sections of the book or dive into a single essay covering one specific issue in more detail (such as biases, mistakes, foresight, talent, or teams). Either way, readers can assess if they agree with the approaches I offer or favor different perspectives. If the latter, they may wish to discuss the issues with some colleagues informally during a break or use it more formally to co-invest in team building and raising the group's strategic IQ. Sampling the collected subsections and chapters (whether in small bites or as one read-through) will help managers refine their own approaches to strategic thinking and leadership. Also, it may help align them better with colleagues or partners who come from different backgrounds, functional responsibilities, or cultural orientations. To add some levity, I start each chapter with a cartoon

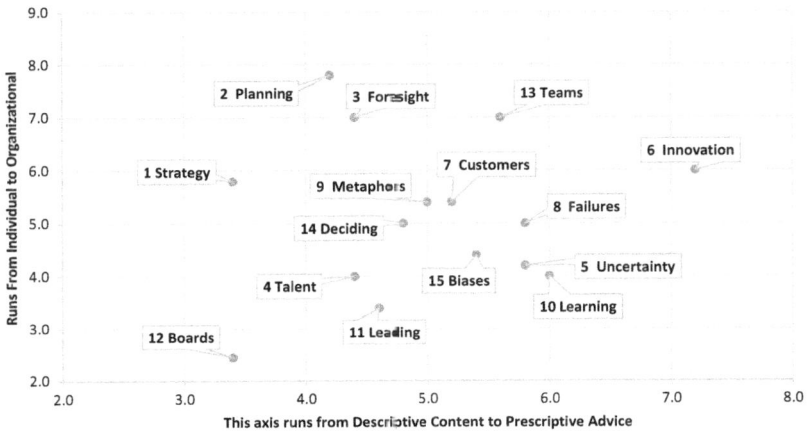

Figure axis labels: Y-axis: "Runs From Individual to Organizational" (2.0 to 9.0). X-axis: "This axis runs from Descriptive Content to Prescriptive Advice" (2.0 to 8.0).

Plotted items: 2 Planning, 3 Foresight, 13 Teams, 6 Innovation, 1 Strategy, 7 Customers, 9 Metaphors, 8 Failures, 14 Deciding, 4 Talent, 15 Biases, 5 Uncertainty, 10 Learning, 12 Boards, 11 Leading

that creatively underscores some key point addressed. Great cartoons excel in depicting issues succinctly with a humorous twist, especially in the hands of such gifted artists as Gary Larsen and the cartoonists at the *Harvard Business Review* I drew on.

It will become apparent to readers that my overall approach to business problems is very much behavioral. This means that I start an essay by identifying important management problems in a realistic business setting. Before offering any conceptual perspectives or prescriptive advice, we need to better understand the behavioral context of any problem. This case approach is also used to provide practical insights, tips, or even full solutions, but not until the essence of the problem and its broader organizational and cultural contexts are sufficiently understood. I have learned the hard way, after decades of strategy and management consulting, that offering prescriptions without first getting well-grounded behaviorally tends to result in failed interventions. Normative advice that is mostly drawn from text books or remote abstractions, rather than real slices of life, often amount to shadow boxing with figures on the wall rather than the real issues. As such, this book aims to illustrate for managers, leaders and teams how to frame thorny management issues by (i) clearly defining a distinct business problem, (ii) viewing it through multiple lenses, and (iii) creatively exploring pragmatic solutions.

Reframing complex issues at the start is quite typical for most essays of this book. In some cases, the reframing may entail a conceptual shift in perspective (e.g., when discussing biases or mistakes) while other sections may offer a step-by-step approach to tackling a complex subject (in say innovation or managing customers). I hope this smorgasbord approach will appeal to a broad array of readers, from academics and students to managers and other professionals. My intent is to offer readers diverse intellectual flavors and examples, so as to satisfy discriminating palates worldwide.

END NOTES

1 Our 2000 Wiley book *Wharton on Managing Emerging Technologies*, co-edited with Professor George Day, outlines the promises and challenges that emerging technologies hold for established firms.
2 When I joined Inc.com in 2012 as a regular columnist, its articles were freely available online. In 2020, however, Inc.com instituted a subscription model. I served as an unpaid columnist, in contrast to many paid columnists there, in order to maintain my independence. I published over eighty posts from 2012 to 2022.
3 https://en.wikipedia.org/wiki/Inc._(magazine)
4 Appendix D lists which articles I drew upon from my column at Inc.com for this book.

PART I: STRATEGY, PLANNING, AND UNCERTAINTY

CHAPTER 1

STRATEGIC THINKING

"Our VC firm takes a two-tier approach: first the seeds, then the money."

1.1 DEVELOP STRATEGY FROM THE OUTSIDE IN

The two most important questions for leaders looking to take their business to the next level are: "How can we play our current hands of cards better" and "How is the world changing around us and why?"

Both questions are essential for identifying a successful business strategy and eventually need to be tightly integrated. But where you start may influence greatly where you end up.

Let me explain: The first question represents an inside-out approach to strategy since it starts with your own strengths and weaknesses. Naturally, it's good to know this, but if you focus too much on your own internal issues, you could miss the bigger picture—along with any chance of fostering radical innovation and disruptive strategies.

So, in addition to that question, the second question is even more important since it forces you to look outside your business. That outside-in approach has the advantage of making you scan wider and not prejudge whether some external changes are good or bad. Here are two ways to adopt outside-in strategies.[1]

Start with Outward-Focused Questions

In traditional planning sessions, a company's leader may ask "how can we serve our customers better" or "how should we improve our products?" Both are highly relevant questions, but they are not the best ones to start with. Instead, save them until the end of your meetings, since these questions bring the discussion back to yourself and help close the loop.

At the start, it is better to ask "why are many customers not buying from us" or "in which ways do our competitors offer superior products?" These questions force you to look at your company from the outside in. Research shows that an external market-driven orientation leads to superior results because it overcomes such common human tendencies as myopia and confirmation bias.[2] By asking why customers don't always favor you, the team puts itself in the customer's shoes.

The answers will likely not be about product features, relative costs, or capacity utilization. Instead, words like "trust," "long-run relationships," "superior benefits," "solutions," and "valuable partner" may come to the fore. Your team will be thinking about the changing needs of your customers as well as your competitor's intentions and capabilities.

Bake the Policy into Your Strategy Sessions

Jeff Bezos, founder and CEO of Amazon.com, showcased the outside-in business philosophy when he said, "rather than ask what we are good at you ask who are our customers? What else do they need? And then you say we are going to give that to them regardless of whether we have the skills to do so"[3]

Your company may already have practiced outside-in thinking by "stapling yourself to a customer order" (to imagine what they experience), role-playing your toughest competitor, or undertaking a review of lost sales. Most likely, however, these are only occasional forays into the customer's world, rather than practices deeply baked into your company's mindset.

Some firms can sustain themselves with inside-out thinking for a long time, especially if competitors think the same way or if they have a very good hand of cards to play. But this is not a safe approach in turbulent markets where new competitors are challenging conventional wisdom, offshore entrants are arriving with deeply discounted prices or technological changes disrupt the business model.

Effective responses demand fresh outside-in thinking that understands the turbulence better. Eventually, the outside-in questions must be connected to the inside-out ones as well in order to become actionable. Just make sure you start with the outside-in approach since internal organizational forces usually pull the discussion inward anyway.

1.2 SEEING EXTERNAL CHANGES AHEAD OF TIME

Great strategic thinkers have a gift for seeing threats and opportunities before anyone else. Here's what they look for and how they approach it.

To get a business going, you need entrepreneurial vision. To keep it performing at a high level day to day, you need intense operational focus. But to survive for the long run, you need a different kind of skill, one that I consider a core attribute of true strategic leaders. In my book with George Day, we call it peripheral vision.[4]

Sad to say, most companies aren't very good at this. When new threats or opportunities emerge on the periphery of their usual business environment, they fail to notice them or misinterpret their import. Most leaders have a hard time with the weak and ambiguous signals that are often the only early warning signs of impending change.

What Leaders Failed to See Coming

There are many examples: Coors failed to see the trend toward low-carb beer until it was too late. Michelin overlooked the crucial role of service stations for their new Flat Run tire. Mattel's Barbie was blindsided by the popularity of the Bratz doll.[5] Another notable case is Lego, which responded poorly to the electronic revolution in toys and gaming, and then went on to underestimate the squeeze that Walmart Grocery and China would put on its pricing power.

As a business owner, you always face the temptation to focus on managing your current offering in the immediate business environment. Someone has to do this, to be sure, and giving unwavering attention to operations will often pay off in short-term performance. But by zeroing in on what's in front of you, you naturally lose peripheral vision—and that can threaten your company's long-term survival.

Having peripheral vision means that you monitor what is happening around the edges of your business: You keep tabs on other industries, distant markets, new research, emerging business models, and remote demographic data that may seem to have little relevance to your portfolio. But strategic peripheral vision is about much more than simply anticipating change. It is about sensing where to look more carefully for clues, understanding how to interpret weak signals, and having the courage to act when the signals are still ambiguous.

Mastering the Art of Anticipation

How do you master the art of anticipation? Our study of over 160 senior executives found that a vigilant attitude is the most important trait of strategic leaders who are good at anticipating and exploiting change.[6] To break that down into a set of practices, we've found that such leaders do nine things well. They

- look for game-changing information at the periphery of their business,
- search beyond the boundaries of current, prevailing views,
- recognize potential changes before the competition does,
- connect the dots of incipient trends by triangulating weak signals,
- entertain multiple hypotheses about the causes of change,
- encourage mavericks in their company to say what they really think,
- organize "paranoia sessions" to tap wisdom inside their company,
- build wide networks inside and outside the organization, and
- remain vigilant and curious about signals from many spheres.

It is important to note that there are two ways you need to look at your periphery. One way, just described, is to "mind" the periphery. This requires *divergence* and means that you need to pay attention to actions across many areas and connect the dots among diverse signals of possible threats or opportunities.

Don't just "mind" the periphery. "Mine" it, too.

But there are other sources of threat and opportunity you need to watch. Sometimes they originate in a well-defined part of the periphery, such as pending regulations or a specific technology. In such cases, you want to thoroughly "mine" for knowledge. In other words, only a very close examination reveals the key insights, usually after triangulating multiple sources of information. This requires a strong *convergent* focus on a specific part of the periphery and rapidly developing the capacity to respond to it.

The good news is that failures of strategic anticipation aren't always fatal. After Lego experienced a deep crisis toward the end of the last century, the company changed its approach.[7] It improved communications with retailers and customers, viewing them as strategic radar and sources of new ideas. Lego teamed up with outside inventors to create new products. Other outside parties helped it create T-shirts, movies, books, toys, and games. Lego also developed robotic kits to replace its 1998 product, emphasizing intelligent bricks, a new programming language, motors and sensors, starter models, and teaching materials for schools.

It was a happy ending, as it turned out. But it would have been much better if leaders had anticipated key changes before they nearly destroyed the company. And if you are serious about being a strategic thinker at your own company, that is a main part of your job.

1.3 HOW TO KNOW IF A NEW STRATEGY WILL WORK

The hard, cold reality is that many strategic projects fail and so we need to learn from those.[8]

Other chapters in this book address factors that can cause strategic initiatives to derail, ranging from team composition, talent, and leadership. Here, I'll examine what for many managers is often the harder risk to assess: is the strategy sound in the first place?

No matter how good your team is, a flawed strategy is hard to implement well. Yes, you can make some adjustments as obstacles arise and engage in tactical corrections midway. But it is far better to assess upfront if the initiative is doomed from the start. Here are the main risk factors to consider:

To what extent does your strategic initiative or key project plan actually:

1. Help your organization serve customers better (internally or externally)?
2. Integrate important activities across organizational boundaries?
3. Align properly with the organization's broader goals and values?
4. Helps hone core capabilities deemed critical to overall success?
5. Identify explicitly critical assumptions underlying the approach?
6. Monitor early indicators of the project faltering or derailing?
7. Allow for reviews and mid-stream corrections in case needed?
8. Coordinate well with other projects underway, in support?
9. Has the necessary senior support and priory of your leader(s)?
10. Consider the impact on other stakeholders and partners needed for success?
11. Reflect the role of competitors in case this project concerns them?
12. Offer a good return on time and investment for all concerned?

No matter how good your team is, a flawed strategy is hard to implement. Gather your team and run through these questions one by one in terms of relevance. Modify them if they don't apply to your strategic initiative and add new ones if necessary to reflect your unique situation. Then start to score the revised list on a scale from 1 (=fatal flaw) to 7 (=very favorable) and see if the total exceeds 60% of the maximum possible. Ideally, you want a score of 80% or better; anything below 30%, may be unduly risky or even mission impossible (since your scores may be too optimistic). Once you understand the project's strategic weaknesses, try to work the system to get better support, additional resources, more realistic targets, or whatever it takes to end up a winner.

The first rule of strategy is only to fight battles you can win. The second is to be thought out enough to see trouble coming before you get knocked over. The third is to have enough courage and flexibility to adjust midstream. As they say in the military, no plan survives contact with the enemy. Or as boxer Mike Tyson put it: Everybody has a plan until they get punched in the face. Being strategic means not getting too many of those hits, especially from opponents like Mike Tyson.

1.4 CREATE DOUBT AND MANAGE IT WELL

—With Wijnand Nuijts*

The renowned physicist Richard Feynman knew that "Doubt is not a fearful thing, but a thing of great value." The philosopher Charles Peirce, the father of American pragmatism, extolled the virtues of doubt since in his view little useful inquiry happens without it.[9] And yet, in business, doubt often has a negative connotation.

That's the wrong way to look at it. What's critical in management is how doubts are cultivated, explored, and resolved. Great leaders know when to question false assumptions, insist on better evidence, and how to encourage team members to engage in critical introspection in order to develop deeper insights. This is not easy, given that feelings of doubt are seldom pleasant. Most action-oriented managers want to bring closure to business problems, be viewed as decisive, and move on. Doubt can be a welcome break, though, whenever premature consensus rises or overconfidence creeps in.

The U.S. Department of Justice recently started to recognize the value of doubt in expert testimony based on an FBI analysis of the accuracy of hair-sample evidence used at trials.[10] The study examined 268 criminal cases and found errors in 95% of the hair-sample analyses. During the 15-year study period, more than a dozen of those convicted in these cases were executed or died in prison. Stung by such expert overconfidence in the courtroom, the Justice Department recently issued new guidelines aimed at injecting some doubt in expert testimony about matching hair, fingerprint, DNA, or handwriting samples. Specifically, claims of "zero error rates" are now banned. The adversarial nature of the courts, which relies on prosecution and defense making their strongest cases, may naturally suppress doubt among hard-driving attorneys. In business, similar dialectic processes will be at play whenever managers have to advocate one-sidedly for their viewpoint. However, doubt is a good lubricant whenever we need to see the world anew.

Allow Room for Hunches and Dissent

One approach is to encourage colleagues to give voice to their hunches, which often manifest themselves weakly at first in the form of fear, irritation,

---

* Head of Department Governance, Behaviour and Culture of the Dutch Central Bank (personal view).

boredom, or perhaps even feelings of guilt. Doubt is a sense that not all is right and that too much is unclear. It is a feeling that casts a large shadow of discomfort over current courses of action, without knowing necessarily what is amiss or how to fix it. As Locke et al. phrased it,[11] "when we nurture hunches, we cultivate the generative potential of doubt." Once doubt exists, the crucial process of inquiry and testing can start, ideally driven by deep curiosity about new questions and challenges. A large bank, for example, was deciding whether to acquire an international competitor. On purely financial grounds, this acquisition seemed very profitable. Yet, at the same time, there was a vague, poorly articulated feeling among some executives that something was overlooked in the analysis. This "hunch" caused the bank's leaders to postpone the decision and explore the feelings of discomfort further. Several rounds of deep discussions revealed that the incipient feelings stemmed from previous acquisitions gone wrong. After being of two minds for a while,[12] the bank decided to table the acquisition due to valid concerns that various regulatory risks could not be well managed.

Managing Doubt Effectively

Apart from surfacing hunches, leaders can induce doubt by exploring surprises that catch them off guard. The surprise may be that other people do not see a problem the same way as you do, or that they deem a certain action to be a big mistake. Since nearly every mistake, misread or surprise has a potential silver lining in hidden lessons, managers need to work hard to mine them for deeper insights. This means orchestrating learning cycles that run the gamut from surprise to doubt to inquiry to learning and action. Once various iterations of this loop have yielded multiple benefits in an organization, its culture will start to view doubt, if managed well, as a valuable business asset deserving of respect. Most complex decisions need both intuitive and analytical examination, and doubts expressed at the right time can help accomplish that.

To illustrate, leaders in the midst of a complex business model transformation had to decide which business activities to outsource and where to push for more internal innovation. However, several board members privately harbored doubts about this approach. Rather than suppress these faint stirrings, some voiced them and the board then embarked on a disciplined process to dig deeper. Each private reservation was explored by asking board members to rotate such roles as defending or challenging the issue of concern. The board learned, over time, that the quality of dialogue could be much enhanced by respecting people's experiences and intuitive feelings, and now accepts that the state of "not being sure" is an essential part of a good decision process. In essence, the board now views latent doubt as a valuable counterweight to overly analytical approaches when solving complex organizational or strategic problems.

1.5 WHEN THINKING BIG ISN'T BIG ENOUGH

The pressures of doing business today, such as beating the last quarter and making the next, are often an impediment to deeper strategic conversations that your organization needs to have. You need to see the big picture, and in too many organizations, the big picture isn't big enough. To develop a much broader view, ask associates to write down their ideas about the following questions. Make it clear that responses may be shared (either anonymously or with personal attribution) to stimulate group discussion about topics that the executive team really should be addressing.

1. *What strategic issues are of most concern to you in your current position or more broadly for our organization as a whole?* Speaking truth to power is difficult, as the grandson of former Secretary of State George Schultz learned when he questioned bold claims by start-up Theranos about using tiny blood pricks to screen for an array of diseases.[13] Nearly everyone tried to muffle him, including his grandpa, who got him a job there and served on the board. In contrast, when Alan Mulally became CEO at Ford, he instilled a culture of brutal honesty, with great success.[14]
2. *What is your typical time frame for strategic decisions and long-term planning? How many years out are you thinking and what is the business scope you normally consider, from local or regional to global?* Leaders have to know since they, and their boards, need to think longer term and farther afield than the management team; if not the leaders, who will? When I was at Shell's planning group in London decades ago, our global scenarios looked 10–20 years into the future, even though executives got reposted every 5–7 years.
3. *What would constitute some very bad external developments or scenarios for the business, including social, political, economic, ecological, legal, and regulatory forces or technologies that are beyond your control?* As Jeff Immelt wrote after becoming CEO of General Electric in 1991 "I could never have forecast so many tail-risk events hitting: 9/11, Enron, Hurricane Katrina, Fukushima, the global financial crisis."[15] It underscores that farsighted leaders should look for black swans, and weak signals and think the unthinkable.

4. *Conversely, what especially good external developments or scenarios could plausibly happen over the next five years, covering perhaps the same but also different topics, forces, themes, or issues?* Good news scenarios are psychologically easier to envision but can still easily be overlooked or misconstrued. Few economic analysts, for example, anticipated the high synchronized growth rates among major economies around the world around 2018, which propelled equity markets to record highs.

5. *More fanciful yet, if you had a crystal ball, what would be the top three questions you would ask in order to help you better perform your current leadership responsibilities and/or help the company overall?* As Voltaire counseled: "Judge a man by his questions rather than his answers." For example, in financial services, what future surprises might be as big as PayPal or Apple Pay, or the various regulations imposed after the Great Recession? Or in terms of new technologies, will Artificial Intelligence have more impact than say space exploration by 2040 in your business?

6. *What are some current or upcoming strategic decisions for which some of the above scenarios and/or uncertainties are especially relevant, and why?* Suppose your big upcoming decisions are about opening a new office, launching a new product, or entering a promising strategic partnership. You now need to examine how these possible moves play out under a really good versus bad scenario and some in-between cases as well. In short, try to stress test your choices. For example, how thoroughly did IBM examine possible setbacks in AI when making that promising technology a "strategic imperative" decades ago[16], with applications in healthcare and beyond?

7. *Which external issues are the most important for you to track over the next 12 months, either for your own area or the organization more generally? What metrics would you ideally monitor?* Forward-looking measures are clearly better than rear-view mirror ones. Your early warning dashboard should be tied to both your strategy and external scenarios. If you want to track shifts in consumer preferences or service quality, for instance, look at customers you lost and why. If you ask them, and know how to listen with a third ear, you can learn a great deal from them, your rivals, and your own people.

8. *What significant external developments were spotted too late in the last five years by you or the organization; why do you think these blind spots occurred? Also, what important developments did you spot ahead of time; what helped you or the firm stay abreast of these undercurrents?* Over a decade ago, one major European chocolate maker (Ferrero) was totally blindsided by the merger of Mars

and Wrigley. As usual, various weak signals foreshadowed this surprise, but due to poor information-sharing, the dots were not connected. In contrast, Adobe sensed in 2008 a shift of packaged software to the cloud because its new CEO Shantanu Narayan excelled in peripheral vision, curiosity, and challenging conventional wisdom.[17]

Once the right issues are surfaced, various approaches can then be followed to develop suitable responses, such as resolving pressing choices near term or developing a sharper strategic vision for the long term. The leader's imperatives here are to start the strategic conversation from the outside in, make room for diverse and even unpopular inputs, develop an inclusive process, and respect uncertainty by not trying to predict what is unknowable. Then, test the robustness of any decision or strategy against multiple scenarios of how major external uncertainties could play out. The broader these uncertainties are, the more flexibility should be built into your strategy, say by using an options approach when making large investments. Relatedly, leaders need to reward alertness to external changes and foster organizational agility, so that quick actions can be taken when needed. The game today for any executive team is learning how to see sooner and act faster to stay ahead in an increasingly turbulent and uncertain environment.[18]

END NOTES

1 Day, George. "The yin and yang of outside-in thinking." *Industrial Marketing Management* 88 (2020): 84–86.

2 Kumar, Vikas, et al. "Is market orientation a source of sustainable competitive advantage or simply the cost of competing?" *Journal of Marketing* 75.1 (2011): 16–30

3 Why Bezos Was Surprised by the Kindle's Success (newsweek.com)

4 Day, George S., and Paul JH Schoemaker. "Scanning the periphery." *Harvard Business Review* 83.11 (2005): 135.

5 Fugate, Jessica Burns, Ronald Kuntze, Erika Matulich, Janette Carter, and Kristen Kluberdanz. "Bratz dolls: Responding to cultural change." *Journal of Business Cases and Applications* 12 (2014): 1.

6 Schoemaker, Paul J. H., and George S. Day. "Determinants of organizational vigilance: Leadership, foresight, and adaptation in three sectors." *Futures & Foresight Science* 2.1 (2020): e24.

7 Robertson, David, and Bill Breen. *Brick by Brick: How LEGO Rewrote the Rules of Innovation and Conquered the Global Toy Industry.* Currency, 2014.

8 Edmondson, Amy C. "Strategies for learning from failure." *Harvard Business Review* 89.4 (2011): 48–55.

9 Psillos, Stathis. "An explorer upon untrodden ground: Peirce on abduction." *Handbook of the History of Logic.* 10. North-Holland, (2011): 117–151.

10 Justice Dept. to Tighten Rules on Testimony by Scientists. *The New York Times* (nytimes. com).

11 Locke, Karen, Karen Golden-Biddle, and Martha S. Feldman. "Perspective—Making doubt generative: Rethinking the role of doubt in the research process." *Organization Science* 19.6 (2008): 907–918.

12 Sanfey, Alan and Luke J. Chang. "Of Two Minds When Making a Decision." *Scientific American*, June 3, 2008.

13 Boni, Arthur A., and Stephen M. Sammut. "'The Good, the Bad, the Ugly': Leadership Lessons From Two Companies-Amgen and Theranos." *Journal of Commercial Biotechnology* 24.4 (2019), pp 67–73.

14 http://www.newsweek.com/247-wall-street-interview-ford-ceo-alan-mulally-79611

15 https://www.economist.com/business/2014/06/27/a-hard-act-to-follow.

16 https://www.dailymail.co.uk/sciencetech/article-6001141/IBMs-Watson-suggested-inaccurate-unsafe-treatment-recommendations-cancer-patients.html.

17 Gupta, Sunil and Lauren Barley, "Reinventing Adobe," Case 9-514-006, Harvard Business School, January 20, 2015.

18 Day, George S., and Paul J. H. Schoemaker. "Adapting to fast-changing markets and technologies." *California Management Review* 58.4 (2016): 59–77.

CHAPTER 2

BUSINESS PLANNING

Here is a good one, 'listen to your employees'

2.1 HOW TO PREPARE FOR THE UNEXPECTED

Maybe you've set aside a small rainy-day fund—just in case you have a month when your cash flow slows to a trickle. Or you've devised an ad hoc Plan B in the event that your carefully laid marketing plan flops. Both are great ideas.

But what about the truly unexpected—the black swans you'll never see coming? Or the gray swans that you are somewhat aware of but can't really get a fix on or understand well enough. It might sound counterintuitive, but you can plan for those too.

People who get good at strategic thinking tend to notice the unexpected sooner than everyone else because they have developed semi-prepared minds. They've done some form of scenario planning, and as a result, they've developed a better sense for what may come in the future.

So, if you've felt bamboozled by too many costly surprises and industry changes, read on.

The Makings of Smart Scenarios

Scenarios are well-crafted narratives about the future that tell very different stories about what might happen. A few scenarios are usually enough to define a broad range of potential fates—though the more volatile your recent past has been, the broader you're going to need to think. Your focus should be on things you can't control or predict in order to put some boundaries around the range of possible worlds you may have to deal with (whether you like it or not).

Good scenarios provide competing intellectual windows on a complex phenomenon and challenge how you think about it. For example, if U.S. automakers had more seriously examined various globalization and technology scenarios a few decades earlier, they might have switched their design and manufacturing strategies much sooner.

The aim is to stress test your current strategy and make sure your plans contain enough flexibility that you will win no matter what the future brings.

How to Do It

Let's see how scenario planning works in a simplified case.[1] Your company is a small business with a mostly unionized workforce manufacturing street sweepers for municipalities around the country. Here is how might do scenario planning in six basic steps

1. *Define the issue.* Lay it out in terms of time frame, scope, and decision variables. So, if you make street sweepers, you might want to know, for example, what your industry might be like five years from now in terms of product prices, new competitors, and regulations.

2. *Make a list of what you know.* What current *trends* will affect your industry five years from now? In this particular example, you know that union power is declining, the workforce is aging, and overseas competition is stiffening. Briefly document these trends and explain why each exerts a significant influence.

3. *Identify what you don't know.* These are the *uncertainties* whose outcomes will significantly affect your industry, such as the strength of the U.S. dollar (which affects imports) as well as new safety regulations before Congress. Briefly explain why and how these uncertain events matter, and examine how they are potentially interconnected.

4. *Construct multiple scenarios.* Brainstorm different outcomes for the top uncertainties. For example, suppose the tide turns against you: You're hit with onerous new regulations and a strong dollar, making exports hard while inviting overseas manufacturers. How would you rebound?

5. *Assess the plausibility of each scenario.* Identify where and why your scenarios may be inconsistent. Is it plausible that a strong dollar, perhaps the result of Republicans being in power in Washington, would also bring about tighter regulations?

6. *Eliminate combinations that are implausible.* Maybe it's unlikely that both weaker union power and higher wages would happen at the same time in your shop. So, in that case, you might remove it from your first scenario draft, correcting the inconsistency so that you end up with a few diverse but plausible scenarios (at least three). Also, make sure your final scenarios cover a wide range of possibilities you might face.

The above list is a bare-bones version of scenario planning. More detailed examples can be found in my recent scenario book as well as earlier academic papers.[2] The methodology matters less than the ability to come up with interesting, coherent, and diverse views of the future that challenge people's mental models to varying extents while also stimulating deep dialog among team members, the C-suite, and the Board. As they used to say at Royal Dutch/ Shell, one of the pioneering companies in the field of scenario planning, the aim is not just planning but surfacing mental models.[3]

2.2 BEWARE THE LIMITS OF SWOT ANALYSIS

When autumn arrives, many companies carve out time for their annual strategic planning sessions. A common corporate go-to is SWOT analysis, in which you assess your company's internal *strengths* and *weaknesses*, as well as external *opportunities* and *threats*. But be careful: SWOT analysis has some inherent limitations. Sometimes, it can even do more harm than good. Here are five common pitfalls to avoid:

1. *Too much navel-gazing.* The first trap of SWOT is that it focuses all the attention on yourself from the get-go. Assessing your own strengths and weaknesses can easily degenerate into a laundry list of items, mixing truly strategic areas (such as your top core competences) with mundane issues (such as payroll processing). Also, labeling an item as a plus or minus entails a value judgment in which your current strategy becomes the implicit reference point. For instance, "excellence in chemical emulsion photography" was once a core strength for Kodak before the digital imaging tsunami hit the industry. In the end, Kodak's chemical prowess proved to be its undoing. As Malcolm Gladwell emphasizes in *David and Goliath*, your current strength may be your future weakness once reframed (or vice-versa).[4]

2. *Imprisoned by the status quo.* The status quo trap is even more insidious when you get to the second part of SWOT, in which you assess external opportunities and threats. The very language of O and T inadvertently forces you to prejudge whether some external change is a positive or a negative, with the current strategy as a natural reference point. It is much better to use neutral language, such as asking what external forces or issues could impact your business. Any of these could be good, bad, or neutral, depending on how you respond to them. Remember that strategy is about winning no matter what happens in your business environment. In turbulent times, this requires much more than playing your current hand of cards better. Often, you have to change that hand by trying new things and perhaps changing your business model entirely.

3. *Insufficient systems thinking.* Mapping out how social, technological, economic, environmental, and political forces may impact your business is hard. The world outside your company walls is more complex and less understood than what's going inside. Grasping how external trends and uncertainties may be changing your playing field requires systems thinking or understanding how each piece affects the whole.

As futurist Alvin Toffler warned, trends are meaningless when examined in isolation; trees do not grow to the skies.[5] Strategic thinkers will ask when key trends might stop and why over what time frame key uncertainties could play out, and how the major pieces of the puzzle interact. At an even deeper level, they will wonder how stable (or unstable) the system is, where black swans may be lurking, and how unintended consequences could shape the future in surprising ways.[6]

4. *Poor outside-in analysis.* In most planning sessions, internally focused topics often get too much attention, and time may run out to do justice to the outside world. As discussed in Chapter 1, to escape this trap, you need to start your discussions by exploring how the world is changing around you. For example, a leader may first ask, "How can we serve our customers better?" or "How should we improve our products?" Both are relevant questions, but they're not the best ones to start with. Instead, ask, "Why ***aren't*** more customers buying from us?" or "In which ways do our competitors offer superior products?" These questions force you to look at your company from the outside.

5. *Little "future-back" thinking.* One weakness of SWOT analysis is that it reduces complex strategy questions to lists of items that in isolation are hard to assess. Systems thinking helps overcome this reductionism by looking at connections among the many items and thus encouraging more integrative perspectives. But this may still not be enough. Strategic leaders also need to be guided by strong future-oriented visions (as Elon Musk is doing with electric cars and space travel). By reimagining how an entire market can be served better and developing multiple scenarios about how the future might unfold via back-casting, strategic leaders can better discern which actions today will create new options for tomorrow.[7]

SWOT can be a good tool if used wisely. It offers a shared framework and agenda for strategic planning. But in the wrong hands, it can also damage by reinforcing a status quo mindset. That's why it should be supplemented with newer strategy tools, including scenario planning, options thinking, dynamic capabilities analysis, and exploratory strategic leadership.

2.3 HOW WELL DO YOU HANDLE VUCA?

The U.S. military coined the acronym ***VUCA*** in the late 1990s to signal a profound shift in its operating environment toward Volatility, Uncertainty, Complexity, and Ambiguity.[8] During the Cold War era, military leaders were accustomed to long-term, multifaceted conflicts with clear enemies of known strength. But after the collapse of the Soviet Union, the environment changed toward diffuse, asymmetric warfare, with agile, dispersed opponents motivated by ethnic and religious causes not always fully understood—consider the "War on Terror."

Similarly, businesses may be seeing the end of a relative stability period, in which chip advances reliably followed Moore's Law, peaceful trade relations were stable, and the dominance of OECD economies appeared unassailable. Business leaders today function in a multi-polar environment that is threatening the liberal world order (think Brexit, Ukraine, or Gaza). Tariff wars were brewing under Trump, China's economic influence is growing, and nationalism—inflamed by immigration—is causing turmoil in many nations. These changes may require a quantum shift in how leaders approach strategy, innovation, and competition, with VUCA being an apt label for the environment they encounter as well. The acronym's four letters refer to conditions that may be closely related, but they are conceptually distinct.

The V of **volatility** applies when external variables, such as the stock market or interest rates, exhibit high amplitude. Volatility usually entails risk but not always; a sine wave flashing on an oscilloscope, for example, exhibits predictable patterns. The U of uncertainty applies when filing a new patent or predicting an election outcome in politics. Uncertainty usually entails unknown outcomes but this need not imply volatility per se. In a patent application, for example, there may be just two outcomes—approval or rejection—but the chances of either occurring may be very unclear. The C of **complexity** applies when variables are highly interconnected, as seen in weather systems or a modern open economy. Finally, the A of **ambiguity** refers to a lack of clarity about the nature of the problem overall or about the key components such as the options, their outcomes, and probabilities.

Even though VUCA has become a widely used acronym, its underlying components often overlap in real-world cases, be it war, business, politics, or science, and this makes it hard to connect the letters one-to-one with unique strategies. Furthermore, leaders may not know what situations lie around the corner for their companies, so they need to develop capabilities that can handle multiple combinations of the four letters.

This transformative skill is not easy, as Blockbuster, Kodak, Nokia, Philips, GE, Samsung, and many others have experienced firsthand. One strategy is to cultivate ambidextrous leadership, the ability to manage a stable business as well as one in the midst of upheaval.[9] Researchers have examined how some firms and leaders manage to thrive in high-velocity environments like Silicon Valley.

The key is to operate in real time, with relatively simple decision rules, explore options in parallel (not just sequentially), and consensus building. Another important strategy for VUCA environments is to systematically build systems that enable managers, and not just leaders, to sense change sooner, seize opportunities ahead of rivals, and transform the organization when and where needed.[10]

Taking the Long View

Few managers in business, public administration, education, science, or the arts deal with VUCA environments daily, and neither does the military, except during times of combat and other crisis situations. Still, senior leaders must take a longer view that very much includes VUCA conditions to avoid being ill-prepared when surprising events occur. Leaders who came of age during more stable times often struggle with how to handle the kind of turbulence common in our digital age. They are accustomed to gradual changes by known rivals within clear industry boundaries rather than rapidly scaling businesses relying on light assets, novel business models, and little respect for traditional market boundaries (think Amazon or Uber).

Old timers will continue to cling to extrapolative planning, which limits their line of sight to steady projections emanating from standard planning and budgeting systems. They may also continue to manage for risk (quantifiable) when they should manage for deep and at times even radical uncertainty.[11] Companies that successfully navigated waves of technological disruption include Adobe, when it moved to the cloud and Netflix, when it shifted from a video mail order business to online streaming and original content, which fueled its exponential growth.

Successful leadership in the VUCA world is less about developing detailed plans and more about continually testing hypotheses about emerging technologies and changing markets in order to learn faster. MasterCard did this stealthily, while operating in the shadow of Visa, by exploring growing market segments ignored by its main rivals.[12] It zeroed in on consumers wedded to cash, recognizing that at times, they still wanted mobile payment options, for example, when barely catching the tube or bus in London. Amazon elevated such broad exploratory strategies to high art, from its humble start as an online bookseller to a retailer of nearly everything, to being first in breaking the trillion-dollar valuation ceiling. In its wake, more than 60 companies became collateral damage including such well-known names such as Barnes & Noble, Costco, Best Buy, GameStop, Macy's, Nordstrom, Sears, Target, CVS Caremark, Rite Aid, and even Walmart.

Disruptive strategies generally call for different kinds of leaders, ranging from highly visionary entrepreneurs to operationally focused managers who can bring about practical change when necessary. VUCA conditions typically require a hybrid form of entrepreneurial leaders who can devise new organizational capabilities that stimulate innovative offerings and streamline new business models geared toward the next big upheaval. As such, VUCA should not be used to slice and dice the external environment but to determine whether you are entering a game-changing future that will require new strategies, leadership models, and organizational capabilities.

2.4 WAYS TO ENVISION UNCERTAIN FUTURES

How can your company better anticipate ways in which the world is changing around you? This is a challenge for every organization functioning in what the military has termed a "VUCA world," as discussed above. The acronym refers to an operating environment characterized by Volatility, Uncertainty, Change, and Ambiguity. For decades now, we have worked with senior executives to help their organizations spot, anticipate, and remain resilient in the face of VUCA challenges. Here are two main ideas that work broadly and in many settings.

Reduce Your Blind Spots

Nearly all organizations we work with, small and large, acknowledge having missed important external developments. For example, the board of a community foundation had to decide what to do with several acres of land that were donated to them. While contemplating this largesse, an energy company approached them about leasing rights for hydraulic fracturing (fracking). The extra income on offer would benefit the community, so the board decided to take a deeper look. To help them, the local staff staked out what parts of the tract might be leased.

But after the board and some key leaders trekked out, in boots and coats, to take a closer look at the donated land, they ran into an ambush of sorts. To their surprise, word got out rather quickly about the fracking option under consideration, and various community groups organized to stop it. The board then temporarily abandoned any lease options because the reputational costs and pushback were too great. After some further education, research, and community meetings, the foundation eventually signed a non-surface lease that provided financial support to the community while limiting the impact on the land.

The above is a simple example of why peripheral vision takes work. Everyone in this situation tried to be thoughtful and act with care including doing some due diligence. Their clear-eyed operational focus on the land itself, however, came at the price of reduced peripheral vision, which requires a wide-angled look to prevent blind spots. Most weak signals of trouble or opportunity are first visible at the edges of your business. Waiting for them to appear at the core means you are too late.

The corporate world is littered with examples of companies whose failure to foresee threats or opportunities proved costly. For example, the personal computer revolution that blind-sided IBM started outside the mainframe business: with small companies, graphic artists, and other specialty players. Likewise, the LED revolution that forced such giants as GE, Philips, and Sylvania to get out of the light bulb business in the U.S. started in flashlights and exit signs—far away from their profitable core segment offering bright, warm lighting to illuminate home or office spaces.[13] Other classic examples include Kodak and digital photography, the Encyclopedia Britannica being overtaken by CD ROMS or RIM's Blackberry. As is typical in technology domains, the threats in these cases came out of left field and were seen too late by senior leaders and the board.

The Need for Scenario Planning

To see the future sooner, leaders need to scan the horizon systematically, look for weak signals, connect various dots, and then communicate the insights via compelling narratives to get others engaged. The donated land controversy highlights the importance of thinking through multiple scenarios when making strategic decisions. Leaders of other community foundations have expressed concern to us that they are not fully grasping how societal polarization, significant funding decreases by the federal government, discontent with elites, troubling questions about social media, AI, concerns about privacy—and other looming issues—will affect the roles, functions and social perceptions of foundations.

During such discussions, I was reminded of a 2016 environmental scan we did with the Knight Foundation to map out how social, economic, political, and technological forces might create deep, unwelcome fissures in American democracy.[14] The mission of the Knight Foundation, headquartered in Miami, is to help foster a well-informed and fully engaged U.S. citizenry through grants, education, and investments. As insightful as we thought our scenarios were, based on considerable desk research and expert interviews, we still misread the fallout of the Trump 2016 election and the accompanying

Facebook backlash—prompting calls for stricter regulations of social media. It clearly takes special, ongoing, and rigorous leadership efforts to see around corners and to develop strategic responses to these external developments that may otherwise rock their world.

The good news is that this daunting challenge is not about being the smartest executive in the room or even having collected the brightest group of people around you. Above all, it's about having the right approach and mindset. Many practical tools and proven success stories are ready for use by vigilant leaders, as described in my 2019 MIT Press book with George Day titled *See Sooner—Act Faster*.[15] It is based on research we did with global companies as well as non-profits that are trying to stay abreast of external changes in the environment as well as the problems festering right under their own noses. Just as each family is unhappy in its own way, as Tolstoy famously wrote in *Anna Karenina*, each organization has its own blind spots and systemic weaknesses. Unlike families, though, corporations have the means to audit their past misses and hits in order to reveal the root causes. Once the underlying organizational issues have been surfaced, a plethora of tools exist to tackle them, as our new book lays out.

2.5 WHY YOU CAN'T PREDICT THE FUTURE

Most big events foreshadow themselves, but often faintly and in fragmented ways. As Winston Churchill quipped: "People sometimes stumble upon the truth but quickly pick themselves up and hurry about their business." As we discussed earlier, vigilant companies try to spot and interpret anomalies as they arise in functions, departments, or business sectors.

The future whispers to us in faint signals rather than full sentences. The signals often come as disjointed snippets of information distributed across time, space, and people without clear meanings. The key question: How well you or your organization is listening to these faint stirrings? The problem is that it is seldom just one weak signal that will reveal the full story. At best, it is a soft warning bell or puzzling piece of data or seemingly white noise. You will have to look for more than one needle in the haystack; you find a bunch, and you may need to work hard to connect and arrive at new insights before others do.

Embrace Anomalies

Drug maker Organon (part of Akzo Nobel) stumbled on a new antidepressant after surfacing a rather small curiosity—and explored it further. The research team running clinical trials for a new antihistamine was failing to prove the drug's efficacy as a treatment for hay fever and other allergies. As it would happen, a secretary involved in registering trial participants for periodic medical check-ups noted that some of them were particularly cheerful. This casual observation would, in most companies, remain buried at the registration desk. Thanks to a culture of broad information sharing, an alert secretary was able to bring her curiosity to the attention of managers, who explored her observation further. The trial's leaders soon realized that the patients in the treatment group tended to be in better moods than those in the control group. Through chance and exploration, they discovered that their new drug might actually be an effective treatment for depression. Organon successfully developed and marketed the drug as Tolvon (mianserin hydrochloride) after it failed as an antihistamine.

Vulnerable organizations typically ignore information that doesn't fit their current way of thinking. Vigilant firms, in contrast, **seek out** anomalies and view them as possible early warning signals. Intuit calls this approach "savoring the surprise." This happened, for example, after the company launched an online money management service called Mint, which was designed for young professionals.[16] Alert team members noticed that some new users weren't behaving quite the way young professionals are "supposed to." Some of the new users were different in terms of amounts transferred, time of day, or kinds of other services they used. Rather than just celebrating their successful new launch, the team dug deeper and found that these anomalous users engaged Mint to manage their self-employment income and spending. Many, it turned out, were Uber or Lyft drivers operating in the expanding gig economy at odd hours. Embracing this market insight, Intuit designed a variation of Quick Books specifically for such self-employed workers—which in turn became its fastest-growing product.

Avoid the Pitfalls

Interpreting anomalies surfaced by keen observers at the periphery can be difficult to interpret when the organizational frame of mind is ill-prepared for the unexpected. A classic example of this vulnerability occurred on the morning of December 7, 1941. The captain of the destroyer **USS Ward**, which was patrolling outside of Pearl Harbor, heard the sound of muffled explosions coming from the Hawaiian mainland. The **Ward's** commander had just fired on an unidentified submarine barely visible at the surface and then dropped depth charges when that vessel submerged. He was pretty sure he had sunk the intruder. Despite firing what was probably the first American shots in the Second World War, his peacetime frame of mind caused him to misinterpret the sounds of explosions. He turned to his lieutenant commander and said, "I guess they're blasting the new road from Pearl Harbor to Honolulu."[17]

Mental frames can distort important signals that seem obvious in hindsight. This happened recently, for instance, to Facebook and other social media companies, who badly misread the growing concern about personal data violations, hate speech, and fake news. Leaders such as Facebook's founder and CEO Mark Zuckerberg viewed their companies as mere communications platforms, rather than publishing houses, and thus took little responsibility for content flowing through their conduits. This lax view opened the door for hijacking by Russian operatives, extreme fringe groups, and other nefarious players, resulting in a huge social backlash against the companies and additional tightening of regulations in the U.S. and elsewhere.

Our book, *See Sooner—Act Faster*, explores how vigilant firms can develop greater foresight than their rivals and outlines why vulnerable firms often miss early signals of external threats or internal organizational challenges. Charles Schwab, for example, was early to see and act on the promise of "robo-advisors," whereas Honeywell stumbled, letting Nest Labs launch the first "smart" thermostat. The role of leaders is critical in how organizations develop vigilance capabilities and cultivate foresight throughout the entire enterprise. Our book drew lessons from a wide range of cases, including Adobe's move to the cloud, Shell's investments in clean energy, and MasterCard's early recognition of digital challenges for cash users.

Importantly, we also describe how to allocate that very precious resource of leadership attention in order to detect weak signals sooner, both outside and inside the organization. As the self-inflicted wounds of Volkswagen, Wells Fargo, and Boeing remind us, problems can fester for a long time inside the organization's belly but eventually become ticking time bombs. Vigilant leaders use the right tools and mindsets to defuse them before they explode, either on their own or with the help of other farsighted leaders in their industry through self-regulation.[18]

The payoff for exploring anomalies and other weak signals inside the firm as well as outside is enormous. Leaders who can truly listen to what other people are telling them, or to what the future is whispering in their ears, will be amply rewarded. Research shows that such firms will enjoy stronger market positions, higher profits and growth, better-motivated employees, and enhanced organization longevity.

END NOTES

1 This example was taken from Schoemaker, Paul J. H., "When and how to use scenario planning." *Journal of Forecasting* 10 (1991): 549–564.

2 Schoemaker, Paul J. H., "Multiple scenario development: Its conceptual and behavioral foundation." *Strategic Management Journal* 14 (1993): 193–213; Schoemaker, Paul J. H., *Advanced Introduction to Scenario Planning*. Edward Elgar Publishing, UK, June 2022, 176 pp.

3 Van der Heijden, Kees. *Scenarios: The Art of Strategic Conversation*. John Wiley & Sons, 2005.

4 Gladwell, Malcolm. *David and Goliath: Underdogs, Misfits, and the Art of Battling Giants*. Little, Brown, 2013.

5 Toffler, Alvin. *Future Shock*. Bantam, 1984.

6 Aven, Terje. *Risk, Surprises and Black Swans: Fundamental Ideas and Concepts in Risk Assessment and Risk Management*. Routledge, 2014.

7 Dortmans, Peter J. "Forecasting, backcasting, migration landscapes and strategic planning maps." *Futures* 37.4 (2005): 273–285.

8 Who first originated the term VUCA (Volatility, Uncertainty, Complexity and Ambiguity)?. USAHEC Find Your Answer (libanswers.com).

9 The Ambidextrous CEO (hbr.org).

10 Teece, David J., Gary Pisano, and Amy Shuen. "Dynamic capabilities and strategic management." *Strategic Management Journal* 18.7 (1997): 509–533.

11 Kay, John, and Mervyn King. *Radical Uncertainty: Decision-Making Beyond the Numbers*. WW Norton & Company, 2020.

12 Mastercard: The Best Kept Platform Secret—Digital Innovation and Transformation (harvard.edu).

13 Schoemaker, Paul J. H., George S. Day, and Govi Rao, "Converting Strategic Ambiguity to Competitive Advantage: How Philips Lighting Solved the Challenge of LED Technology Disruption." *Strategy & Leadership* 48.2 (2020), pp. 10–17.

14 Imagining the future(s)—Knight Foundation.

15 Day, George S. and Schoemaker, Paul J. H., *See Sooner–Act Faster: How Vigilant Leaders Thrive in an Era of Digital Turbulence*. MIT Press, 2019, 186

16 Geoff Colvin, "How Intuit Reinvents Itself" Fortune. (November 1, 2017), 77–82.

17 Wohlstetter, Roberta. *Pearl Harbor: Warning and Decision*. Stanford University Press, 1962.

18 Donaldson, Thomas, and Paul J. H. Schoemaker, "Self-Inflicted Industry Wounds: Early Warning Signals and Pelican Gambits." *California Management Review* 55.2, Winter (2013): 24–45.

CHAPTER 3

FOSTERING FORESIGHT

"He's in a good mood today.

He found out the New York Times is keeping an obituary on file for him."

Tom Toro

3.1 WHY YOUR BUSINESS IS GOING TO CHANGE

When thinking about the future of innovation, it is instructive to look back since it shows that significant innovations have occurred in the process of innovation itself. Companies moved from inside-out innovation, where firms build on core strengths to conquer adjacencies, to open innovation. P&G is a prime example of this deep trend.[1] In the past, nearly all innovations came from inside P&G; now, most new innovations are sourced from the outside using an approach called "connect and develop." This trend will continue plus a few others highlighted below.

Quantum Innovation

Google's approach is a prime example of "quantum innovation," which is defined as out-of-the-box thinking that is disruptive to competitors and even the company itself. The paradigm shift underlying moonshot innovations seldom fits the current business model or the organization's structure. It usually starts with a very broad sense of purpose and audacious goals, such as Google's desire to organize the world's knowledge or Tesla's goal to make electric cars commonplace. This is what entrepreneurs like Richard Branson (Virgin), Elon Musk (SpaceX and Telsa), Sarah Blakey (Spanx), and John Mackey (WholeFoods) excel at. Cancer Treatment Center of America is doing this as well by reimagining the world of cancer care, with the patient placed foremost in everything that happens.[2]

New Organizational Forms

The traditional 9-to-5, Monday-through-Friday work environment of old is giving way to many new organizational forms. We now see virtual companies, internal and external networked partnerships (think Uber and Airbnb) and companies that spin off new startups. Other new forms include ambidextrous organizations, which can focus on existing products while also keeping an eye on creating new products or markets. And so-called "front-to-back" companies that place the customer at the center of all of their activities. Finally, there are "sense-and-respond" companies such as Zara, a retailer that quickly translates fashion trends into a shipment of new products twice a week. This flurry of innovation in organizational forms will continue to be fueled by technology and changing approaches to work-life balance.

Reverse Innovation

Globalization and outsourcing have also led to "reverse innovation." The world is no longer a one-way outsourcing street moving from West to East. While the

West still exports many high-end products and services to developing nations (and still sources cheap labor), innovations in emerging markets are now flowing back to the West as well. This is happening with Brazil, China, and India across such diverse fields as biofuels, IT, and medicine. New approaches to making cheap artificial hips in India, for example, are finding their way back to the U.S. and Europe. Plus, reverse innovation often means frugal innovation, which is welcome in a world where access to capital, land, labor, and natural resources has become a pressing strategic business issue tied to sustainability.[3]

Harvesting Mistakes

Many breakthroughs came out of a sequence of mistakes or failures. Clearly, not all mistakes are bad; many are portals of discovery. Adopting a more tolerant mindset about mistakes opens the way for testing new processes and projects, even ones that may not look promising initially. Many successful innovations do not become so until they are nourished at an early stage and endure many setbacks, failures, and adjustments.[4] As Honda's founder noted, "Success is 99 percent failure." Rather than wait for brilliant mistakes to occur by happenstance, cutting edge companies may actually encourage deliberate mistakes, defined as testing beyond your belief system—just to see. Such experiments cannot be justified using rational cost-benefit analysis. Instead, they require leaders and a culture that views mistakes as a portal of discovery.[5]

How to Innovate for the Future

When the world is changing at breakneck speed, innovation becomes an organization's most important weapon. History offers a few key lessons about how to wield that weapon in the future:

o The world is a big place: don't limit yourself to just innovation from within your company.
o Aim high: otherwise, incremental innovation can cause you to miss out on breakthrough opportunities.
o Experiment with new organizational structures that are agile and horizontal.
o Practice frugal innovation and learn from the bottom of the pyramid as well as the top.
o View mistakes as portals of discovery: every failure has learning as a silver lining.
o Cultivate leaders who thrive on uncertainty, take the long view, and champion change.

3.2 GETTING BETTER AT LOOKING AHEAD

—With George Day*

Jack Welch identified "seeing around the corner" as a mark of great leaders.[6] He said they must have a sixth sense about what may lie ahead. First, this means asking broader questions than those covered by operations dashboards. Second, these questions should be viewed as "thought starters" to explore parts of the picture beyond where others focus.

Follow these rules to get your mind pointed into the future:

Learn from the past. A natural starter question is, *"What have been our blind spots?"* Studying actual as well as near "misses" helps reveal patterns of systematic vulnerabilities in the organization. Next, see if there are instructive analogies or precursors from another industry or geography. One nanotechnology firm, for example, began looking more deeply at the genetically modified organism (GMO) debacle in Europe (remember Frankenfoods) for sources of public resistance to new technologies.[7] The firm's leaders felt that GMOs and nanotechnologies have some worrying similarities: both technologies may pose health hazards and both were developed by faceless global firms viewed with suspicion. Also, in both cases, the public could easily imagine unpleasant risks while the benefits were mostly indirect.

Another insightful guiding question about the past is: "Who in our industry has a strong track record of seeing sooner and acting faster?" What is their secret? This prompted one packaging technology firm to copy a rival by launching an outpost in Japan, expecting relevant innovations to appear there first. Examining your own past, as well as best practices elsewhere, can help reduce your own vulnerability to surprises. This is a good start although seeing around corners entails more than just learning from the past.

Canvas the present. Most surprises have antecedents, often appearing as anomalies—something that deviates from what is normal or expected. A competitor may start hiring a different kind of talent, for example, or a customer complains about a tightening of labor supply. An early focus on anomalies was central to how Ford CEO Alan Mulally set out to challenge the insular and vulnerable mindset of his leadership team. He made it culturally acceptable for Ford executives to raise concerns or even admit that they had no good answers, starting with his own doubts and questions.

---

* Professor of Marketing, The Wharton School.

Much can be learned from mavericks and outliers in an organization. They may be tolerated for their specialized talents, but their broader insights are seldom sought. As Intel CEO Andy Grove, the famed proponent of healthy paranoia found, most mavericks within the company had difficulty explaining their visceral concerns and feelings to leadership.[8] Vigilant organizations try to listen carefully to employees at multiple levels by encouraging openness to ideas and addressing festering problems. This goes far beyond suggestion boxes since it includes regular meetings, formal recognition, and encouraging feedback about how leaders responded to warnings that had been flagged earlier.

Another rich source of probing questions is complaining customers, especially those who walk away. Lost sales and postmortems on contracts won by competitors are revealing, but only if those doing the pathology are open to digging deeply. Smart firms monitor blogs, social media sites, and chat rooms for signs of trouble in order to take rapid, remedial action. Some go further and examine edge cases. One company asked, for example, what are some new types of jobs that did not exist two years ago? The answers they found included: indoor farmer, synthetic tissue engineer, and virtual fashion designer. Most of us can roughly guess what these are about and decide if a trend watch is warranted. But other jobs that surfaced, such as "bot wranglers," are less obvious and may require a deeper investigation.

Scan the future. Asking good questions about the long term can be greatly aided by the construction of scenarios. These are alternative future narratives that reflect how important uncertainties—from socio-economic to technological—could play out in the years ahead. What is the next oil shock or market disruption? Try to include at least one "impossible" scenario, such as what happened to Arthur Andersen and Enron. By explicitly entertaining the "unthinkable," such as leaders going to prison (Enron and Tyco) or the business model collapsing (Kodak and Nokia), leaders might confront scary scenarios before they actually happen. Without such shock cases, the organization may simply rationalize away important early warning signals.

And try this for a thought starter: How would you attack your own business if you were a new market entrant using a disruptive digital business model? The aim is to surface and exploit all internally known weaknesses of the current business (and then fix them). This approach is a variant of the "red team" exercise widely used by the military in which internal teams role play key decision makers inside the enemy.[9] Red teams can likewise surface weaknesses in a new strategic initiative, such as launching a new product or integrating a merger. The red team would be asked to systematically collect any signals suggesting that the plan is wrong, thus allowing for timely correction perhaps.

A final imaginative, guiding question asks, "What future surprises could really hurt (or help) us?" For example, what future surprises might be as big as PayPal, Dodd Frank, or Crypto currencies in financial services? Also, what would be an idealized future[10] that we should try to make happen? A global advertising agency explored how new digital technologies could change marketing. The company examined how the role of the Chief Marketing Officer would change and how media decisions would be made differently. Such probing questions helped them see around the corner a bit more, which may just be enough. After all, in the land of the blind, one eye is king.

3.3 STANDING STILL MEANS LOSING GROUND

Navigating the unknown can be thought of as voyaging, like Columbus or Hudson, into uncharted terrain. The explorer would do well to prepare mentally for surprises, remain agile, minimize heavy baggage, practice acuity and vigilance, and maintain good communication with the home base. The key is to develop an organizational ability to anticipate well in advance and to respond to unforeseeable exigencies in a timely and resolute fashion. Here are some of the main components underpinning that approach.

Bold Moves. When times are unstable, the payoffs associated with strong moves—especially when rivals are paralyzed—can create significant economic opportunity. These moves can take the form of launching disruptive technologies (e.g., Netflix), a quantum shift in the business model (Uber), or ecosystem transformations (Apple's iPhone). They may call for new arrangements with governments or the sharing of industry wide risks in say banking, nuclear power, cyber security, gene therapy, or offshore drilling. Such ecosystem moves require a shift away from just a firm-focused view of strategy to an industry-wide perspective aimed at preventing systemic risks or other catastrophes that can inflict broad collateral damage.[11]

Clarity of purpose. In times of uncertainty, when many people are unsure or even paralyzed, effective leaders imbue their organization with a strong sense of purpose. People must know what they are fighting for and find legitimacy in the underlying rationale. In the fog of battle, clear principles can serve as beacons for high-integrity organizations, in addition to opportunism, street smarts, or scrappy hustling. When Boeing was at its peak long ago, its vision was crystal clear: build the best airplanes possible. Managers need to know what sets their company apart, as Steve Jobs did in the 1980s when emphasizing that Apple built personal computers that start with people—in contrast to IBM's machine-first orientation.

Adaptive Capabilities. As the lure of new treasure propels organizations into the unknown, they better arm themselves with flexible and reconfigurable capabilities. A multi-purpose Swiss knife will be better than some sophisticated high-power drills for making small holes only in titanium materials. When the fog is thick, focus on your resources and capabilities, as opposed to only end markets and products. Honda did this early on when emphasizing three core competences: excellence in engine design, manufacturing, and power transmission. Honda then adroitly leveraged each of these in cars, motorcycles, lawn mowers, etc. Since core competencies take time to develop, they will be very hard to imitate or transfer, thus bestowing *sustainable* advantage.

Network Mindset. Most other organizations can only achieve their goals through alliances, partnerships, and horizontal network strategies. Apple created an entire ecosystem to develop its winning iPod, starting with digital rights management software known as FairPlay. This got music owners and app developers on board in creating a walled garden for song buying to counter illegal downloads. Apple further leveraged its iPod success into the iPhone and iPad and thus conquered the world. Network models are common in nature, from lower organisms like insects and complex primates. Business textbooks, however, still favor a physics mindset than a biological one. Fortunately, common terms such as organizational DNA, mutations, and symbiosis are changing the metaphor.

Ambidextrous Leadership. The more uncertainty organizations face, the less likely it is that the current strategy will succeed without major adjustments. So, leaders must know when and how to change the plan. Netflix did this successfully by expanding its mail-order business for DVDs to online streaming of videos and then developing its own content. In a sense, leaders must be both classical musicians, for the part of the script that is robust, as well as jazz performers who can improvise. This calls for ambidextrous leadership that is quite different from General George Patton barking directions sitting atop a white horse. Humility, shared decision-making, and flexibility are more crucial today than the ability to direct the troops top-down.

Organizational Vigilance. None of the above will matter unless the organization possesses sufficient capacity to spot changes in its business. This means surfacing anomalies, exceptions, surprises, and customer complaints. P&G did this well after launching Febreze, a spray that eliminates unpleasant odors in the home or clothing. Rumors started in chat rooms that Febreze might kill canaries and other birds kept in homes. Being very sensitive about its brands, these rumors were quickly picked up, independently investigated, and then successfully countered by the company. Vigilant organizations are highly alert about changes in their environment, both external and internal.

The irony is that usually, some people inside the company are aware of signals that their leaders are missing. But they may not realize that leaders are overlooking these early warning signs. Better communication is the main safeguard against companies getting blindsided. Although there are no foolproof analytical methods against blind spots—a fool with a tool is still a fool—leaders need to work hard to uncover the traps and biases that hold back their organization. This means fostering an inquisitive culture since faster learning is the only durable competitive advantage in times of upheaval and change.

3.4 FIND THE FUTURE BEFORE IT FINDS YOU

—With Govi Rao*

The early signals from emerging technologies are often weak and hard to interpret. The possible disruptions envisioned may fizzle—or scale rapidly when new entrants launch novel business models. In such cases, entrenched players must assess whether to wait and see, invest in strategic options, or get ready to exit vulnerable business segments before it is too late.

The lighting industry's response to the gradual rise of light-emitting diodes (LEDs) over decades is instructive here. The Dutch company Philips Lighting used three key strategies to figure out what to do.[12] First, its leaders probed the challenges and opportunities of LED technology early on, starting in the 1990s. Second, they formulated and tested competing hypotheses about LED applications as well as market trajectories. Third, they used these insights to develop multiple scenarios to test their strategies as well as educate their organization and the industry about potential market quakes ahead.

The Lighting Industry

Philips, Sylvania, and General Electric (GE) constituted a long-standing oligopoly, followed by several tier 2 regional OEMs (Original Equipment Manufacturers). The three main players held about 65% of the U.S. lighting market, especially in lamps and controls, before the new millennium. But around 2000, industry leaders became increasingly concerned about the potential disruptions that LEDs might pose. Would the 100+ year-old lighting paradigm created by Thomas Edison in 1880 finally come to an end?

---

* Former leader of Philips' LED unit; CEO of Phase Change Solutions

In early 2003, the major stakeholders in the lighting industry joined forces to map out the future of the business and launch a drive for market transformation. They developed wide-ranging scenarios about the future of lighting, some scary, and others more promising. The scary scenarios were intended to shake the industry out of its complacency, assuming that shock therapy now would be better than waiting for major disruption later. Philips' in-house projections served as a starting point for the "Bridges in Light" initiative at the Lighting Research Center (LRC) to foster an industry-wide perspective. These scenarios were later used by a major trade group, the National Electrical Manufacturers Association (NEMA), to launch an education effort along with a broad marketing program to help the industry adapt to LED. One positive outcome was that LED technology became part of its standards setting around 2005.

How Philips Responded

The impact of LEDs depended on several factors beyond the technology itself, such as changes in customers' buying behavior and needs, emerging regulations, and the overall focus on energy efficiency. CEO Gerard Kleisterlee set up a separate LED business unit in 2005 to break away from the established industry rules. He placed the unit in the U.S., as the LED market was most advanced there and sufficiently removed from headquarters in the Netherlands. This new unit entered into unusual partnerships from 2005 to 2010, teaming up with players from adjacent industries, traditional OEMs, and even a few competitors.

Some early marquee projects undertaken by Philips, such as lighting up the Saks Fifth Avenue building façade for the holidays in 2005, required partnering with a small upstart LED company that did not have sufficient resources to scale its innovation. Building on the success of these forays, the new business unit embarked on bolder projects, such as converting the lights in the New Year's Eve ball in Times Square from halogen bulbs to LEDs. This headline-grabbing initiative at the end of 2008 likewise required collaborating with another small, innovative design-and-technology company to create the desired lighting effects using LEDs. It was a smashing success, covered the world over, and gave LEDs even more prominence.

However, this striking success move by the LED unit dismayed some traditional lighting advocates within Philips who wondered "why help accelerate a disruptive technology that may put us out of business?" Fortunately, Philips' overall organizational culture continued to offer a supportive context by launching deeper inquiries and fostering constructive doubt. Even though many traditional lighting managers were skeptical, and the lighting industry remained hesitant, a few senior executives devised internal avenues to explore LEDs further.

To acquire the necessary manufacturing capabilities, Philips entered into several joint ventures (JVs), starting with Lumileds, which is co-owned with Agilent Technologies. Philips then acquired the remaining 47% of Lumileds from Agilent in August 2005. These and other technology investments benefited from Philips' well-known brand and broad channel access to markets globally. The new LED business unit allowed Philips to forge ahead of the industry even though the internal process of debate to resolve conflicting priorities was often laborious and bureaucratic. Indeed, the board had to throw its weight behind the new internal LED group at times to fight uphill battles against powerful traditional business units within Philips that favored investments in conventional technology.

Scenarios for LED

Around 2005, Philip's leaders became especially interested in two key uncertainties whose outcomes could significantly shape their future business environment. The first uncertainty was about how quickly the shift away from conventional lighting—where Philips was strong—could happen. The second uncertainty selected was the market's adoption rate of integrated digital solutions for existing or new applications.[13] LED technology would likely enable genuine lighting innovations due to its small size, long life, low voltage, and wide temperature range. This meant it could be embedded in all kinds of materials or applications, such as lighting urban landmarks, enhancing medical applications, or enabling military technologies.

In the most challenging scenarios envisioned by Philips, hardware controls for lighting—such as fixed switches on walls—gave way to digital controls operated from anywhere. Lighting controls would be transformed into software applications offering features far exceeding traditional hardware controls. Architects, designers, and interior decorators would gain market clout once new versatile digital controls reached attractive price points for consumers. This switch toward intelligent, integrated lighting solutions could use very little of the old analog systems, and it would amount to a brave new world for many traditional players.

The End Game

By 2013, LED-related sales accounted for around one-third of Philips Lighting's total, having risen by 75%. This growth put Philips in the lead LED position compared with traditional rivals. But Philips' leaders also realized that LED would profoundly disrupt the old lighting industry and decimate the long-standing oligopoly. The low gross margins of LEDs, due to cheap manufacturers in China and a shrinking light bulb replacement business, made it an unattractive business for Philips, a company accustomed to high margins. It saw the bleak future sooner than its main rivals thanks to early probe-and-learn strategies followed by disciplined strategic scenario analyses. All this required strong support from the CEO and board, starting with forming a stand-alone LED unit and then shielding it from legacy business units determined to protect turf. Leadership vigilance is ultimately what allowed Philips to see the gathering LED clouds sooner than GE and Osram, which gave it a longer time window to divest its traditional lighting assets.

The strategic question for Philips became how best to exit, and when, before the other two major players would do likewise. Philips started to explore the sale of its lighting business in 2014, which resulted in a two-part divestiture in 2017 while keeping a minority stake in a new company called Signify.[14] This company continued to market the Philips brand for some time, while the Philips itself shifted its focus further toward the consumer health and medical systems world. GE took notice and started to unload its lighting business as well, in the face of steadily dropping profits. Osram followed suit in part but decided to stay in some key market segments, such as automotive LED lighting. In short, the powerful lighting oligopoly has largely folded its cards after many decades of being on top.

Playing the end game well when markets quake deeply, due to digital disruption, regulatory changes, or other exogenous factors, remains a key leadership challenge for many firms. Social media companies, like Facebook and Google, are still struggling with new privacy regulations and nefarious players hijacking their platforms. Remaining vigilant requires heeding the lessons from those who failed to see ahead, such as Kodak, Wells Fargo, Nokia, or Boeing, while also developing internal capabilities to let the company see around corners and act on early warning signals in a timely manner.

3.5 AVOIDING SURPRISES

—With George Day and Kirsten Sandberg*

Why are some companies surprised less often and better able to manage the unexpected? Most leaders can usually handle small surprises such as the bankruptcy of a minor supplier by just winging it. But big surprises, such as regulatory trouble, a big new competitor a shift in consumer behavior, or a new technology, require a more systematic approach.

---

* Marketing Professor at Wharton; Writer, Editor & Consultant in New York *city*

Survey the Landscape

Start by examining your past surprises (both the threats and missed opportunities) since each will tell a different story about where your organization can improve. Each surprise has a silver lining in the form of new lessons about what you missed and why.

Ask whether the issue mushroomed inside your company or outside your walls. External surprises—such as the health of the economy or emerging technologies—typically involve numerous moving parts and may be especially complex to grasp fully for a single company. But many other eyes, including journalists and academics—are likely tracking these as well. Take advantage of their research.

Internal surprises, on the other hand, are ones you really need to be on top of yourself. These may include festering scandals or missed innovations. Although closer at hand, these issues may be obscured by wishful thinking, turf battles, political maneuvering, myopia, or rationalization.

The intriguing part of surprises is that somebody in your company probably knew about them but failed to tell you. Most surprises foreshadow themselves through weak signals. The issue is not a lack of information; it's the people who miss tripwires they should have noticed. Below are four different strategies for preventing surprises better.

Finding the Threats and Opportunities

1. *Sniff out the rotten apples (internal threats).* From internal trading scandals like Libor, phone hacking by London tabloids, sexual misconduct, or outright fraud, there are usually many warning signals before something goes surprisingly wrong. When retail giant Target got hacked, and millions of consumer records were stolen, the retailer actually had an extensive cyber security system in place. But this system had cried wolf so often that IT personnel didn't spot the massive theft until weeks after the fact. To defuse such ticking time bombs, leaders need to develop deep and wide communication channels across the company and foster an internal culture of high integrity. There will always be malware, but those surrounding it can help surface internal dangers. For this strategy to work, leaders need to *syndicate the risks*—that is, give more people a stake in detecting and fixing any dry rot that might undermine the company.

2. *Canvass the neighborhood (external threats).* Studies show that most companies get hit by about three major external shocks every five years. Mattel's Barbie doll got a black eye when an edgy doll named Bratz sneaked up and took a third of the market share. Blackberry, IBM, and Nokia were badly blindsided by Apple and Samsung in mobile phones. Although you can't see all external surprises early you can scan the periphery and amplify weak signals. The warning signs may be right under your nose. Someone in your own company probably knows about a threat but doesn't realize its importance or feels uncomfortable sharing the information. To detect early warning signals, leaders need great curiosity. Ask many questions and develop wide and diverse external networks. *Collect all the rumors* and paranoia that blow around and separate the signal from the noise.

3. *Look for treasure in your attic (internal opportunities).* Most companies house a wealth of new ideas that never make it into plans and budgets. When leaders conduct internal innovation tournaments, they are often surprised by the many ways to improve their organization, products, and services or their strategy. Successful bottom-up innovations include 3M's famous *Post-it* notes, faster luggage off-loading in London for British Airways, and even Viagra. To tap into rich but dormant veins of creativity, leaders must be open to suggestions from below, incentivize teams to take appropriate risks, encourage fast and cheap learning, and create cultures where well-intentioned mistakes are celebrated, not punished. Don't let your suggestion box turn into a black hole where bright ideas go in, but nothing useful ever comes out. Be an idea-driven organization that values fresh thinking inside the company. *Energize your employees* and emphasize that not all insight or wisdom resides at the top.

4. *Walk in your customer's shoes (external opportunities).* Often, companies miss opportunities right in their own backyard. Entrepreneurs like Richard Branson or Elon Musk see sooner and farther because they think outside in. They explore the outside world as P&G does through its "connect and develop" strategy, where employees search for new product ideas beyond P&G's core markets. The majority of P&G's innovations now come from external sources. Open innovation is a welcome antidote to the prevailing "not invented here" syndrome. To see the world through your customers' eyes, staple yourself to a purchase order. Follow it throughout your company to experience what the customer experiences. Practice what anthropologists do so well: *observe without filters* or prejudice and let the data speak.

Know Where Your Strengths and Weakness Lie

To get better at seeing around corners, list examples of when your company anticipated threats and opportunities—and when it missed them. Look for examples in each of the four areas from your own company. These will show you where your vigilance is strong and where you are vulnerable. Once you've identified these strengths and addressed your weaknesses, create mechanisms to leverage your vigilance in other parts of the company or through your extended network of partners. Although you won't prevent all problems or catch every opportunity, you should be able to increase your vigilance and reduce unwelcome surprises.

END NOTES

1 Huston, Larry, and Nabil Sakkab. "Connect and develop." *Harvard Business Review* 84.3 (2006): 58–66.

2 Calvo, Jorge. *Journey of the Future Enterprise: How to Compete in the Age of Moonshot Leadership and Exponential Organizations*. Libros de Cabecera, 2020.

3 Govindarajan, Vijay, and Jim Euchner. "Reverse innovation." *Research-Technology Management* 55.6 (2012): 13–17.

4 Maxwell, John C. *Failing Forward: Turning Mistakes into Stepping Stones for Success.* HarperCollins Leadership, 2007.

5 Schoemaker, Paul J., and Robert E. Gunther. "The wisdom of deliberate mistakes." *Harvard Business Review* 84.6 (2006): 108–115.

6 Jack Welch quote: You talk about seeing around corners as an element of […] (azquotes.com)

7 Welchman, Jennifer. "Frankenfood, or, Fear and Loathing at the Grocery Store." *Journal of Philosophical Research* 32. Supplement (2007): 141–150.

8 Only the Paranoid Survive: How to Exploit the Crisis Points That Challenge Every Company: Grove, Andrew S.: 9780385483827: Amazon.com: Books.

9 Red Team: How to Succeed By Thinking Like the Enemy – Kindle edition by Zenko, Micah. Politics & Social Sciences Kindle eBooks @ Amazon.com.

10 Ackoff, Russell Lincoln. *Re-creating the Corporation: A Design of Organizations for the 21st Century*. Oxford University Press, 1999.

11 Schoemaker, Paul J. H. "Managing systemic industry risk: The need for collective leadership." Chapter 9 In Howard Kunreuther, Robert J. Meyer and Erwann O. Michal-Kerjan (eds.) The Future of Risk Management. University of Pennsylvania Press, 2019, pp 149–170.

12 For further details, see chapter 5 in Day, George S., and Paul J. H. Schoemaker. See *Sooner, Act Faster: How Vigilant Leaders Thrive in an Era of Digital Turbulence.* MIT Press, 2019.

13 Schoemaker, Paul J. H., George S. Day and Govi Rao. "Converting strategic ambiguity to competitive advantage: How Philips Lighting solved the challenge of LED technology disruption." *Strategy and Leadership.* 48.2 (2020): 10–17.

14 The parent company Philips reduced its ownership in Philips Lighting by $600 million via a stock share sale. *Reuters.*

CHAPTER 4

MANAGING TALENT

"We're looking for someone with the wisdom of a 50-year-old, the experience of a 40-year-old, the energy of a 30-year-old, and the pay scale of a 20-year-old."

FROM *HARVARD BUSINESS REVIEW*, MAY 2012. CARTOON BY RANDY GLASBERGEN.   © HBR.ORG

4.1 SIX WAYS TO ATTRACT AND KEEP TOP TALENT

—With Thomas Johnston*

Even if you have a brilliant strategy and the best laid-out plans, it does not mean a thing if you don't have the right team to deliver the goods. Your company is in a war for talent, and in that war, just about everyone is your enemy. When Bill Gates was asked a few years ago who Microsoft's main competitors were for top employees, he replied McKinsey and Goldman Sachs. These days, he would likely add Google and any of the scores of promising startups.

In other words, great employees have many choices, even in today's economy, and they aren't just limited to your industry. To attract top-flight intellects, you need to build a persuasive case as to why your opportunity is not just the best of your competitors but the best of all potential employers, including the one he or she works for now. How do you do that?

- *First, get your team aligned.* Start with some deep self-examination about what your company truly needs, and make sure everyone on the team agrees. A major turnoff for top job candidates is to hear the job profile described differently by different employees involved in the search.
- *Make a good first impression.* When the ideal candidate walks through your front door, what does he or she see? Have you created an appealing place to spend 50–60 hours a week? What does the work environment tell the candidate about you and your company? A bad first impression makes it very hard to entice a strong candidate to your payroll.
- *Draft Why Docs.* The main (and usually the most important) question every candidate will be thinking is Why? Why should I join you, and why do you want me? Everyone in the process needs to be able to answer both questions. They should all be able to explain why the move to your firm will indeed be in the candidate's best interest.
- *Remember it's not all about you.* Avoid the temptation to spend all your time selling the candidate on how great your company is without first understanding what really matters to the candidate. Learn that first, and then build the WhyDoc to address your candidate's desires.

---

* CEO of SearchPath, an executive search firm.

- *Get out and hunt.* When there is a critical need to fill, take the initiative and call key people whom you respect. Ask them for the names of top performers they know or have worked with. And don't stop with your circle of contacts. Have your whole team generate a slate of candidates.
- *Stay flexible.* The more you can offer, the more likely you are to win the heart of your candidate. It is never just about money. Top candidates want growth, development, opportunity, recognition, and lifestyle. They want to feel passion, but they often want balance as well. No one wants to put in 75-hour weeks and then get "the look" when they want to leave early on a Friday to coach their child's soccer team.

You cannot win the war for talent by being passive. Involve everyone in the process, and remember that top performers always have choices. You will win only if the role at your company fulfils their desires—and it is a big win for them, too.

4.2 TO HIRE WELL, THROW AWAY THE JOB DESCRIPTION

The traditional way to hire is to decide what Mr. or Ms. Right looks like for the various positions you feel you need to fill and then find the closest match. There may be a better way if you are willing to make some mistakes up to a point.

In my book *Brilliant Mistakes*,[1] I chronicled scores of missteps and supposedly doomed experiments by the likes of the Wright Brothers, Albert Einstein, Steve Jobs, and J.K. Rowling—all of which led to great breakthroughs. But "brilliant mistakes" aren't limited to iPods, science, and flying machines. They can also be useful in the curious mating ritual known as hiring new staff. The basic challenge in hiring, as in dating, is to find a suitable match efficiently in an ocean of possibilities. It's all about knowing what you want—right?

Well, only up to a point.

Whether they care to admit it or not, hiring managers, like most people, suffer from tunnel vision, unconscious prejudices, and a far narrower range of experience than they realize. Thinking they know what they want, they shut themselves off to innovative possibilities. For that reason, a smart approach to hiring would be to sample widely beyond your usual selection criteria.

Maria Dahvana Headley, a 20-year-old NYU drama student, took this notion to the extreme in the dating game. After too many fruitless forays into New York's night scene, she decided to try a bold and outrageous experiment. She resolved to say "yes" to any man who asked her out on a date (except convicted felons).

Her memoir, *The Year of Yes*,[2] describes how this policy led to dates with her building's maintenance head, a homeless man, a Microsoft millionaire who still lived with his mother and a career woman. She finally accepted a date with a playwright, divorced, many years her senior with kids, whom she fell in love with and married. She never would have given him a second glance before this experiment.

This is a great example of a brilliant mistake. Surely, dating at random sounds like an idea doomed to failure, but setting a narrow filter is perhaps even more so. Her approach is the opposite of searching with strong preset criteria: in evolutionary terms, she pursued a strategy equivalent to random mutation.

By permitting many mistakes in dating, Headley created more variance and was able to learn faster about what she truly wanted in a partner. What Headley realized is that our typical way of experimenting—developing a preconceived idea of Mr. or Ms. Right and finding someone to fit the part—does not always lead to the best decisions. Making more mistakes, as Headley did in her "year of yes," can really speed the process of learning.

Although few companies would embrace hiring anyone who applied, many have benefited from expanding their approach beyond the ordinary. A former CEO of Philips in Holland would take senior prospects on challenging hunting trips to see how they managed adversity. Nordstrom hires salespeople from a wide spectrum and then quickly separates the wheat from the chaff. Mark Fidelo, the creative director of Young & Rubicam, took a risk hiring Festus Mbuimwe from Kenya who responded to a job opening he was clearly underqualified for. But Fidelo liked the draft advertisement Mbuimwe submitted and hired him for a five-month internship. Mbuimwe, now an editor at a Nairobi-based website, brought a perspective that Young & Rubicam could never have obtained from the standard candidate.

So, how might you do likewise?

1. Go ahead and set some selection criteria, but don't let them become a straightjacket.
2. Occasionally interview someone who doesn't fit your criteria and perhaps hire one or two.
3. Experiment intelligently: limit the downside risk while giving the upside a chance.

Do you have the nerve to try searching beyond your narrow filters? It takes smart mistakes to survive in the business jungle, especially if your strategy is all about innovation. My contrarian advice is to induce variance in your hiring process rather than reduce it. Do that, and evolution will be on your side. Good luck.

4.3 ARE YOU SABOTAGING YOUR OWN HIRING PROCESS?

—With J. Edward Russo*

Hiring new employees is a multi-stage process. First, you have to find promising candidates. Then, you have to screen them, conduct interviews, perform due diligence, negotiate terms, etc. But a long hiring process can create potential stumbling blocks for smart managers, particularly when information about potential candidates trickles in piece by piece.

Research at Cornell[3] and other universities has shown that, in situations like this, people tend to form opinions early on based on partial information. It may just be based on a phone call, suggestions from colleagues, a friendly tip, or just a short bio. Then, as new information comes in, people tend to unknowingly play up new data in support of their initial leaning while at the same time downplaying new information that runs against that tentative view.

How Sticky Leanings Happen

Here is a simple illustration of how this information distortion can affect hiring decisions. Let's say you've narrowed the field down to just two candidates: A and B. You have a natural leaning toward one of them. You then receive additional information: A has 10 years of experience with related products, and B has five years with a competitor in the same product category. The way this new information affects your opinion of A and B should be the same, whether you had been leaning toward one or the other.

But this is not the case in real life. If you happened to be leaning toward A, you will tend to interpret the new information as more favorable to A than to B (and vice versa for those who lean toward B). The people who like A say things like "experience really matters," while the B supporters conclude from the same new information that "B understands our rivals and their products better." This common interpretation bias happens unconsciously: The people involved truly think they are interpreting new information objectively.

This bias sets in the moment a personal leaning has been formed, and it is hard to shake this, even when presented with clear unambiguous information to the contrary. The effect is quite strong, ranging from a 10%

---

* Professor of Management, Cornell University.

to 40% distortion on average, whenever new evidence is presented. The exact magnitude depends on the specific circumstances, but the effect has been demonstrated in numerous studies with sales reps, jurors, physicians, accountants—and entrepreneurs.[4]

Luckily, there are a few steps you can take to reduce this bias in your hiring process so that new information will speak more fully for itself, with less filtering.

How to Become Less Sticky

1. *Reserve judgment.* Don't look at information about prospective hires piece by piece. Wait until the file is more complete, and then decide whether to set up an interview. The fewer interim judgments you have to make, the smaller the chance of distorting the new information to support your leaning.

2. *Don't compare people.* Try to evaluate each candidate in isolation from others. Ask how well A or B would fit your job opening without comparing them to each other. Focusing on the job fit prevents you from leaning toward one candidate or the other and frees you up mentally to look at new information more objectively.

3. *Document the pros and cons.* Throughout the hiring process or any important decision, for that matter, force yourself and everyone else involved to document their reasons for or against a particular candidate. Also, emphasize as a leader that new information should sometimes change people's minds.

4. *Pick out the worst candidate.* Instead of focusing on the best candidate, start by eliminating the worst of the lot. The contrast between good and bad will focus on both the positive and negative attributes of each and at the same time instill a critical mindset conducive to challenging your own thinking.

5. *Groups can help (but sometimes hurt).* Working in groups can eliminate the bias entirely if there are differences of opinion in the group about whether Candidate A or B looks better so far.[5] But be warned: Once everyone in the group deems one candidate superior, the stickiness bias gets magnified greatly. If it is hard to get a group together, asking just one well-informed, strong person to play devil's advocate will help.

4.4 CONDUCTING A GOOD PERFORMANCE REVIEW

—With Josh Klayman[*]

An article in *The New York Times* described Amazon as a company determined to tell employees clearly and directly where they stand, but also a company whose approach to performance feedback is brutal and intimidating.[6] We can't assess the company's methodology here, but Amazon would be far from unique in having difficulty getting performance feedback right. Many companies just aren't very good at this, which is too bad because it can hurt both the company and the employee. After all, the purpose of the often-dreaded performance review is to help people get better at their current job or the next one.

So, it seems logical to first present the facts about an employee's recent performance and then to discuss why some aspects were strong and others might need improvement. But research by management psychologists in the U.S. and Australia shows that such discussions seldom foster a shared view between the employee and supervisor.[7] Rather, they usually result in defensive behaviors, disagreement about the causes of excellent or poor performance, and bad feelings that actually undermine improvement. There are several explanations for this unfortunate and all too common result, which effective leaders manage to circumvent.

1. *Attribution Bias.* When we evaluate others, good or bad, we tend to attribute their performance to enduring personal traits such as ability, personality, motivation, etc. When we evaluate ourselves, however, we blame bad performance on unfortunate circumstances—time constraints, lack of resources, ambiguity about goals, poor guidance, or those idiot co-workers. In contrast, when results are good, we flip the explanation and credit our effort, our smarts, and overall competence. Of course, your employees will do the same. Such self-serving attributions are ubiquitous and often unconscious whenever there is causal ambiguity. They can also be strategic, however, which explains why success has many fathers and failure is an orphan.

2. *Ambiguous Signals.* Facts need to be put on the table, but they seldom are. Different people enter the meeting with their own facts, values, experiences, and explanations. The best approach is to put each

---

* Professor of Behavioral Science, University of Chicago.

other's presumed facts on the table before trying to reach a shared understanding of what happened and why. But people may tiptoe around sensitive issues, share just some of the relevant information, or suppress their true feelings in order to preserve harmony, at least temporarily.

3. Managers may mistakenly try to improve the tone by emphasizing the credit they give for the subordinate's success and by going easy on blame for failure or by being deliberately ambiguous in their attributions. These strategies only interfere with learning and fall apart when the manager gets the impression that the subordinate just isn't getting the message.

4. *Strategic Behavior.* Self-serving excuses for sub-standard performance are to be expected. Employees want to keep their jobs, get raises, and eventually be promoted. Consequently, they'll have a selective memory when it comes to factual information they share with the boss as well what explanations they offer or refute. Likewise, bosses may not freely share all relevant facts and promote explanations that are just as self-serving. If some of the poor performance is truly due to factors beyond the employee's control, bosses may not wish to admit this to cover their own hides. Such strategic posturing often exacerbates disagreements about causes, contributing to bad feelings and a loss of trust—to the detriment of younger talent and the organization at large.

5. Given the above biases and distortions, it is better not to diagnose the many causes underlying good or bad performance too extensively. The difficulty of untangling the multiple causes of performance is confounded by the noise in the channel: competing agendas, deep psychological biases relating to self-serving attributions, memory distortions, and defensive rationalizations. So, it is often unwise to delve deeply. As the song says, Let It Go. Especially in cases of bad performance, it's important to avoid the blame game. Instead, zero in on why the results don't measure up (being as fact-based as possible) and then move on to what's going to be needed to improve the situation.

6. *Focus on the Future.* Rather than debate the past, focus your limited time and energy on engaging the employee in finding creative solutions to overcome important problems. This will expand the employee's view of what can be accomplished, generate positive feelings of agreement, and build motivation for the employee to perform at a higher level. Once trust is restored, the employee may be more open to coaching

and more willing to ask for he_p. Both managers and employees may then be able to avoid the kind of defensive routines and strategic distortions that so often reduce performance reviews to uninformative or even divisive rituals.

4.5 HOW SEASONED LEADERS REDIRECT ATTENTION

Hiring smart people is great but you may need to provide them guidance about where to focus. Managers often solve the wrong problem due to lack of information, or may focus on the left when the threat or opportunity is coming from the right. Seeing around corners is hard in business as well as in our personal lives. We all have limited mental resources and therefore need to block out signals deemed irrelevant at times

Teaching people how and where to pay attention may sound odd, but it's fundamental to success. We often don't do it well and one key is to stay away from attention sinkholes. As Nobel laureate Herbert Simon forewarned that "a wealth of information creates a paucity of attention."[8]

The Psychology of Attention

Attention research examines what people notice as well as what they filter out in terms of seeing, hearing, feeling, smelling, and tasting. If a few random digits are fed into your left ear and different ones into your right at the same time, which side will get more attention (in terms of your recall later)?

Deliberate as well as automated processes are involved in attention. We can surely decide at a cocktail party whom to speak to or not. But when shown an object and asked to describe its shape, we cannot ignore its color because this is instantly processed by our minds. When asked not to think about an elephant, for example, it is already too late to banish this image from your brain.

Attention involves a complex interplay between sensing and interpreting; what we see is often determined by what we expect to see. When people are asked to remember five playing cards that are briefly shown to them, most will fail to notice that some had the wrong color, such as a red spade or a black heart. We can be so focused on a single task that we fail to recognize things in the periphery.[9]

In a widely seen short video, people are asked to count how often a basketball is passed among various players. Then a person dressed in a gorilla outfit slowly walks through the basketball play and less than half notice it.

Northwestern professor William Ocasio defines organization attention as the socially structured pattern of focus by decision makers within the organization.[10] Unlike individual attention, it is not easy to turn the head of an organization in a different direction. As Thomas Davenport and John Beck noted in *The Attention Economy*,[11] "Before you can manage attention, you need to understand how depleted this resource is for organizations and individuals."

What Leaders Can Do to Manage Attention

1. Use available digital technologies to measure where organizational attention is high and low.
For example, by analyzing work-related emails in a firm, suitably anonymized, leaders can track what issues are trending. Such text analytic approaches are widely used to assess consumer sentiments in the travel industry or for early detection of shifts in the appeal of political candidates. Sentiment analysis software can handle massive amounts, from everything published in the popular media about a person to emails, intranets, or other corporate communications formats. One downside is that many may view this as overly Big Brother.

2. Recognize that prior knowledge shapes and constrains the creation of new knowledge inside a firm.
New information can only create value if it connects with existing know-how, akin to a new drug needing to bind with cell receptors to work. If not, it will be in one ear and out the other. The richer a firm's existing knowledge base is around a topic, the finer will be its sieve for catching new information.

If leaders feel that more attention should be paid to customer service, regulatory compliance, or some promising new technology, they need to train people in those domains. This will enhance the firm's absorptive capacity in those areas and draw organizational attention there.

As Louis Pasteur noted, chance favors the prepared mind, and various techniques—such as scenario planning, scanning exercises, and war gaming—can help prepare the corporate mind to get lucky or smarter.

3. Know that although focused attention is crucial in comprehending new information, too much of it can backfire.
Focusing intently on one area comes at the price of highly reduced peripheral vision about things happening elsewhere. To avoid walking around with blinders, or running through red lights, leaders must create slack to explore beyond the firm's narrow fields of vision.

One way is to encourage curicsity about interesting topics seemingly removed from present concerns. Another is to create task forces that counter the prevailing focus areas of the organization, such a red team tasked with challenging whether a new strategy is really working or a special scouting trek to explore a potentially disruptive technology that most others are ignoring.

4. Encourage managers to develop a third ear or eye, which is all about noticing hidden cues or soft signals that matter.

When meeting with customers or external partners, also pay attention to what is not being said and learn how to read between the lines. The brilliant fictional detective Sherlock Holmes did that when, examining the murder of a horse trainer, he asked a local constable about the curious incident of the dog not barking. Holmes deduced from this missing clue that the dog knew the murderer.

A more disastrous example of not spotting missing data occurred when NASA examined a data chart of previous shuttle flights the night before the scheduled launch of the Challenger shuttle in 1986.[12] The concern was that low temperatures could cause O-rings to fail, but the chart showed no correlation between past O-ring damage and ambient temperature. However, the chart did not include flights with zero O-ring damage, and including those would have clearly established a link. NASA proceeded with the launch, and a few minutes later the shuttle exploded midair, killing all aboard.

END NOTES

1 Schoemaker, Paul JH. *Brilliant mistakes. Finding success on the far side of failure.* University of Pennsylvania Press, 2011.

2 Headley, Maria Dahvana. *The Year of Yes.* New York: Hyperion, 2007.

3 Russo, J. Edward. "The predecisional distortion of information." In Evan A. Wilhelms and Valerie F. Reyna (eds.), *Neuroeconomics, Judgment, and Decision Making.* New York, NY: Psychology Press, 2014, 91–110.

4 Russo, J. Edward, Kurt A. Carlson, and Margaret G. Meloy. "Choosing an inferior alternative." *Psychological Science* 17.10 (2006): 899–904.

5 Boyle, Peter J., Dennis Hanlon, and J. Edward Russo. "The value of task conflict to group decisions." *Journal of Behavioral Decision Making* 25.3 (2012): 217–227.

6 https://www.nytimes.com/2015/08/16/technology/inside-amazon-wrestling-big-ideas-in-a-bruising-workplace.html?_r=0.

7 Humanly Possible, Inc.

8 Herbert A. Simon "Designing Organizations for an Information-Rich World." In Martin Greenberger (ed.), *Computers, Communications, and the Public Interest.* Johns Hopkin Press, 1971, 37–52.

9 Schoemaker, Paul J. H., "Attention and foresight in organizations." *Futures & Foresight Science* 1 (2018): 1–12.

10 Ocasio, William. "Attention to attention." *Organization science* 22.5 (2011): 1286–1296.
11 Davenport, Thomas H. and John C. Beck. *The Attention Economy: Understanding the New Currency of Business.* Harvard Business Review Press, 2001.
12 Starbuck, William H., and Frances J. Milliken. "Challenger: Fine-tuning the odds until something breaks." *Journal of Management Studies* 25.4 (1988): 319–340; Vaughan, Diane. *The Challenger Launch Decision: Risky Technology, Culture, and Deviance at NASA.* University of Chicago Press, 1997.

CHAPTER 5

NAVIGATING UNCERTAINTY

"Good heavens! What if they've come seeking market share?"

FROM *HARVARD BUSINESS REVIEW*, OCTOBER 2014. CARTOON BY PATRICK HARDIN. © HBR.ORG

5.1 SEVEN WAYS TO APPLY SCENARIO PLANNING

—With Arjen van den Berg*

Whenever you face high uncertainty, you need to be creative as you navigate uncharted waters. But you also need a prepared mind. This is where scenario planning can really help.[1] As explained step-by-step in Chapter 2, you need to identify your top external uncertainties and then weave these into three or four plausible stories about how the future might unfold in different directions.

This essay focuses on what to do with your scenarios once you have developed some good ones. But let's first make sure your scenarios are indeed relevant by answering the following questions:

- Does your current strategy implicitly or explicitly "bet" on the occurrence of just one of the various scenarios you developed?
- Would you change your strategy if you knew for sure that another scenario was in fact going to happen (as opposed to the one assumed)?
- Do the scenarios challenge some commonly held assumptions in your company or industry; do they stimulate deep dialog?
- Do your scenarios surface new risks that you need to protect against more fully or new opportunities that thus far were overlooked?
- Do the scenarios point you toward important early warning signals that you need to monitor so that you can see around the corner?

The more you said yes to the above five questions, the better your scenarios are. So, suppose you got at least three yes answers, how do you now connect the scenarios with upcoming decisions or perhaps your overall strategy and business vision? Based on numerous scenario projects we did with clients around the world, they can serve the following important purposes.[2]

1.Stress-testing your strategy
Many organizations use scenario planning to test the robustness of their current strategic plans against a wide range of alternative scenarios. It is the equivalent of putting an airplane wing in a wind tunnel to see at what point it fails as pressure builds up. Stress testing helps companies minimize potential negative consequences and be better positioned to seize opportunities.

2. Platform for innovation
Companies on the move often use scenario analysis to expand their geographic footprint, explore adjacent markets, invest in new technologies,

---

* Managing Partner, London Office, Decision Strategies International.

explore new partnerships, or reach beyond their industry boundaries. Because multiple scenarios force them to consider a wider range of futures, they may see many new opportunities on the horizon as well as looming clouds perhaps.

3. Go deep

Don't think of scenario planning as just a corporate activity conducted by futurists and staff people. Savvy organizations translate the scenarios across multiple organizational levels to connect better with those managing functional and business strategies. For example, how will the scenarios impact talent management, IT requirements, financial (budgeting) processes, or legal requirements?

4. Monitoring key uncertainties

Organizations in fast-moving markets often use scenarios to monitor early warning signals in the external environment. This lets them see sooner than rivals which way the wind will be blowing. Effective monitoring requires systematically scanning leading indicators and the ability to link key signals to tactical or strategic adjustments of your plans.[3]

5. Rebalancing your options portfolio

Smart organizations have developed a portfolio of projects that can be adjusted whenever the tide turns. They follow a stage-gate process that starts with small investments that are later scaled up or dropped as needed. As with your personal investment asset allocation, you may need to rebalance your options portfolio in business whenever the world changes for you.

6. Creating organizational agility

Agility requires that your strategic intent is flexibly combined with a portfolio of actions that will make your strategy happen. Some initiatives in this portfolio will prove robust across scenarios; others will be highly scenario dependent and therefore fragile. For the fragile ones, you need to be vigilant in monitoring key uncertainties and then acting on key signals in a timely way. This requires adaptive leadership as well as a good strategic radar.[4]

7. Stakeholder management

Once the key elements of scenario-based thinking are in place, an agile organization will use various tools to manage its key stakeholders strategically. This means sharing your views, discussing trade-offs, and building support for key strategic initiatives. Also, use your scenarios to explain your strategic choices and build support inside your company and well beyond.

5.2 WHY DEEP DOWN WE DON'T LIKE UNCERTAINTY

Uncertainty is that unwelcome, unsettling feeling we experience when we don't know what the future may bring. It can range from small scale—like being unsure when dinner guests will arrive while preparing their meal—to something much greater.

And there was no larger-scale uncertainty recently than COVID-19, which has laid bare our anxieties, trepidations, and lack of caution. In early 2020, most of us suffered from fear and willful blindness; by mid-year, we were on knife's edge, either cowering or throwing caution to the wind; and then later on, we felt exuberant about miracle vaccines. Not everyone experienced quite this sequence, and some people may want to crawl under a rock again if nasty new COVID-variants or other pandemics emerge.

But why do we handle uncertainty so poorly? Behavioral research suggests that nearly all of us desire some control over our lives,[5] and uncertainty is an unpleasant reminder that we often can't. Many events we just cannot control—from the weather, other people's behaviors, and perhaps our own emotions.

The need for control is only one side of the story, however, since humans also have a deeply rooted need or desire for variety and surprise. Life would be pretty boring if we could predict or control everything. That's why we embark on adventures and explore unknown terrains. Or why Las Vegas exists. But few would consider COVID-19 a welcome diversion or interesting episode unless perhaps they are research scientists.

To sort out our conflicting emotions, it helps to understand the different kinds of uncertainty, from financial and social to physical and moral. Our risk tolerances likely differ among these domains. Some people are willing to risk life and limb for fun, like a conservative accountant enjoying the thrill of bungee jumping. Each of us needs to find the right balance by taking less risk in some areas and more elsewhere.[6]

When COVID-19 was thrust upon us, most people countered it by reducing risk-taking elsewhere. Once the pandemic subsided in the U.S., we embraced more risk again, socially and otherwise. As we continue to rebalance our risk portfolios, try to keep the following pitfalls in mind.

Our Risk Perceptions are Biased

Researchers studying risk perception asked people to rate the risks, from low to high, of a broad cross section of activities, such as skiing, driving a car, living near a nuclear power plant or being exposed to X-rays at the dentist. The researchers then contrasted laypeople's responses with those of experts in those domains.[7] Where the experts focused primarily on the statistical profile of any given risk, laypeople were unduly influenced by:

- Whether they could control the risk (yes for cars and no for airplanes),
- how much they knew about the risk (soccer injuries vs. radon exposure),
- whether the risk strikes people in clusters (earthquake vs. losing a wallet),
- a risk's societal image or dread (catching Ebola vs. tripping in a shower).

Vivid risks—such as shark attacks or explosions—leave a strong imprint and are typically feared disproportionately to their actual probability of occurring. The car trip to the ocean is usually riskier than swimming in it, even where occasional shark attacks do happen, such as in coastal Florida. Another mental factor is how readily we can imagine plausible pathways to a catastrophic outcome. It is much easier to imagine your airplane falling from the sky (due to engine failure or pilot error) than to envision getting stomach cancer or being accidentally electrocuted at home.[8]

COVID-19 is a risk over which we have some control through how we behave, and we learn more about it every day, even though the new variants remain scary. The disease can occur in clusters (like retirement homes) but also strikes randomly. As more knowledge was gained, societal dread declined in the U.S. and Europe although not in all quarters due to lockdown protests, antivaxxers, QAnon, and other social media charlatans. Also, the shifting advice of public health officials, reflecting the changing nature of the virus and its prevalence, has heightened some people's fear of the virus. Clearly, risk is not just about statistical numbers but also about feelings and indeed politics.[9]

Flawed Choices Involving Risk

In addition to distorting the estimates of probabilities and consequences, research shows that people are often inconsistent when making choices involving risk, even if the probabilities and consequences are properly assessed. Here are four major biases[10]:

First, we tend to be risk averse for risks involving gains but less so when it comes to losses. For example, most of us would prefer $100 for sure over flipping a coin to receive either $200 or nothing. But when given the mirror image choice on the loss side, many would opt to flip the coin (risking losing $200 or nothing) rather than accept a sure loss of $100. In general, humans tend to be risk averse for gains but may double down to avoid sure loss, which suggests rather inconsistent risk attitudes.

Second, we tend to factor probabilities into our choices in distorted ways by overweighting low probabilities and underweighting high ones. Consider this inconsistent set of choices: Most of us prefer a guaranteed $100 over an 80% chance of getting $120 and 20% of getting nothing. But when both these choices are reduced equally by a factor of four in likelihood, people will switch preferences. They will opt for a 20% chance at $120 over a 25% chance at $100, which is a flip-flop of the previous choices. If you like an apple better than a pear, you should also like a small chance of getting an apple over an equally small chance of getting a pear.

Third, people often treat any given risk in isolation from other uncertainties they face and thus fail to adopt a portfolio perspective. Flipping a coin once may seem risky. But flipping it many times will reduce the risk due to the law of large numbers. With many flips, the possible payoffs will start to resemble that famous bell-shaped curve of statistics, known as the Normal or Gaussian distribution. For example, flipping a weighted coin that offers you a 60% chance of winning $100 and a 40% chance of losing $100 just one time may be unattractive. But flipping that weighted coin a hundred times likely is attractive since it offers you a $2,000 net gain on average with just a small chance (less than 3%) of having lost money after those hundred flips.

Fourth, people tend to prefer known risks over ambiguous ones, even if these cases are statistically identical. Suppose you can draw a ball from an urn containing 50 red balls and 50 white ones versus an urn in which the ratio of red to white balls is unknown to you. Suppose, further, that you get $100 if you draw a red ball blindfolded—which urn would you rather pick one ball out of? Most people favor the first urn even though the second one, with an unknown ratio of red to white, will on average—in the absence of any further information—also offer a 50% of drawing red. Indeed, people will not even prefer the unknown urn if they are allowed to choose which color to bet on! This illustrates our innate aversion to ambiguity, which can be detrimental when choosing between jobs, investments, or life experiences.[11]

5.3 KNOW WHAT YOUR CUSTOMERS WANT FIRST

—With Steve Krupp[*]

The number one worry we hear from our clients today is this: "I need to understand my customer better, but it's getting harder, not easier." Why is

---

[*] Managing Partner and CEO of Decision Strategies International.

this particular uncertainty so foremost on many entrepreneurial minds? Let us count the ways:

- Customers are less loyal and far less trusting than they used to be. This is especially true in industries whose reputations suffered during the financial crisis—including banking, pharmaceuticals, energy, airlines, and media. But even if you're in an unrelated industry, you're likely to feel some of the same effect.
- Consumers have more power than ever before, thanks to social media, comparison shopping online, and a proliferation of choices plus advice.
- Customer diversity continues to increase, putting a premium on micro-segmentation and deep customer insight.
- By increasing the noise-to-data ratio, the data deluge occasioned by the Internet can actually make it harder to understand your customers.
- Economic uncertainty and data overload confuse customers as well, making them less interested in products than in flexible, adaptive solutions.

To get close to this more demanding client, you really need to get inside his or her head. Here are five ways to do that[12]:

- *Stand in your customer's shoes.* Look beyond your core business and understand your customer's full range of choices, as well as his or her ecosystem of suppliers, partners, etc.—of which you may be part. This exercise will also deepen your understanding of competitors and help you better anticipate their moves.
- *Staple yourself to a customer's order.* Track key customers' experiences as they traverse your company's pathways and note where the experience breaks down. Some hospitals ask interns to experience the check-in process as fake patients. One client asked managers to listen in on its call center. If you can't exactly put yourself through a customer experience, try role-playing exercises at all points of the customer's experience with your company.
- *Field diverse customer teams.* One bank added members of the back-office support group to its customer team, supplementing the usual customer-facing roles. IBM sends senior teams from different disciplines into the field to meet customers and develop a deep understanding of how to serve them better.

- *Learn together with customers.* GE invited its top customers in China, along with local executives and account managers, to a seminar on leadership and innovation. Doing so not only helped GE executives better understand the mindset of Chinese counterparts; it also helped them to influence that mindset.
- *Lean forward and anticipate.* Focus on what customers will want tomorrow, as Steve Jobs and Richard Branson did so exquisitely. Try to envision different futures through tools like scenario planning and then explore how underlying market shifts may affect your customers.

Remember that sometimes you need to get out of your own way to really understand your customers. Psychologists know, for example, that you're likely to listen for problems that fit your own offerings and to discount others. That bias alone can cause you to miss important opportunities or to get blindsided later.

So, try to listen with a third ear, as an anthropologist would, to what your customers are saying to you and also to what is not said. If you can truly hear them, they'll tell you all you need to know.

5.4 THINK YOUR THINKING IS SOUND? TAKE THIS TEST

Our increasingly uncertain world places a great premium on critical thinking, which is about asking the right questions, challenging assumptions, seeing more angles, and being aware of thinking biases. For instance, put yourself in the shoes of NATO leaders as they ponder continued Russian attacks on Ukraine or the continuing turmoil in the Middle East. Closer to home, should supply-chain managers rethink their adherence to just-in-time inventory in view of protracted supply gridlocks during COVID? And did you consider high U.S. inflation in 2023 to be transitory—linked to fiscal stimuli and COVID-related economic dislocations—or something more structural and lasting?

That's a lot to ponder. So, to sharpen your critical thinking skills about uncertain issues, here are seven test questions. My answers and explanations follow.

1. A mother reads a scientific study that 17-year-old boys in the U.S. have fewer automobile accidents per 1,000 trips than 16-year-old boys. This prompts her to wait a year before letting her just 16-year-old son drive to make him safer. Is her reasoning correct?
2. Earlier U.S. Census studies have found that the number of annual divorces filed equals about half the number of new marriages registered

each year. These findings have been the basis for the commonly claimed fact that about half of all new marriages will end in divorce. Is this inference correct?

3. You play a game of tennis against a slightly better opponent and decide to put some money on the match. You are both equally fit in terms of stamina and physical endurance. Are your chances of winning the match the same whether you play just one set or the best out of three?

4. You attended a large conference where one of the European speakers had an accent that sounded more Swedish than German to you. But you were not quite sure, so you make a bet with your friend about whether the speaker is from Germany or Sweden. Assume the accent is all you have to go by, since you don't recall the speaker's name nor any other biographical information. Which nationality do you bet on and why?

5. You are playing golf and reach an interesting par-three hole where the tee is 10 feet higher than the green below, which happens to be completely flat. There is no wind, fog, or rain. How should you play it: Hit the shot as if the green is level with the tee area? Or try to identify all the factors that could affect the shot's eventual length due to the 10-foot difference in elevation. You may recall from physics that a ball or bullet will follow a parabolic trajectory if there is no air friction.

6. Several studies about the benefit of bicycle helmets have shown that fewer severe head injuries occur—for most falls or spills—if you are wearing a helmet. Does it follow therefore that making helmet use mandatory will further reduce head injuries in cycling?

7. During the early part of World War II, many English bombers were being shot down by the Germans. To reduce their high casualty rate, the Royal Air Force (RAF) decided to reinforce its bombers with armor. But where? Since metal was scarce, they had to be smart about which surface areas to strengthen. Their statistical analysis of the bullet holes in planes that returned revealed a very uneven pattern of locations where planes had been hit. Should the RAF reinforce its bombers where bullet holes were most numerous, evenly throughout the plane or elsewhere?

Answers:

1. We don't know if the driving improvement is due to 17-year-olds being more mature or due to them having an extra year of driving experience under their belts. If the latter, waiting a year won't help. Probably both effects operate, so waiting may be wise.

Lesson 1: Always consider multiple hypotheses when explaining a fact.

2. In a stable population with zero growth, the cross-sectional statistic on divorces filed in any one year may be a good estimate of the chance that any random marriage will end in divorce. But if the population is growing, or if values and marital expectations are changing, and if the ages or income levels at which people marry shift, then the cross-sectional data may be misleading about the longitudinal pattern of divorce.

Lesson 2: It is easy to lie with statistics; are you comparing apples and oranges?

3. The longer you play, the more the final result will conform to the law of averages. Since this favors the better tennis player, your chances decline if you play three sets. If you were to play Roger Federer, say, your best chance to beat him is to play just one point and hope he misses. And even that is a long shot; so just forget about playing any further than one point.

Lesson 3: Lay your bets according to the underlying statistics; consider base rates. The race may not always go to the strongest or fastest, but that is nonetheless the way to bet.

4. Since Germany is more than eight times larger than Sweden (84 million people versus 10 million), you should bet on Germany unless you are very sure about your impressions about the accent you heard or have good reasons why German speakers would be less common.

Lesson 4: Understand the law of averages and be sensitive to sample size: As an old proverb goes, one swallow does not bring in summer.

5. First, you should hit a golf shot that does not go as far as normal since the ball will travel longer in the air and thus farther. But other, mostly secondary, factors may also come into play due to the effect of the altitude difference. For example, the ball will hit the green at greater speed and thus will bounce up higher (especially if the green is cold and hard). Also, since the angle of impact on the green will be steeper, the horizontal length of subsequent bounces may be less. Finally, any backspin your swing may have produced will reduce how far the ball travels through the air. Even though most of the factors mentioned suggest that you should aim your ball less far horizontally, your optimal aim will depend on the size of these other factors, some of which are correlated.

Lesson 5: Multiple effects usually operate in complex cases; try to consider all.

6. Over the decades, helmet use has increased in the U.S. but head injuries did not decline as much as expected. Possible explanations include: improved bikes make riders go faster; wearing a helmet creates a false sense of security and more risk-taking on the road; riders wear their

helmets incorrectly (too much forehead exposed); the type of people riding bikes may have shifted; and traffic and road conditions may have changed. Experts especially blame the false sense of security that helmets give to bikers and car drivers. For example, cars will pass closer when bikers wear helmets than when they don't.[13] Behavioral changes often lessen the benefits of safety actions, as has been seen with seat belt laws, insurance, diet advice, anti-smoking remedies, and COVID-19 vaccinations. Humans may suffer from unconscious risk-homeostasis, as captured in the adage that the sum of sins tends to remain constant.

Lesson 6: Look for unintended consequences that may undermine your initial goal.

7. The initial thinking was to reinforce the areas with the most bullet holes. But when the RAF asked esteemed statistician Abraham Wald to examine the surviving bombers for damage patterns, he came to a different conclusion.[14] Wald reasoned that the surviving planes had not been damaged fatally by the random bullets and thus suggested reinforcing in places showing the fewest bullet holes. These were the most vulnerable, he argued since few bombers apparently survived those bullet shots. The RAF followed his counterintuitive advice and improved the survival rate of its bombers and crews.

Lesson 7: Ask what data you aren't seeing and why. There could be a selection bias, in this case known as a survivorship bias.

5.5 WHAT YOU DON'T KNOW COULD KILL YOUR COMPANY

"We never saw it coming." That could be the epitaph of many companies that have faded into history: Studebaker, Sears, Shearson Lehman, AltaVista. But why couldn't they see the dangers lurking in the not-too-distant future? And it is not just companies that get blindsided but governments, NGOs and non-profits alike. Consider the legions who were unprepared for COVID-19 or Russia's invasion of Ukraine, and the ensuing supply chain crises, inflation and further splintering of existing world orders.

Organizations benefit disproportionately if they see looming threats or embryonic opportunities sooner than rivals. To do so, however, requires leadership teams that orchestrate *vigilance* at all levels of the enterprise. Many management consultants justly emphasize the growing need for agility, mindfulness, resilience, and vigilance. However, few address how to achieve this in practice—even though that is where the rubber hits the road. When I was interviewed about what vigilance is and how you develop it, here are some of the Q&As that followed.

Q1: What are some telling external and internal surprises you have studied?

External surprises related to digital disruption really tripped up Kodak, Nokia, Blackberry, and many other IT firms. Likewise, many executives were unprepared for the serious supply disruptions that followed the COVID-19 outbreak in 2022, from Peloton's exercise bikes to most automakers.[15] Facebook is another example of being unprepared when nefarious actors abused its platform, followed by media and PR storms.

Notable *internal* surprises that made it to the front pages occurred at Theranos, Volkswagen, and Wells Fargo—with layers of fraud detected far too late. We also saw notorious cases of high-profile CEOs abusing their power for years, like Harvey Weinstein at Miramax and Roger Ailes at Fox News, further fueling the "me too" movement. Keep in mind that the leadership skills needed to avoid internal surprises, like safety violations, may be quite different from those required to see external ones, such as regulatory changes.

It's useful as well to distinguish between threats and opportunities since these also entail different competencies. Leaders who are good at seeing the promises of new distribution channels, emerging technologies, or ecosystem enhancements will not excel, necessarily at handling threats related to abuse of power, discrimination, fraud, espionage, kickbacks, cyber risks, rogue operators, or any other problem festering inside the firm.

Still, there are some traits that generalize across most cases, such as being curious, open-minded, listening to weak signals, and showing courage when pursuing potentially unwelcome news.[16]

Q2: Why are leaders often last to know about negative surprises?

The root problem here is "distributed intelligence" where one part of the system doesn't know what another side knows, which is why systematic "knowledge management" is so important. But then, organizations may run into the problem of information overload as the Nobel-winning economist and political scientist Hebert Simon noted when he said that "a wealth of information creates a paucity of attention."

There is also the problem that bad news doesn't always travel well—especially upward. Who in Russia's top echelon is going to tell President Vladimir Putin upfront that his military strategy is deeply flawed or that his sense of history is slanted and self-serving? Not me, comrade.

Great leaders are able to surface weak signals, such as rumors of a pending merger or new legislation gaining traction. Weak signals can easily be overlooked or dismissed as white noise. To interpret them properly usually requires finding more dots and connecting them. This is why vigilant leaders must tap into informal channels as well, from water cooler conversations to what people talk about in grapevines outside the company.

More controversial methods exist as well for this, such as codifying all e-communications (anonymized for privacy as needed) and then use AI-based text analysis to mine for subtle shifts in organizational attention and sentiments. The paradoxical bottom line here is that any big thing that surprises an organization typically has multiple precursors; nearly always, there were weak signals, and some people were in the know. Surprises seldom come out of the blue, although early warning signals typically first appear at the edges of the business. That is why leaders need to scan the periphery and look around corners for faint stirrings.

Q3: What factors set vigilant organizations apart from others?

The issue is not just seeing sooner but also acting faster on that information while still keeping your options open. Vigilant organizations have to be self-learning enterprises that build a collective vigilance capability and mindset buttressed by curiosity, candor, and interest in diverse inputs. This also requires a cultural willingness to challenge superficial assumptions and outdated conventional wisdom. Vigilant leadership teams invest in tools and training so that managers will act faster when the time is right. Leaders who fail to foster such vigilance are typically late in comprehending early warning signals and are often forced to react in haste. By then, they will have lost valuable degrees of freedom to maneuver and are at risk of choosing from inferior options.

Our own research surfaced the following drives as most crucial for organizational vigilance.[17]

Leadership commitment to vigilance, demonstrated by an openness to weak signals from diverse sources, while also encouraging others in the organization to explore issues beyond their immediate domain and think outside the box.

Investments in foresight are often made through centralized units for scanning and using strategic dashboards to monitor plausible future scenarios. It also includes training managers and staff about the multiple methods available in the foresight literature.[18]

Strategy-making processes have to be flexible and agile by adopting "outside-in" thinking and "future-back" analyses. Outside-in thinking starts with understanding how the outside world is changing rather than focusing on the current plan. Future-back thinking asks what it takes to win long term and how to plant sufficient seeds ahead of time to succeed.

Coordination and accountability when interpreting weak signals is key as well, supported by an organizational norm of sharing information readily across silos. This last driver is what it takes for the other three drivers to flourish.

Q4: Do vigilant organizations actually outperform their rivals?

A longitudinal study of 85 European multinationals in 2008 by Rohrbeck and Kum[19] assessed the "future preparedness" of each using a detailed organizational survey. The researchers then waited seven years to assess each firm's gain in market capitalization and profit. For the 36% of firms judged to be highly vigilant in 2008, the average gain in stock price was 75% in 2015— nearly double the stock gains of the more vulnerable firms. These vigilant firms were also 33% more profitable in 2015 than the others. There is further corroborating evidence, using other outcome-based field research, that building vigilance indeed pays off with the right investments, attitudes, and tools.[20]

It is crucial that leaders are committed to fostering a culture in which weak signals are spotted early, shared quickly, and acted upon in a timely manner. To understand this culturally, we studied Mastercard's remarkable transformation under CEO Ajay Banga.[21] First, he encouraged overly comfortable managers to take thoughtful risks and develop the courage to decide with imperfect information. Second, he fueled constructive paranoia to avoid being blindsided by rivals. Third, he emphasized the need to develop a more global view reaching well beyond current boundaries. To help change Mastercard's culture, he promoted mavericks, developed new partnerships, explored underserved segments (such as people preferring cash over credit cards), and invested in better understanding the next generation of consumers (especially adolescents and children).

It worked, raising Mastercard's game significantly against its main rival, Visa. Vigilant leaders are change agents who empower managers and teams to become the eyes and ears of the organization. They also train people in the gentle art of *reperceiving* their business, from products and services to customers and partners, in search of joint gains. And finally, they empower these teams to pursue new opportunities beyond the confines of traditional procedures, routines, and mindsets. In a word, they excel at *revitalizing* their organization so that managers will be ready and able to navigate future turbulence.

END NOTES

1 Schoemaker, Paul J. H. "Scenario planning: A tool for strategic thinking." *Sloan Management Review* 36.2, Winter (1995): 25–40.

2 Schoemaker, Paul J. H., *Profiting from Uncertainty: Strategies for Succeeding No Matter What the Future Brings.* Free Press, July 2002.

3 Schoemaker, Paul J. H., George S. Day and Scott A. Snyder, "Integrating organizational networks, weak signals, strategic radars and scenario planning." *Technological Forecasting & Social Change* 83 (2013): 815–824.

4 Alessandro Di Fiore, "Planning doesn't have to be the enemy of agile." *Harvard Business Review*, September, 2018.

5 Langer, Ellen J. "The illusion of control." *Journal of Personality and Social Psychology* 32.2 (1975): 311.

6 Schoemaker, Paul J. H., "Determinants of risk-taking: Behavioral and economic views." *Journal of Risk and Uncertainty* 6 (1993): 49–73.

7 Slovic, Paul, Baruch Fischhoff, and Sarah Lichtenstein. "Rating the risks: The structure of expert and lay perceptions." *Risk in the Technological Society*. Routledge, (2019).pp 131–156.

8 Tversky, Amos, and Daniel Kahneman. "Judgment under Uncertainty: Heuristics and Biases." *Science* 185.4157 (1974): 1124–1131.

9 Slovic, Paul. "Risk perception and risk analysis in a hyperpartisan and virtuously violent world." *Risk Analysis* 40.S1 (2020): 2231–2239.

10 Tversky, Amos, and Daniel Kahneman. "The framing of decisions and the psychology of choice." *Science* 211.4481 (1981): 453–458.

11 Kovářík, Jaromír, Dan Levin, and Tao Wang. "Ellsberg paradox: Ambiguity and complexity aversions compared." *Journal of Risk and Uncertainty* 52 (2016): 47–64.

12 Day, George S. *Innovation Prowess. Leadership Strategies for Accelerating Growth*. University of Pennsylvania Press. 2013.

13 G. J. S. Wilde, "Critical issues in risk homeostatis theory," *Risk Analysis* 2.4 (1982): 249–258.

14 Mangel, Marc, and Francisco J. Samaniego, "Abraham Wald's work on aircraft survivability." *Journal of the American Statistical Association* 89.386 (1984). pp 259–267.

15 Phadnis, Shardul S. and Paul J. H. Schoemaker, "Visibility isn't enough – supply chains also need vigilance." *Management and Business Review* Vol 2.2,(2022) pp 49–59.

16 Day, George S. and Paul J. H. Schoemaker, "How Vigilant Companies Gain an Edge in Turbulent Times." *MIT Sloan Management Review*, Winter 2020.

17 Schoemaker, Paul J. H, and George S. Day. "Determinants of organizational vigilance: Leadership, foresight, and adaptation in three sectors." *Futures & Foresight Science* 2.1 (2020): e24.

18 Schwarz, Jan Oliver. *Strategic Foresight: An Introductory Guide to Practice*. Routledge, 2023.

19 Rohrbeck, René, and Menes Etingue Kum. "Corporate foresight and its impact on firm performance: A longitudinal analysis." *Technological Forecasting and social change* 129 (2018): 105–116.

20 Schoemaker, Paul JH, and George Day. "Preparing organizations for greater turbulence." *California Management Review* 63.4 (2021): 66–88.

21 Andrew Shipilov, "How Does Digital Transformation Happen? The Mastercard Case," INSEAD (Case Center 318-0049-1, 2018); "MasterCard's Ajay Banga: Why 'Yes If' Is More Powerful Than Saying No", *Knowledge@Wharton* (July 24, 2014).

PART II: INNOVATION, FAILURE, AND LEARNING

CHAPTER 6

IMPROVING INNOVATION

"Diane, please keep it professional. This is no time for selfies."

6.1 WHY FAILURE IS THE FOUNDATION OF INNOVATION

Honda's founder, Sochiro Honda, said it well: "Success is 99% failure." Many winning products have their origin in failure. This included classics such as McDonald's Hula Burger (1962), Apple's Lisa (1983), Coca-Cola's New Coke (1985), or Corning's DNA Microarray (1998) and many others.

Mistakes allow for variation far beyond what was expected—you make a wrong turn but find a better road to your destination. Thanks to mistakes, we now have such medical innovations as penicillin, smallpox vaccine, pacemakers, Viagra, and many others, all well documented in the book *Happy Accidents*.[1] It argues that half the advances in medicine had an accidental origin.

This is why it's so crucial for companies to foster a culture that celebrates productive mistakes, the kind that can stimulate thoughts and generate new paths. If leaders do not allow for some failure, they also kill innovation. But as my own book *Brilliant Mistakes* emphasizes,[2] to get those productive failures, you need to tolerate some silly and even stupid ones as well in your mistake portfolio. As with stocks, if you want to get a few big returns, you need to be willing to accept losses as well.

The Truth About Failure

James Joyce noted poetically that "mistakes are our portals of discovery." They stimulate us to look beyond our narrow cocoon and encourage lateral thinking. They invite a fuller exploration of the periphery, that vast domain outside our area of focus where treasure may be hidden. Thomas J. Watson, Sr., who founded IBM, understood this deeply when he said: "So, go ahead and make mistakes. Make all you can because that's where you will find success: on the far side of failure."

But these great examples are the exception to the rule. Research shows that most people and organizations are not very good at accepting failure or loss. Most would like to eliminate errors altogether from their lives since losses loom much larger than gains psychologically.[3] This is why most managers pray at the altar of success rather than innovation and its periodic losses.

Think about it: Do you promote your employees on the basis of results or their process, even if the outcome isn't so good? One very successful options trading company, the Susquehanna International Group, evaluates its traders not on how much money they made for the company each month but on how sharp their reasoning was going into the various trades they made.[4]

Successful companies know how to strike the right balance between performance and learning cultures. A key obstacle to overcome is our deeply ingrained aversion to failure. Your psyche just registers pain more strongly than loss. So, we need to work on reframing failure, perhaps as "time-released" success. View it as the bitter medicine that we need for innovation, then take a few gulps, and see if over time the benefits outweigh the costs.

Different Ways of Handling Failure

So, honestly, what is your typical attitude toward mistakes? I have listed five mutually exclusive responses below. Select the one that comes closest to how you actually feel and behave when confronted with setbacks or failures. If you doubt your ability to be honest about this sensitive matter, just ask others which answer below most closely describes how you typically behave.

1. I hate mistakes, hide them quickly, learn little from them, and will likely repeat the same error again in the future.
2. If I can't hide the mistake, I do try to analyze what happened and whom to blame; so, some learning occurs, but it is mostly finger pointing and ego protection.
3. I generally welcome well-intentioned mistakes in myself and others; I strongly feel we should give recognition awards at work to people who failed for the right reasons.
4. I rank long-term learning higher than short-term results and fully accept that embracing mistakes is part of the package; I try to celebrate insights gleaned from errors.
5. I have actually made mistakes on purpose at times, by trying things that went against my best judgment, just to see if my thinking was perhaps flawed in this case.

The higher the number you circled, the better you are in dealing with failure in a positive way. To provide some benchmark data from a survey we conducted at Wharton Executive Education, people's choices were distributed as follows: 3%, 32%, 42%, 22%, and 1%. Most people (74%) circled answers near or below the middle of the scale, namely 2 or 3. Clearly, many managers still have some ways to go, with few having reached the highest plateau of making mistakes on purpose to learn something really new.

6.2 HOW TO UNLEASH CREATIVITY—POLL THE CROWD

—With George Day*

Want to tap into real business growth through innovation? Ask not what you can do for your company but what your company can do for its customers. Keeping your focus trained on what is going on beyond your company's borders could mean the difference between just chugging along to steaming past the competition.

High-growth companies (and those that want to be) are best served when taking an external, or "outside-in," view to running their business. Here are four broad benefits of looking outward:

Anticipation. Outside-in thinking naturally asks questions about how the outside world is changing and unleashes creative thinking about the implications. The payoff comes from seeing opportunities and threats sooner. You will be less vulnerable to surprise attacks by competitors, and new products will be more successful. The early mover invariably has an edge over the reactive responses of later entrants that have fewer degrees of freedom.

Adaptation. When everyone in the company is attuned to the customer experience and its pain points, there is more likely to be a wide-ranging and ongoing search for pain relief. Are deliveries either too early or too late for the customer? Are customer service reps watching the clock and leaving callers frustrated? Examining this carefully is the essence of continuous improvement, or Kaizen approaches, and, as Toyota showed, this is a powerful way to grow.

Alignment. When outside-in thinking is embedded in the organization, there are fewer turf battles and more collaboration; resources are used more productively. Customers applaud because they benefit from clear accountability for their welfare. They aren't left in limbo while navigating among your silos. Everyone in your company shares the same information, so you can readily identify the most valuable customers to nurture and retain, all of which help you grow.

Alliances. The more your organization is focused outside, the more opportunities you will spot to partner with suppliers, large customers, and even rivals (in the spirit of 'coopetition'). To do well in a highly networked world, you need to co-create with partners and jointly shape an ecosystem in which all of you can grow. If your partners do well, so will you, and vice versa.

---

* Professor of Marketing, The Wharton School.

The benefits from anticipation, adaptation, alignment, and alliances are hard to realize fully in practice. They can easily be subverted by complacency ("we have mastered the recipe for success") and short-run performance pressures that put inside-out thinking in control. It takes vigilant market-driven leaders to keep making the case that your customer's interest be put first and next the well-being of your strategic partners. None of that will happen unless your organization really starts to think outside in.

6.3 STAYING AHEAD OF CUSTOMERS

—With Steve Krupp and Vivek Kumar[*]

As an entrepreneur, you strive to develop deep, lasting, and meaningful relationships with your customers. But in a fast-changing marketplace, this is no easy task. Market forces beyond your control can change the landscape drastically. Just consider how Google has seriously impact the healthcare field and Tesla, the automotive industries, or the way social media has changed how companies engage with customers. No company is immune to the risks and disruption inherent in a world of VUCA (one that's volatile, uncertain, complex, and ambiguous).

Successful companies combat these forces by shifting their strategy from just providing a product or service toward offering total solutions. If done well, this shift can help you build deeper customer relationships that increase their lifetime value for your company and might help you withstand the gale winds of creative destruction better.

Here are four techniques that will allow you to stay ahead of the curve.

1. *Scan wider.* Look at your marketplace through an external lens, from the outside in. Instead of focusing internally on levers you can control, such as investments and initiatives, start by examining the major external forces of change in your industry. This broader view will help you spot signals of change sooner so you can get a fresh angle on serving your customer even better. News articles, industry publications, and even customer interviews are rich troves of external clues about impending change, especially if you incorporate them into your strategic planning.[5]

---

[*] CEO and Senior Consultant respectively at Decision Strategies International.

2. *Map your customer ecosystem.* Don't just gather information through your own interactions with customers. Create a map of all potential connections that exist in your ecosystem. As you develop this map, make sure you include your customers' suppliers and their customers, industry regulators, political influencers, and other key stakeholders you may not have direct interactions with today. Creating this map enables you to see the broader picture of potential drivers changing your customers' businesses beyond what your current limited, narrow view would allow.

3. *Identify top customer business drivers.* With external market forces identified and your customer ecosystem mapped out, focus on determining those business drivers that have the highest impact on your customers. Is it operational efficiency, expanding product lines, or better marketing that is critical to your customers' success? Expanding the conversation beyond your own products or services (and showing genuine interest in your customers' businesses) will result in deeper relationships.

4. *Collaborate with your customers.* Once you have started a strategic dialog, you can then shift the focus toward co-creating win–win solutions. Even if you are not currently providing products or services in new growth areas, this is how you get your customers' attention. For example, if operational efficiency or innovation are becoming critical customer success factors, discuss changing what you offer them and how. By exploring and investing in areas of mutual interest, you will signal how serious you are about your customers' future success.

It may not be easy to shift traditional mindsets and embrace the four approaches sketched above. But once you prove that you can help your customer beyond the tried and true, your company will reap many benefits as well.

6.4 WANT TO ACE YOUR START-UP? MASTER THE FIVE MS
—With Charles Robins[*]

Most technology start-ups fail. Yet the prospect of doom hardly discourages entrepreneurs because the rewards are disproportionately great for those who do succeed. What sets the winners apart? They score well on the five key Ms: Market,

---

[*] Managing Director, Fairmount Partners, Conshohocken, PA.

Model, Moat, Management, and Momentum. Although your original business plan may change over time, it is still an important starting point to attract talent, capital, partners, and customers, which collectively provide a platform for growth, change, and scale. Here is what investors, employees, business partners, and board members look for in deciding whether to back a new venture.

Market: Assessing the size of your opportunity is critical, even though many entrepreneurs give this short shrift. They simply base their plans on top-down statistics and then hope to get X% of the overall market segment. When Dirt Devil introduced a new-generation, high-powered handheld vacuum cleaner in 1984, it was the first of its kind.[6] But if the company had positioned Dirt Devil to take even a small share of the broader vacuum market, it would have been met with much skepticism. Instead, it created a new market segment: quick cleanup at home or in minivans. Consumers bought 23 million units in the first few years because the company pursued guerrilla tactics, such as selling through K-mart and Walmart. Dirt Devil carved out a niche "wedge" in a large, established global market, selling 100 million vacuums a year.

Once you have a clear, distinctive offering, try to set reasonable sale prices and growth targets. Typically, "your" market will start very small, given your unproven offering and your initial position as an aspiring pioneer. But your plan should still try to support more than $50 million of annual sales within five years. As a rule of thumb, your long-term "baseline" plan should assume not more than 10%–15% ownership of the overall target market, though an upside case could be higher, perhaps 30%. Seldom will a new firm conquer much more than that. Also, penetrating an existing market usually costs you a multiple of the revenue your share will generate.

Model: The all-important business model includes the assumptions underlying revenue estimates, plus your ability to meet demand and growth.[7] Investors may want to see the business model presented using three different cases: conservative, expected, and aggressive. These diverse scenarios will illustrate the full potential of the business around a credible "baseline" operating strategy. This multiple-scenario approach will also help set benchmarks for monitoring and adjusting the business.

Ideally, the model's projections should cover at least five years because investors typically evaluate their returns over that period. They may give you up to two years to build out the new venture, perhaps another year to reach profitability, and then they expect to see solid growth and profitability. This will allow them to calculate ROI metrics in, say, the fifth year as a basis for assessing the firm's value. Institutional investors will need this for their exit plan and to achieve their portfolio's target returns.

Moat: New businesses must also be able to play defense and create barriers to competition. First, you must build the case that you have indeed a "minimally viable product" (MVP) that is saleable. Ideally, the product has at least a two-year lead over any potential rivals offering a solution similar to yours. Your competitive edge can be a combination of invested R&D, domain expertise, intellectual property, team quality, partnerships, first-mover advantages, etc. To persuade skeptics, develop a clear picture of your current competition and what it might become in the future. If successful, "your" market will no longer be yours alone and quickly attract new entrants as it grows in size.

Start-ups sometimes fail to consider future market dynamics, including how they will sustain their initial lead as the market grows. Often, pioneers don't win the race because fast followers improve the offerings, leaving the original innovators behind with arrows on their backs. This happened to Friendster, Palm, Netscape, TiVo, and many others before.[8] Large competitors can take the wind out of a young company's sails by commoditizing or marginalizing their offering. Your moat should include a product roadmap that lays out how and where to invest in the future so that you can protect your competitive edge against imitators and disruptors. This roadmap should cover your internal innovations as well as acquisitions. The latter may call for extra funding as a key part of your business model.

Management: None of the above matters if you don't have the right people on board. It starts with committed managers who can execute day-to-day. Entrepreneurial drive, conviction, and ambition are all necessary ingredients when starting a new business. The personal motives of the management team also merit attention—they should entail much more than money. A focus on sales is especially important early on, with a strong leader clearly in charge of generating the revenue that helps keep the doors open. Attracting and retaining seasoned talent is also critical; they understand the learning curve of a new business.

The core team should be guided by people with vision, experience and strong connections, at senior levels. Flexibility is fundamental since new ventures may have to pivot their business model multiple times before becoming successful. This is where a strong board of directors is crucial to provide the experience, oversight, and governance needed to anticipate, recognize, and correct problems, as well as to keep many moving pieces, including strong personalities, in their proper balances. The board failed to do this when ousting Steve Jobs in 1985 from Apple in favor of John Sculley. Not surprisingly, Jobs fired almost the entire board after having been invited back as CEO in 1996, following a decade at Pixar and NeXT.[9]

Momentum: Strong margins, steady growth, and attractive operating leverage—flow down to the bottom line—are your goals. Investors, partners, and employees love a business where profits grow much faster than revenues as the business scales. The key here is demonstrating momentum since there can be a vast gulf between the theory of a business and its execution. Once your flywheel is in motion, it will power a conveyor belt of talent. Top people like to see their equity grow in value. Apart from sales increases, you can perhaps demonstrate momentum via other metrics, such as growth in your sales funnel, retention, and customer satisfaction.

Sustainable growth requires money since few growth companies can rely on internally generated cash alone. Additional funding can come from multiple sources, such as friends and family (angel investors) or venture capital firms (VCs), whose sieve is usually very fine. A VC may review 1,000 business plans each year and invest in just five. Whatever your funding sources, remember that all key players involved will likely use the 5Ms to assess their level of interest in your venture as well as its market value.

6.5 VIGILANCE: A STRATEGIC WEAPON FOR ENTREPRENEURS

Kodak and digital cameras, Nokia and the smartphone, Sears and online retailing: the pages of business history are crowded with examples of companies that missed the boat. And you can expect more chapters to be written, considering the unprecedented levels of change and uncertainty today. It's become even harder to spot early warning signals, making vigilance an ever more critical leadership capability Are you truly vigilant? And just what does that take?

We researched this issue by comparing vigilant and vulnerable companies.[10] We wondered what is really the difference between say Charles Schwab, which was early to see and act on the promise of "robo-advisors," and Honeywell, which stumbled when Nest Labs debuted an internet-enabled thermostat? Or why did GM embrace autonomous cars before its traditional rivals?

We did not just want to understand why companies spotted or missed external opportunities but also why some leaders got blindsided by internal problems that festered for years. Why did Wells Fargo, Volkswagen, Facebook, or Boeing miss the trip wires or run through red lights that were flashing before scandals and disasters unfolded?

Whether it's a missed opportunity or threat, from either inside or outside the organization, the root cause is usually a lack of organizational *vigilance*. We all miss signals due to limited attention, competing priorities, and, often as well, a lack of curiosity. What manager has not said "My plate is full," then ignored a signal of a potential problem, and later regretted it? In our book *See Sooner—Act Faster*, co-authored with Wharton professor George Day, we identify the key skills and practices of vigilant organizations and leaders.[11]

Fostering Organizational Vigilance

Traditional methods of strategic planning, risk analysis, and decision modeling are less effective today due to increasing uncertainty. This may seem odd, given the growing information processing capabilities available. But there is just too much uncertainty at the periphery and too little stability at the core in most business segments.

To deal with this new reality, you need a new set of skill-building tools, including how to allocate the scarce resource of attention, detect weak signals and separate them from white noise, and respond strategically ahead of competitors. You can use the diagnostic survey at the end of our book to calibrate and benchmark current levels of vigilance in your organization. Then, follow the leadership agenda below to systematically build vigilance and agility throughout your organization.

The following key steps can help you spot early warning signs sooner in order to act faster.

1. Scope to Determine How Widely to Look
One way to set the scope is to assemble a diverse team of independent thinkers from both inside and outside the company. As one of our clients phrased it, "tap into the organization's paranoia." (Intel's late, great co-founder, Andrew Grove, titled one of his books *Only the Paranoid Survive*). Invite everyone to voice hunches, concerns, doubts, or intuitions that would otherwise remain dormant. The leadership team can then spotlight issues that seem negligible now but may emerge as big ones over the next few years. Adopting a three- to five-year time frame will allow leaders to peer farther ahead than rivals, especially when few clouds are visible on the horizon now.

2. Focus Organizational Attention Via Guiding Questions
Organize your questions into three categories: (a) learning from the past, (b) interrogating the present, and (c) anticipating the future. Ask your team, "Which rivals have a consistent record of seeing sooner and acting faster?" and "What is their secret?" Many companies interrogate the present by monitoring blogs, social media sites, and chat rooms for signs of brewing trouble with customers,

but they may not really see ahead. Truly vigilant organizations, in contrast, track market changes by studying "edge cases" that signal opportunities or threats—in engineering, the "edge" refers to cases that purposefully push the limits. Leaders should also develop different future scenarios that capture how today's major uncertainties might jointly play out in years to come.

3. Actively Scan to Explore More Deeply

Active scanning is built on the scientific method: you start with a set of hypotheses, which are then tested and revised further based on new data obtained. Active scanning is rooted in a deep sense of curiosity and exploration. Doing this type of scanning, however, demands that you encourage diverse—and even contradictory—inputs to ensure that all sides of a complex issue are surfaced. To stimulate scenario planning, for example, leaders should pose such questions about the future as "What surprises could really hurt us (or help us)?" and "What future disruptions may be as big as those that we experienced in recent decades?" This means the organization must learn how to think from the outside in rather than remaining captive by the status quo.

4. Decide Which Signals to Amplify and Clarify

Through active scanning, organizations frequently identify many more signals than they can possibly digest. So, leaders need to develop ways that highlight the most interesting weak stirrings. Canvasing the wisdom of crowds is one approach. Research has shown that groups are often better than individuals at making accurate judgments.[12] The reason is that individuals have at best partial information, which often allows diverse groups of people to be smarter than even the most informed in the team. A truly diverse crowd will reflect the varying experiences and views of numerous people, which thus helps cancel out random noise.

Each organization must craft its own approaches to becoming more vigilant. Google co-founder Larry Page, for example, challenged his teams to anticipate the future not just by asking what will likely be true but also what could possibly be true, even if totally unexpected. Such guiding questions are a productive way to launch a broad scoping dialogue; his question gives the team permission to challenge conventional thinking without negative repercussions.

General Electric's senior healthcare group created a task force to process a wide array of weak signals about new opportunities for healthcare in India. These signals foreshadowed several nonlinear shifts, including a shortage of doctors and hospital beds, growing unmet patient needs, and an underdeveloped health insurance industry. But the team also highlighted growing digital connectivity and other emerging opportunities in India for GE. Unfortunately, GE failed to foster such prescience in its power division, which contributed to its recent mega struggles.

Procter & Gamble pursued yet a different approach to stay abreast of external changes. The company offered select retired executives in Europe a part-time retainer so that they would periodically report on interesting developments in, for example, private label or branded products. For P&G, this is a natural part of its "connect and develop" approach to innovation, which is about reaching far beyond its traditional networks for new insights. This approach helped it, for example, launch a highly successful rotating toothbrush years ago, inspired by lollipops for children in India that used a tiny toy battery to rotate the stick in their mouths.[13]

These kinds of initiatives—and many others elsewhere—start with curious leaders asking penetrating questions beyond the usual drills and then empowering teams to explore them thoroughly. Over time, this will imbue vigilance into the fabric of your organization and hone its capacity to look around corners for new threats or opportunities.

END NOTES

1 Meyers, Morton A. *Happy Accidents: Serendipity in Major Medical Breakthroughs in the Twentieth Century.* Simon and Schuster, 2011.

2 Schoemaker, Paul J. H. *Brilliant Mistakes: Finding Success on the Far Side of Failure.* University of Pennsylvania Press, 2011.

3 Ariely, Dan, Joel Huber, and Klaus Wertenbroch. "When do losses loom larger than gains?." *Journal of Marketing Research* 42.2 (2005): 134–138.

4 Schoemaker, Paul J. H., and Philip E. Tetlock. "Superforecasting: How to upgrade your company's judgment." *Harvard Business Review* 94.5 (2016): 73–78.

5 Day, George S. and Schoemaker, Paul J. H., "Scanning the Periphery." *Harvard Business Review*, Nov. 2005, 135–148.

6 Seabrook, John. "How to make it." *The New Yorker* September 20 (2010): 66–73.

7 Zott, Christoph, and Raphael Amit. "Business model design: An activity system perspective." *Long Range Planning* 43.2–3 (2010): 216–226.

8 https://www.usatoday.com/story/money/2018/07/11/50-worst-product-flops-of-all-time/36734837/.

9 When Steve Jobs Got Fired By Apple – ABC News.

10 Schoemaker, Paul J. H., and George S. Day, "Determinants of Organizational Vigilance: Leadership, Foresight and Adaptation in Three Sectors." *Futures & Foresight Science* 2.1 (2019): 1–16.

11 Day, George S. and Schoemaker, Paul J. H., *See Sooner–Act Faster: How Vigilant Leaders Thrive in an Era of Digital Turbulence.* MIT Press, 2019, 186 pp.

12 Surowiecki J. 2005. The Wisdom of Crowds: Why the Many Are Smarter than the Few and How Collective Wisdom Shapes Business, Economies, Societies, and Nations. London: Little, Brown.

13 Sakkab, Nabil Y. "Connect & develop complements research & develop at P&G." *Research-Technology Management* 45.2 (2002): 38–45.

CHAPTER 7

MANAGING CUSTOMERS

"Of course they know you're a dog. Your shopping patterns give it away."

FROM *HARVARD BUSINESS REVIEW*, JUNE 2015. CARTOON BY CROWDEN SATZ.

© HBR.ORG

7.1 THE ECSTASY AND AGONY OF CUSTOMER SERVICE

Getting customers is an important goal—but keeping them matters more. Here are four key lessons from a recent experience I had with the cable company.

If you ever want a quick lesson in customer service, call the phone company which in my case was Comcast in the U.S. which handles phone, tv, and e-mail.

I just experienced the best and the worst customer service when trying to reactivate my Internet, phone, and cable TV service after an extended time away. I had called the company ahead to switch from vacation mode to full service, but when we arrived home again, there was no signal.

The ecstasy part started when a competent and friendly person named Ram showed up on Sunday morning. It took him an hour to string a new coaxial cable, and all three services got activated. Still, some TV boxes did not recognize the signal, so Ram made various office calls, rebooted the signals and bingo, it worked. He did not have to do this but went the extra mile.

Now for the agony: a third cable box, which records TV programs while we are watching others, was still having problems. Whenever I called customer service, I got rerouted to the wrong customer representative. The reason: I have both residential and business services from this company due to my home–office setup. Keeping this straight turned out to be a major challenge for the call center.

When I called the 800 number, I spoke first to residential representatives but then got kicked back to business representatives—creating a loop I could not break without a "warm handoff." After waiting 25 minutes, with many reassuring pre-recorded messages that my call was very important, I finally got through, then got dropped again, had to start over, reached wrong desk etc.

Here are four imperatives that any business owner can pull from this experience:

1. *Keep customers happy all the time.* My provider really excelled at getting a new line set up quickly but crushed the experience when it came to keeping me, an existing customer, happy. If you want to really delight customers, all systems need to integrate and focus on the customer experience rather than your internal needs and departments. Try to maintain a high-quality standard across the entire value chain so that ecstasy on one side is not ruined by agony somewhere else.

2. *Follow through all the way.* On the phone, each agent seemed narrowly focused and would quickly pass the problem on to someone else without staying on the line. They may be rewarded for how quickly they solve a customer problem or pass it on. This is how customers end up in infinite loops. American Express excels at tracking and following customers

across various channels, as do Macy's department stores. You can't hold customers responsible for follow up—this is your task since customers routinely drop or lose the ball.

3. *Know your customer intimately.* Cable and other service providers often suffer from amnesia once a customer is transferred internally. The whole information-gathering routine starts all over. Excellent customer service means having records at every touch point about your customer, including a retrievable footprint. Amazon and Target do this very well in mass retailing. Four Seasons does it well personally—they remember your room, food, and wine preferences.

4. *Put your executives on the front line.* Have executives call in from a regular customer number, with a normal set of issues, so they experience your service the way customers do. Ask execs to do a stint in the call center, stand behind the sales counter, or check-in guests at the front desk if you are a hotel. Don't just smell your own perfume, but reach out to customers as well. Try to staple yourself to a work order (figuratively) so you experience the entire customer buying process.

Above all, don't assume that your customers are a captive audience. Mobile technology and social media are making consumers very smart and nimble. Also, non-traditional competitors (like Apple, Google, and Amazon) will weaken your grip on customers through new technologies that will disrupt your business model.

For company leaders, this means peering into the future through scenario planning, segmenting your business from multiple angles, and running war-gaming exercises to stay ahead of rivals. The aim is not just to delight customers today but to build organizational capabilities to do so tomorrow as well, when a new generation of customers will be in the driver seat.[1]

7.2 HANDLING CUSTOMERS YOU RATHER NOT HAVE

—With Nicole Adam Kraus[*]

Sales are vital to any business, naturally. But sometimes, even paying customers can be too much trouble. A New York City McDonald's franchise once made headlines after employees attempted to shoo away customers who tend to camp

---

[*] Principal at Decision Strategies International.

out for hours on end. Zappos's female teenage customers are throwing "try new shoes" parties, where they order shoes online and then return them for free, thanks to the Web retailer's free returns policy.

Such examples merely scratch the surface of the difficulties small businesses face daily. You obviously want to please customers, but you also need to make a living—and at a time when the economy is still recovering from a major financial crisis, that's not easy.

Decades of reinforcing the message that the "customer is always right" haven't helped, either. A generation of consumers—now armed with social media—is trained to hunt for good deals and at times takes unfair advantage. Suddenly, a change in policy that is perceived by the masses as "anti-consumer" can ruin a company's reputation in minutes. (Remember when Netflix unbundled its mail and online business?)

Things get even trickier for McDonald's franchise owners, in large cities especially, who need to contend with a serious loitering challenge. This is a far greater dilemma, as it includes community, humanitarian, and business issues. Still, the heart of the issue is the same: Can you change your overall customer strategy and still keep a strong relationship with your good customers?

If you're considering changing your relationship with some or all of your customers, try the following:

1. *Define your core customers.* Who are your key, valuable customer segments today? What do they need, and how might that change in the future? This will help to influence both this and future customer-centric efforts.
2. *Understand the bad eggs.* What do some customers get very upset? How do their needs match or conflict with what you offer? Is there something you're doing to encourage their "bad" behavior?
3. *Assess the damage.* How much do the bad eggs cost your business today? What are the potential long-term business and brand implications if it continues? Are there any long-term benefits?
4. *Classify the problem.* Is the problem occasional or endemic? Is it within or outside the control of your business alone? How easy is it to change? What kind of damage might a change cause for your business? What is the upside? Resolving these questions will help you determine what measures to take.
5. *Plan and take action.* Depending on the above, your next steps may be minor or radical. Consider your stakeholders' reactions (customer, employee, broader community, media, etc.) when you decide to enact change. Run small pilots first, to test a variety of approaches, before launching a business-wide change.

Consumer relationships are more personal these days, and consumers feel they deserve a real voice in the corporate arena. Social media is their megaphone.[2] This isn't a bad thing. It just poses new challenges for businesses. When you're running a franchise business like McDonald's, changing the rules for visitors may entail working through major social, ethical, and business implications. McDonald's and other such establishments must consider the broader community and various support systems available to help local business owners thrive while staying sensitive to the needs of the patrons.

What happens if you don't address the issue? Having staff spend time and attention on the bad eggs means that you're neglecting the needs of those people who truly support your business. Unless you are a charity, "bad customers" can seriously drain your profitability and destroy your business in the long run. If you and other firms don't thrive, it means that many more other people will suffer as well.

7.3 BAD CUSTOMER SERVICE HAPPENS, BUT DON'T ACCEPT IT

Many organizations drop the ball when it comes to customer service. They need to reframe such instances as teaching moments and opportunities to build customer loyalty.

Want to create a customer for life? Make sure your customer service operation is always up to snuff and delights the customer as much as possible.[3] Sounds simple in theory, but here are five reasons companies routinely drop the ball on customer service:

1. *They focus too much on new business.* Most companies work much harder at getting new customers than keeping them, even though it costs about eight times more to acquire new customers. Once the fish is hooked, it goes into a different, less-valued bucket. Make sure that this second bucket gets loving care as well.

2. *They treat customer service as a cost center.* Different people work here, often overloaded, usually underpaid and understaffed. It is a natural target for cost-cutting. Each small reduction in service may not be noticed in itself, but three successive reductions may be noticed loud and clear by the customer. Whole Foods, in contrast, manages to make food shopping a very customer-centric experience despite additional costs, such as setting up bike racks and repair centers outside their stores for their cyclist customers.

3. *There are few incentives for reporting complaints.* It might make the customer reps or their managers look bad. So, often, the complaint department is moved to Siberia. Bad customer experiences are shared many more times with others than good experiences. But most people don't share anything at all. So, the reputational damage of bad service may be small to the firm, which may also explain why subsequent complaints might go unanswered. It is smarter, however, to solicit complaints and treat them as free market intelligence.[4] Try to turn every service error into a valuable teaching moment.

4. *They can get away with poor service.* In some markets, there may be just a few providers and less competition, so customers have limited options to switch. Further, customers may be locked in or face high switching costs, and their bad experiences may occur just intermittently. If all customers suffer equally, it may become the norm, as well as fun fodder (like the phone company) for late-night comedy. Consumers will often put up with substandard service amid limited options— but only until a new rival comes along who dramatically redefines service.

5. *Leaders just aren't focused on service.* In many companies, leaders are more focused on improving product features than service quality. In mature markets, however, product features become similar or just standard. The opportunity to shine is greater on the service side, especially because it is harder to assess, deliver, and imitate. But that's not how most higher-ups think. If only their incentives were tied to customer scorecards: service—and loyalty—will surely improve.

Score your own company in terms of how often each cause above contributes to bad customer service. With this profile in hand, approach customer service anew. Align incentives by putting the customer front and center in all your operations. Walk in his or her shoes and view the complaints as great sources of free information. Also, have senior execs listen in on call-center conversations every week to stay on top of emerging customer trends.

In the old days of Detroit, it was a capital sin to drive a foreign car—your tires would likely be slashed or worse. No General Motors employee would dare drive a Honda or Volkswagen to work (too bad, given that they would have learned a lot). Leaders should instead encourage employees to shop at all serious competitors, test their call centers, visit the websites, and then discuss the good, bad, and ugly compared with their own.

7.4 PUTTING RISK MANAGEMENT ON THE MENU

—With Joyce Schoemaker*

During the height of COVID-19, before vaccines existed, we dined at a fine restaurant on a covered terrace. Even though we were outside and the staff wore masks, several things struck us as less than ideal. First, there was essentially no social distancing between servers and patrons. Multiple, masked servers approached our table several times, within ten inches of our faces, to offer water, bread, butter, wine, and take our orders. It felt like business as usual in terms of visits to the table and the friendly small talk, which made us uncomfortable.

Although my area of expertise lies in advising large corporations on decision-making amid uncertainty, it occurred to us while dining out at the height of the COVID-19 pandemic that restaurants can greatly improve their risk management as well. They should learn from big business how to control risk better and from hospitals how to manage infection exposures. Here are some ideas for restaurants and guests to rethink their own risk management.

Having It Your Way

Deadly risk was on the menu during COVID's peak, along with the risotto. Restaurants should offer a risk management menu as well. For instance, a restaurant could offer diners three levels of service to more fully respect their risk tolerances. The first, full service, is what we did in the past. Many restaurants still seemed to consider this *de rigueur* when offering a complete dining experience. Restaurants could also offer a second level: partial service, which would permit contact with a table only when requested by a guest. The third level would entail no close contact at all. The staff would strictly maintain at least six feet of distance from the table, with foods or drinks placed on a separate counter or side table for pick-up by guests themselves.

You could communicate your preference ahead of time when making a reservation or when entering. To make it clear to all, including diners at other tables who may otherwise come over to say hello, a simple traffic system could be added by posting one of three flags at each table. A green flag for full service as of old, with all being welcome. Yellow says that staff should approach a table only when requested, without any chitchat. A red flag stands for zero contact.

---

* Microbiologist and author.

In each case, tables should be prepared with water, butter, bread, olive oil, salt/pepper, etc., just before guests arrive. Also, disposable paper menus with room for written requests should be used (as quite common now), or orders could be conveyed via cell phones or other apps. Guests opting for a red table approach could also remain low-tech by one of them walking all menu choices over to a nearby service counter.

Instituting this kind of signaling system would honor diners' risk preferences and make them more willing to chance an evening out. Levels two (yellow) and three (red) also imply that the host or hostess, as well as the restaurant manager, need to resist the temptation to be extra friendly or hospitable. During our meal, for instance, we experienced several superfluous table interruptions by well-meaning staff who asked if we wanted to try special wines, French cheeses, and some unusual desserts. It was unwise to offer such culinary digressions up close at the height of COVID-19 when social distancing was critical, especially in crowded indoor settings where patrons sit close for hours without wearing masks.

Managing Risk Better

For customers who opt for levels one (green) and two (yellow), the question of risk reduction is still important and perhaps counterintuitive. If you could choose, would you rather have one server handle all of your table's needs or multiple servers sharing the load equally? At first glance, having more people serving your table may seem riskier since you are more likely to be in touch with a COVID-19 carrier. But if one single server does all the work at your table, you will have much more exposure if that person is infected. This issue is akin to deciding whether to keep all your valuables with one person in the group while traveling on vacation versus spreading them around. With eggs in multiple baskets, your chance of having some loss goes up, but the chance that you lose all your eggs goes down. Infectious diseases are more complex, however, since your vulnerability depends on many factors other than exposure time and physical proximity.

Another issue we contemplated was that since our servers tended to be younger and more carefree, they might unknowingly be infected without showing symptoms. Further, when diners remove their own masks once seated, they become like sitting ducks themselves while placing their fellow diners and servers at greater risk as well. Foremost, diners should exercise whatever limited control they have by remaining vigilant. Try to keep your group small, avoid laud laughter (too many air droplets flying), and keep your distance. The main challenge is not to let your guard down, which is especially hard after drinking some alcohol since you will become overly relaxed and far less attentive.

How carefully the restaurant screens its staff is crucial also, including those working in the kitchen. Ideally, the restaurant would disclose to patrons how often the staff is checked for COVID-19 symptoms—and what happens if they have them. Like airlines, restaurants could also publicize their cleaning protocols. Being reminded of these precautions could be an appetite killer for some, but will probably put most guests at ease.

In the midst of a raging pandemic, many people might welcome more structured risk management—or may not risk dining out at all. This is especially true for the elderly and those with preexisting conditions that increase their vulnerability to the virus. Giving diners the final choice about the level of safety they want is the crux of being customer-oriented amid a pandemic.

Considering the economic hardships COVID-19 has inflicted on restaurants, they all need to think outside the box more and institute rigorous distancing between staff and customers. The old norms of lavishing highly personalized services are misplaced at a time when patrons desire friendly distancing above all. Restaurants going the extra mile in reducing virus exposures can tap into a market segment that otherwise will just continue to eat at home. There are other benefits as well, such as developing customer loyalty, avoiding reputational damage, and becoming more adroit in adapting to other disruption scenarios lurking around the corner.

7.5 YOU CAN'T BE CUSTOMER-CENTRIC FROM A DISTANCE

In many industries, companies use dealers or support organizations to deliver products and services. Carmakers rely on independent dealerships, insurance companies have external agents, and cable television companies commonly use private contractors for installations and service.

Such cascaded models, however, make it difficult to remain customer oriented. The customer may come first in the eyes of the cable company, but the third-party technician installing a box in your home might not see it that way. They're usually more focused on those who pay them rather than those who expect quick, competent, and friendly service. That's one of the reasons the net promoter score—a common metric of customer satisfaction—ranks cable companies near the bottom.

A cascaded service model is where good intentions too often meet awful execution. I recently experienced this first-hand when trying to get our home warranty company to repair a broken gas line at our house. A relatively straightforward repair took 45 days. It's not that the company didn't want to get things right. Let's just say things didn't go according to plan.

My home warrantee company is large and one of a number of such firms offering contracts that promise to quickly repair broken electrical wiring, gas fuel lines, plumbing, cooling, and heating systems.[5] Depending on where you live and the type of coverage (gas versus plumbing, say), costs range from $3 to $6 a month. Combination plans allow you to mix and match coverage.

Most companies promise customer service 24/7, no deductibles, and a one-year guarantee on repairs if they are handled by an approved subcontractor. Although repair warrantee plans for appliances have been common for quite some time, consumers care even more about their critical systems like water, heat, gas, electric or toilets. Indeed, failures in any of these can cause a genuine emergency and repair costs exceeding $1,000. Since I was an academic and business consultant at the time and not a plumber, this protection appealed to me and even more so to my wife.

A Good Idea in Theory

The logic of home warrantees is simple: Homeowners shift the financial risks of system failure to the insurer, for a premium. This lets homeowners avoid large losses while securing immediate access to repair companies vetted by the insurer. The insurer earns money by spreading that risk. Moreover, the insurer can arrange better prices by working with multiple contractors. But in return, you give up control over how quickly and well the home emergency is fixed.

And that can lead to trouble, as we recently experienced. Our warrantee company was not equipped to handle a slightly out of the ordinary case. Result: an unhappy customer and the company overpaying for inefficient and slow repairs performed by its own contractor. A lose–lose proposition all around.

Our case concerned the repair of a gas pipeline network, running above and below ground, that provided natural gas to a kitchen stove, a pool heater, and a backup generator—which we need in hurricane-prone Florida. One pipe section started to leak gas, which we could smell outside. We called the municipal gas company, which dispatched a team quickly to turn off *all* of our gas until the leaks were properly fixed. And they were, but a month and a half later.

Some Lessons Learned

Clearly, having to wait for more than six weeks to repair the gas pipe to our kitchen, plus some other essential appliances, qualifies as bad customer service. The twists and turns of this saga involve poor communications, improper diagnosis upfront, overworked subs, unfamiliarity with local codes, and multiple failures trying to fix things. And there was very little we could do about it since we were no longer in the driver seat according to the contracts we signed.

Somehow, our insurer managed to provide lousy service and overpay for repairs it covered due to the role of intermediaries. The process of communicating with the insurer, which in turn communicated with the contractor, was tedious because it was multilayered. Different individuals answered at the insurer's call center (possibly run by an outsourcing company), and none would provide callback numbers.

Also, we needed to sort out issues of jurisdiction, scope of coverage, and repair standards that needed to be met. It was clear to me that the contractor wanted to minimize any additional work and never fully grasped the scope of the issues that needed to be addressed. As a consequence, the insurer paid about $8,000, or more than double what these repairs really would have cost if we had hired private contractors ourselves.

This case example demonstrates how difficult it can be to institute a truly customer-centric business model remotely.[6] The starting point has to be a deep understanding of the customer's situation—and not just the pain points. If only service providers could staple themselves to the work order from start to finish, they would realize how many bureaucratic hurdles the customer has to negotiate to get good answers or service. The company may think it is providing mass customization, with everything running smoothly behind the curtain and customers getting personalized attention. But this is an illusion in many cases.

A key lesson is that the more intermediaries you insert, the more that idea breaks down, as it did in our case and presumably many others.[7] In short, if you want to buy a home warrantee policy, understand that you will lose control of the repair process once it gets started. Of course, if you're on a tight budget or unable to easily handle home emergencies yourself easily, teaming up with a credible repair insurer is often a decent solution. Although by no means a perfect one.

END NOTES

1 Berman, Barry. "How to delight your customers." *California Management Review* 48.1 (2005): 129–151.

2 Grégoire, Yany, Audrey Salle, and Thomas M. Tripp. "Managing social media crises with your customers: The good, the bad, and the ugly." *Business Horizons* 58.2 (2015): 173–182.

3 Weinstein, Art. *Superior Customer Value: Finding and Keeping Customers in the Now Economy.* Routledge, 2018.

4 Knox, George, and Rutger Van Oest. "Customer complaints and recovery effectiveness: A customer base approach." *Journal of Marketing* 78.5 (2014): 42–57.

5 Royal, Sebastien, Nadia Lehoux, and Pierre Blanchet. "Comparative case study research: An international analysis of nine home warranty schemes." *International Journal of Building Pathology and Adaptation* 41.4 (2023): 789–824.

6 Selden, Larry, and Ian C. MacMillan. "Manage customer-centric innovation-systematically." *Harvard Business Review* 84.4 (2006): 108.

7 Albaum, Gerald, and James Wiley. "Consumer perceptions of extended warranties and service providers." *Journal of Consumer Marketing* 27.6 (2010): 516–523.

CHAPTER 8

THRIVING ON FAILURES

"I think we're in good enough shape to start making the same mistakes again."

FROM *HARVARD BUSINESS REVIEW*, DECEMBER 2010. CARTOON BY TERESA BURNS PARKHURST.   © HBR.ORG

8.1 YOU NEED TO MAKE MORE MISTAKES

If you have ever flown in an airplane, used electricity from a nuclear power plant, or taken an antibiotic, you have benefited from someone's brilliant mistake. Each of these life-changing innovations was the result of many missteps and an occasional insight that turned a mistake into a surprising portal of discovery. Even Albert Einstein made at least 23 mistakes in his published scientific publications. Some of these were necessary to achieve his monumental insights about the deeper forces of nature.[1]

Successful people tend to have a different view about mistakes than most ordinary people. Not only are they more tolerant of them (in themselves and others), but also they often embrace them. Steve Jobs celebrated his mistakes during a commencement speech at Stanford, and J.K. Rowling admitted that she could not have produced her astoundingly successful Harry Potter series without having hit rock bottom first. [2] People in the arts and humanities tend to embrace mistakes comparatively easily. As trumpet great Wynton Marsalis put it, if you are not making mistakes, you are not playing jazz—you are not trying. The same mindset can help business.

During the monopoly era, U.S. telephone companies had to provide service to every household in their region, no matter the household's credit history. Each operating company collected deposits from customers with the worst credit history in their state in order to minimize damage to equipment and delinquent bills. A few companies decided to test their credit scoring model by not charging the deposit for several months. This was clearly a mistake by normal business standards. But then they discovered that the "risky" customer segment actually had fewer delinquencies than some of the others, with less damage to equipment. This counterintuitive insight caused them to recalibrate their risk models and charge deposits based on different criteria. The improved credit models added an average of $137 million to the bottom line every year for a decade.

As Chairman and founder of our company, Decision Strategies International, I wondered whether our policy of not responding to Requests for Proposals (RFPs) that came in over the transom was perhaps flawed. We had never responded to an RFP without knowing at least one person at the requesting company, assuming that the prospective client was either price shopping or had already determined its favorite candidate but needed other bids for appearance. Against the better judgment of many, I decided to test this assumption. We took the next RFP that came in and tailored a proposal. To our pleasant surprise, the unknown client accepted our proposal and then hired us for additional projects later, amounting to more than $1 million in consulting fees.[3]

John Wanamaker, founder of the first major department store in Philadelphia, famously said: I know that half my advertising dollars are wasted, but I don't know which half. The same is true for your business assumptions, especially if you are in a changing market, uncertainty is high, your problems are complex, and innovation is your game. In such an environment, a good portion of your assumptions are likely wrong, but you don't know which. The only hope to escape from your self-imposed mental box is to test beyond the scope of what you deem worth testing.

This is quite different from normal experimentation, which you can justify on the basis of expected cost and benefits. When making a *deliberate mistake*, you are spending time and money on tests that conventional wisdom suggests are not justifiable. Deliberately making errors goes against the human grain. But trying too hard to avoid them may be the greatest mistake of all.

8.2 HOW TO MAKE A BRILLIANT MISTAKE

Everyone makes mistakes—every entrepreneur, every business leader, every employee. The mark of a great company isn't that it avoids failures—that's impossible—but that it has the wisdom to take full advantage of them.

Social science tells us that we humans are short-sighted by nature. We are wired to seek out evidence that confirms what we already believe and to ignore evidence that contradicts it. On top of that, we are usually overconfident, thinking we know more than we do and underestimating how much we don't know. This leads to tunnel vision and myopic judgments.[4] The great virtue of mistakes, whether by accident or design, is that they widen your range of experience, shrink your ego, and open yourself to discoveries you would otherwise never make.

Stumbling on Chaos

History is full of such brilliant mistakes. A notable one occurred in the early 1960s at MIT. Meteorologist Edward Lorenz had just completed a large round of simulations of a weather system and wanted to repeat the experiment over a longer time frame. Rather than waste the mainframe's valuable CPU time, he manually typed the final numbers from the results table. To his surprise, the second simulation diverged radically from what he expected. He was puzzled about it for days. Then it struck him: he had entered numbers using a computer printout that rounded all numbers to three decimal places, whereas the computer stores six decimal places. This tiny rounding error pushed the second simulation onto a markedly different path. In that sense, the exercise was a failure.

But the apparent error led Lorenz, after some more deep thinking, to a far more significant discovery. In a complex system, tiny changes in the initial inputs can cause massive changes at a later stage. Lorenz's discovery is now known as the "butterfly effect"—after the notion that the fluttering of a butterfly's wings can ultimately lead to a tornado halfway around the world—and is one of the foundations of chaos theory. For his brilliant mistake, Lorenz was awarded the 1991 Kyoto Prize.

The Lorenz example illustrates the two prime ingredients of a brilliant mistake:

1. Something goes wrong far beyond the range of prior expectations and
2. New insights emerge whose benefits greatly exceed the mistake's cost.

The brilliant part lies especially in condition (2) but also in recognizing that (1) is necessary for (2) to occur. You want to increase the chance of (1) and (2) occurring together. When they do, you could have a brilliant mistake on your hands.

Golden Egg on Your Face

It's not easy to get your business to view failure so positively, but it can be done. The president of an Ann Arbor, Michigan business concocted what he calls the Golden Egg award to make sure his people would extract as much learning as possible from failures. He asked managers to share their mistakes at a monthly meeting, which is not unlike the mortality and morbidity reviews hospitals hold to learn from medical errors. At first, participants were reluctant to open up, but eventually, these confessionals became a favorite part of the session.

The manager who presents the best mistake of the month gets the Golden Egg trophy—a spray-painted L'eggs pantyhose plastic egg. Initially, the trophies stayed in the desk drawer of the (un)lucky winner. But over time, winners became proud enough to place the trophy on their desk for the entire month. This naturally steered conversations with visitors to how managers were able to convert eggs on their faces into omelets rich with insight and learning. In short, the president managed to change the culture from one that hides mistakes to one that explores and even celebrates them. You can do likewise, and your company will reap the benefits.

8.3 MANAGING YOUR EMOTIONS AFTER FAILURE

Everyone makes mistakes, and, typically, emotional turmoil follows. Here's how you can channel those negative feelings into an opportunity to learn and bounce back.

As a dynamic manager leading your company, you will invariably make a few mistakes along the way. It happens to all of us, from missed deadlines and stupid emails to ruffled feathers. (If these things *don't* happen to you at times, start to worry). But the deeper problem is that that no one really *likes* to fail. So, when we do, we often miss key lessons.

Just look at the many expressions associated with mistakes. We speak of people eating "crow," "humble pie," their "hat," and of course their "words." Mistakes are hard to digest and may literally make us sick to our stomach. As Kathryn Schulz wrote in her splendid book *Being Wrong: Adventures in the Margin of Error,* "If being right is succulent, being wrong runs a narrow, unhappy gamut from nauseating to worse than death." [5]

How to Handle Mistakes Better?

First, you need to accept that some people are better at their chosen game than you are in the sense of scoring higher on average. So, at times, you will lose. Second, recognize that how you handle and channel your emotions after you have lost is at least as important for long-run success. Business careers are not sprints but marathons—continual learning is the key.

So, imagine you have made a big mistake. Let's go to that very hard moment when you have realized that mistake, and your heart drops into your stomach. Then, do the following:

1. *Accept that failure produces negative emotions* in you and others, not unlike burning your finger at the stove or tripping on the ice. Hopefully, you are still alive and just bruised, so that you can extract a few lessons for yourself and others.
2. *Identify the mix of emotions* in yourself and others. Are you frustrated? Desperate and angry? Bored? Or confused? Believe it or not, neurologically speaking, these deep emotions actually have adaptive value. So yes, simply *knowing* which of those feelings you are experiencing is a step toward getting over them.
3. *Let things simmer [...] for a while.* Give these mixed emotions some rein since they will probably initiate some self-correction on their own steam.

They set in motion actions and reflections that on their own will start to improve things. For example, frustration leads to change, confusion to search for meaning, and despair or boredom to choosing a new line of work, perhaps.

4. *Redirect your energy.* As Martin Seligman, the father of positive psychology, has shown during decades of research, the key is to focus on what is *specifically* changeable in the problem at hand.[6] Get concrete and zero in on what could be changed the next time. Reframing your thinking optimistically so that you can discover ways toward finding solutions is the key to discovering the silver linings that surrounds every failure.

Lastly, generally speaking, focus only on things you can control and just try to accept the uncontrollable, although a slight illusion of control can actually be beneficial to your mental health (if not your decisions).[7] And most importantly, don't indulge in general negativity about yourself, your co-workers, or the world at large! After bad weather, the sun will start to shine again and seeing it sooner helps restore emotional energy, a sense of purpose and success.

8.4 HOW TO MAKE HAY WHEN THINGS GO HAY-WIRE

You know the concept of dark data? Most companies are sitting on valuable information that either they fail to use or don't realize they have in the first place. One of the most valuable strains of these dark data is mistakes that well-meaning employees make in pursuit of innovation. Usually, your employees will quickly sweep the story of their mistake under the rug to minimize reputational damage. That can be an enormous missed opportunity. As the boss, you want to bring these dark data to light so your company can benefit from their silver linings.

Harvesting Mistakes

Create a mistake bank. John Caddell set up a public website where anyone can deposit their mistakes—anonymously if they wish—so that others don't fall into the same trap.[8] If you do the same internally, make sure to include near-misses, just as the Federal Aviation Administration does, and for the same reason. For example, the Danish company Grundfoss, the world's leading manufacturer of pumps, asks workers on the assembly line to record whenever something almost goes wrong. They learn as much from these near misses as from actual screw-ups—and at a much lower cost.

Run a competition. When I published my book *Brilliant Mistakes* with Wharton Digital Press, the publisher invited people to submit stories of mistakes that yielded a net gain. The focus was mistakes that had fortuitously, or perhaps by design, led to advances that more than made up for the cost of the mistake. Start running such competitions in your own company to foster a genuine learning culture or, in a related vein, try orchestrating *Innovation Tournaments.*[9]

Allow limited sloppiness. The biologist and Nobel Laureate Max Delbrück (1906–1981) recommended what he called the "principle of limited sloppiness."[10] He advised his students to be sloppy enough in their lab experiments to allow for the unexpected but not so sloppy that they could not identify the reasons for any anomalous results. Alexander Fleming's discovery of penicillin is a famous example of the power of limited sloppiness. Fleming let his petri dishes get badly contaminated one summer in 1928 and then noticed that certain spores that had blown in through the open window inhibited bacterial growth at the edges.[11] In essence, he pulled an epic medical advance from his trash can.

Make deliberate mistakes. Bob Galvin, a longtime CEO of Motorola, was renowned for encouraging contrarian thinking. He wanted people to challenge themselves by remaining constantly in motion. If the train goes right and everyone jumps on board, try to make the case why it should go left instead, he would counsel. After projects were ranked for funding and the cut-off line drawn at, say, project 15, he would find funds for projects 16 and 17 as well. David Ogilvy, the founder of advertising giant Ogilvy & Mather, did roughly the same: he would run advertisements that he, his team, or clients did not believe would work just to test their theories. Most of these rejects indeed tested poorly, but a few turned out to be brilliant, such as a classic Hathaway shirt commercial showing a man with one eye patched.

What the Organization Can Do

When giving reviews, make sure to ask your team for examples of learning from mistakes. If people can't supply credible examples, warn them that the next time around this will cost them in their bonus since they clearly are not taking enough risk. Apart from individual reviews, orchestrate team discussions. After one hospital looked into medical errors, they realized that nurses were most likely to make drug mistakes—about the type, dosage, timing, side effects, etc.— when they got interrupted. So now, when they administer medicines, nurses wear a cap or other sign that signals clearly "don't disturb." As a result, drug errors dropped significantly.

Most people don't understand why mistakes can be so valuable or how to learn from them. To make the connection clear, first teach them to frame any mistake as a learning opportunity. A.G. Lafley, when CEO of Procter & Gamble, emphasized that we should view many mistakes as gifts because they tell us something we did not know.[12] Second, emphasize that perfection is not the ultimate goal; learning is. British consultancy Nixon McInnes celebrates its employees' confessions of mistakes at a meeting held every few weeks, which it calls the "Church of Fail."

Mining the dark data of mistakes lurking in hidden recesses of your company is not easy but the rewards can be great. After all, you are trying to change people's minds as well as your organization's culture. Both kinds of change are urgent today. In times of rapid or momentous change, the race no longer goes to the swiftest. It goes to the smartest learners.

8.5 MAKE NO MISTAKE: YOU SHOULD FAIL ON PURPOSE

It may be the most counterintuitive thing you could ever do. But committing mistakes by design could produce more insight than merely waiting for them to happen randomly. The main virtues of failures lie in their ability to enlarge our range of experience, shrink our egos, and increase the chance of discovery. As IBM founder Tom Watson Sr. emphasized "if you want to succeed faster, make more mistakes." If much of what we believe is mistaken, we can either wait for other people to point it out or we can figure it out on our own. The latter route is faster but it also means that you have to test things in what appears to be a time-wasting exercise.

Deliberate Mistakes

My *Harvard Business Review* article "The Wisdom of Deliberate Mistakes" with Robert Gunther offers step-by-step advice for how to select mistakes worthy of testing.[13] Note that these tests are not your typical rational experiments, where you expect a positive investment return on average. They are a special type of inquiry that your rational side would reject because of a negative expected payoff. These counterintuitive tests pay homage to Albert Einstein, who said that "if you have never made a mistake, you have never tried anything new."

A deliberate approach to making mistakes may seem crazy at first, but smart people do it all the time to accelerate their own learning and achieve higher performance. As noted earlier, when trumpet wizard Wynton Marsalis was asked how valuable mistakes are in jazz, he replied, "Very important, because if you're not making mistakes, you're not trying." Even though artists are especially adept at toying with crazy stuff, including deliberate mistakes, the same is true in business and science.

My book *Brilliant Mistakes* examines this counterintuitive thesis in much greater detail.[14] As noted before, shortly after this book appeared, my publisher organized a contest that asked readers to send in their most brilliant mistakes. The winning submissions ranged from an experienced doctor stumbling on a medical insight to a young female performer at children parties finding new ways to mix in balloons, as further detailed in a *Wall Street Journal* article highlighting the learning potential of mistakes.[15]

My aim here is to reorient your attitude toward setbacks and failures since these are usually under-analyzed. A corresponding adjustment is needed for unexpected successes, which are much easier to celebrate and are often over-attributed to brilliance. The bigger opportunities for learning therefore lie on the far side of failure, where we may not want to tread as a team or even when alone.

Suggestions and Lessons

1. Embrace the full learning potential of failure by overcoming the shame and fear that usually turns us away from discovering failure's hidden messages. Rather than forgetting about them, we need to dissect unexpected outcomes with clinical detachment, as in medical post-mortems.

2. To learn from a failure, it's critical to separate your decision-making process—which is the part that you own—from the decision's outcomes, which may have been influenced by random factors you can't reasonably be expected to control, such as pure chance.

3. There is a big difference between silly or stupid errors and truly brilliant failures that contain the hidden seeds of success. It all hinges on the relative costs and benefits of what is at stake. For an inadvertent mistake to become brilliant, your search for the silver linings—in the form of new insights or opportunity—must in the end far exceed the cost of the failure.

4. The highest form of learning is not just to wait passively for random failures to occur (as they will naturally) but to create more room for mistakes and commit them on purpose. Just as random mutations have advanced evolution reactively, clever, well-designed mistakes can open new portals of discovery prospectively based on foresight and imagination.

I sometimes ask executives about what taught them the most in their careers, expecting answers like specialized training, seasoned mentors, new challenges, or colleagues. But the most successful ones often said "my mistakes," which requires intellectual honesty as well as curiosity. The school of hard knocks can indeed be a great teacher but it is also sends in horrific bills. So, you may as well wring each last drop of learning from every hard-won lesson.

END NOTES

1 Ohanian, Hans C. *Einstein's Mistakes: The Human Failings of Genius*. WW Norton & Company, 2008.

2 We ran a prize contest at Wharton, co-sponsored by Inc Magazine, asking managers about their most brilliant mistake; see http://wdp.wharton.upenn.edu/brilliant-mistakes-contest

3 Schoemaker, Paul J., and Robert E. Gunther. "The wisdom of deliberate mistakes." *Harvard Business Review* 84.6 (2006): 108–115.

4 Russo, J. Edward, Paul J. H. Schoemaker, and Edward J. Russo. *Decision Traps: Ten Barriers to Brilliant Decision-Making and How to Overcome Them*. New York, NY: Doubleday/Currency, 1989.

5 Schulz, Kathryn. *Being Wrong: Adventures in the Margin of Error*. Granta Books, 2011.

6 Seligman, Martin E. P., and Mihaly Csikszentmihalyi. *Positive Psychology: An Introduction*. Vol. 55. No. 1. American Psychological Association, 2000.

7 Taylor, Shelley E., Margaret E. Kemeny, Geoffrey M. Reed, Julienne E. Bower, and Tara L. Gruenewald. "Psychological resources, positive illusions, and health." *American Psychologist* 55.1 (2000): 99.

8 https://www.amazon.com/Mistake-Bank-Forgiving-Mistakes-Embracing/dp/0989292002.

9 Terwiesch, Christian, and Karl T. Ulrich. *Innovation Tournaments: Creating and Selecting Exceptional Opportunities*. Harvard Business Press, 2009.

10 Data Deluge: The Principle of "limited sloppiness".

11 W. H. Hughes, *Alexander Fleming and Penicillin*. London: Priority, 1974.

12 Quoted from an interview in the April 2011 *Harvard Business Review*. The entire issue was devoted to exploring the role of failure in business and provides powerful examples of smart CEOs recognizing that you can learn more from failure than success.

13 Schoemaker, P. J. H. and Gunther, R. E. "The Wisdom of Deliberate Mistakes" *Harvard Business Review*, June 2006, pp. 109–114.

14 Schoemaker, Paul J. H. *Brilliant Mistakes: Finding Success on the Far Side of Failure*. University of Pennsylvania Press, 2011.

15 Paul Schoemaker Talks to the Wall Street Journal about Brilliant Mistakes – Mack Institute for Innovation Management (upenn.edu).

CHAPTER 9

POWER OF METAPHORS

"Now can you explain that with a parable?"

9.1 HOW ANALOGIES INFLUENCE YOUR THINKING

It can be quite revealing to tune in to the kind of imagery people use when talking. Consider, for example, how people speak about organizations. Some see organizations through a family frame (as was common at IBM in early days); other may use sports metaphors to convey key messages (like not dropping the ball or stayed focused on winning). Yet, others may liken an organization to an orchestra with multiple conductors, etc.[1]

Metaphors and language matter in how people think and act. Consider, for example, how we talk about fixing the economy. For those viewing the economy as a *complex machine*, fuel injection might make good sense as well as lubrication to get the economic fly wheels going again. Others might view the economy as a *sick person* addicted to debt, oil, special interests and bloated government programs, in which going cold turkey would hold some appeal. But of course, they don't want to kill the patient, so some time may be needed for detoxification.

Yet, other observers or policy makers may view the economy as an unruly *forest or garden* that grows and adapts to survival pressures; if so, pruning would be in order at times. And those more cynical might view political economy more like *contact sport*, in which case various metaphors could spring to mind, from soccer to boxing. Note as well here how the role of leaders, players, strategies, regulations, etc., can differ markedly between sports, say football versus basketball. The former resembles how armies operate with central planning while the latter is more agile and improvisational.

Seductive Simplicity

The great benefit of metaphors is that they simplify; each economic metaphor above touches on an important aspect by analogy. As Lakoff and Johnson explained "The essence of metaphor is understanding and experiencing one kind of thing in terms of another [...]. we act according to the way we conceive of things."[2] The downside is that a strong metaphor can create a false sense of understanding if it fails to capture the essence of a problem situation and its solution.[3]

Metaphors and analogies in general often distort our thinking in hidden ways, by drawing attention disproportionately to what fits and obscuring what doesn't get highlighted in the analogy. As Einstein noted, "we should make things as simple as possible, but not simpler." The question is whether some of your favorite metaphors for thinking about complex subjects, such as the economy, leadership, joint ventures, team work, or competition actually offer you flawed or simplistic analogies.

For example, consider the widely used product life-cycle concept in marketing.[4] This biological metaphor suggests that products naturally arise, grow, mature, and die, just as individuals do. So if managers wedded to this view see a product's sales decline for several quarters in a row, they would naturally think that the product is in decline. And once the product strategy is adjusted to reflect this presumed stage of decline, resources may be withdrawn and decline will quickly follow (as a self-fulfilling hypothesis). Of course, if decline has truly set in, this may be the smart move so money can be spent more wisely elsewhere; why fight a losing battle?

Should Products Die or Adapt?

Procter & Gamble as well as many other companies, however, reject the product life-cycle metaphor as unduly self-limiting.[5] Rather than viewing the product as a single organism proceeding through its life stages, they view the product as the species itself. So, the product must be adapted to changing circumstances to remain viable. In the product life-cycle view, products must be allowed to die. In the "product as species" frame, attempts are made to "mutate" the product so that it better fits its market niche or, perhaps, can migrate to an adjacent segment not yet served well by competitors. Of course, as P&G would readily admit, the downside of the evolutionary view is that managers support a doomed product for too long, and will not let it die when in fact it should.

Are You a Master or Prisoner of Metaphors?

To avoid being imprisoned by poor metaphors, you need to do the following:

1. Be sensitive to what metaphors and mental imagery people use; does the boss always speak in football lingo or perhaps in family terms?
2. Don't buy other people's analogies hook, line, and sinker (including this one) so that you don't get framed. Try to consider alterative metaphors.
3. Recognize that most metaphors highlight aspects of the problem that are valid and deserving of attention (as shown above, this is the easy part)
4. The harder challenge is to figure out where a given metaphors hides, distorts, or totally misses the boat (e.g., sport metaphors assume a zero sum game which business clearly is not; and the rules in business are not fixed in stone).

5. Once you understand the pros and cons of various metaphors, select one that best highlights the issues most essential to the problem and run with it.

6. If no single metaphor can do justice to the crux of matter, try to think in multiple metaphors and integrate their complementary suggestions.

Later in this chapter, I will examine further if stud poker is a good metaphor for new product development (as strongly suggested in the bestselling book *In Search of Excellence*). If you want to test yourself in advance of reading my own take, try to answer questions 3 to 6 above for poker.

9.2 A HEDGE OR BET? A MATTER OF PERSPECTIVE

Much in metaphor hinges on imagery, association and attention since language matters. Consider for example whether a decision under uncertainty qualifies as a hedge or a bet in normal parlance. On one level, the answer is simple. If an investment reduces your risk, it is a hedge. If it increases your risk, it is a bet.

So, now it all depends on how you define risk. Also, there is the tricky issue of whether increases in risk are compensated by higher expected return. And this raises the most vexing question of all, namely how to define the relevant portfolio against which the change in risk in your analysis is to be measured. This question is essential to the Volcker rule which holds that banks too big to fail should not be making big bets with house money since the upside would accrue to Wall Street, whereas Main Street would have to bail out the banks if it all goes sour.[6]

In this regard, it matters greatly how you define what constitutes a bet versus a hedge. Suppose your company can invest $50,000 in return for an even chance of a payoff of $0 or $100,000 (all amounts are stated in net present value terms so that we can ignore the time value of money; let's also ignore taxes). Since the expected value of this investment is zero, you either lose your $50,000 investment or have a net gain of $50,000 (i.e., $100,000–$50,000) with equal chances. By definition, a risk neutral person would be indifferent, a risk-averse person would reject the bet and a risk taker would accept it. But that is only true if we look at this investment in isolation of other risks in play for this person. Once we adopt a portfolio view, things get more complicated because the actuarially fair bet above can either increase or decrease the portfolio's overall risk depending on how its returns correlate with other asset returns in the portfolio.

In the 1950s, Harry Markowitz solved the complex problem of how to optimally balance a portfolio when having to allocate a fixed investment amount across various well-defined securities.[7] Let's suppose that a risk-averse investor used this basic portfolio model to optimally allocate $1 million across n different investments. Next, assume the investor is given the opportunity to reallocate some of these funds into a new investment offering a negative expected return while also offering strong inverse correlations with many other investments in the portfolio? Should any funds be diverted into this new $(n+1)$th security, which on its own would clearly seem to be a risky bet. The answer could well be yes. A risk-averse investor might gladly sacrifice some expected return in the portfolio in order to lower its overall risk. Paradoxically, what seemed a very risky bet at first suddenly becomes a prudent hedge, or vice versa.

The question further arises if this dynamic can also happen at a market level, for companies like JP Morgan whose stocks are traded publicly. The short answer is yes. The path-breaking portfolio work at the individual level subsequently spawned the development of the capital asset pricing model (CAPM) in finance, for which Harry Markowitz, Merton Miller, and William Sharpe were awarded the Nobel Prize in Economics in 1990.[8] The CAPM examines how rational investors should behave when operating in simplified and idealized efficient markets. The model showed that investors would only demand an extra return for systematic risk (measured as beta).

Furthermore, each investor should hold a portfolio composed of just the risk-free asset and the market portfolio. The assumptions of CAPM have since been relaxed, but its portfolio insight remains, namely that investing in negative return options can be quite rational. What seems a risky bet in isolation can be a valuable hedge within a portfolio view. And the reverse can happen as well, for example when JP Morgan Chase's presumed hedges inadvertently increased global risk.[9] To quote from a U.S. Congressional report[10]:

> *JPMorgan Chase has consistently portrayed itself as an expert in risk management with a "fortress balance sheet" that ensures taxpayers have nothing to fear from its banking activities, including its extensive dealing in derivatives. But in early 2012, the bank's Chief Investment Office (CIO), which is charged with managing $350 billion in excess deposits, placed a massive bet on a complex set of synthetic credit derivatives that, in 2012, lost at least $6.2 billion. The CIO's losses were the result of the so-called "London Whale" trades executed by traders in its London office—trades so large in size that they roiled world credit markets.* [Quoted from the original]

Although the technical details of this massive JP Morgan Chase scandal are too intricate to cover here, including what exactly went wrong and why, we know more generally that:

1. Portfolio thinking can be counter-intuitive.
2. Risk depends on how the relevant portfolio is defined.
3. The devil resides in the correlations of risks, especially their systemic components.
4. Complex trading strategies can back fire with unintended consequences as a result.
5. Never mistake models for reality since the latter tends to be more unruly than assumed.
6. Even sophisticated risk managers are often unduly confident in their risk models.
7. Don't be dazzled by complex math, but ask probing questions using common sense.

9.3 IS POKER A GOOD MINDSET FOR BUSINESS?

—With J. Edward Russo*

Poker has gone from smoke filled backrooms to high stakes television shows in recent years. It has drawn the interest of scholars at Harvard and elsewhere to better understand the mind, and educators use it as a way to teach critical thinking and prepare students better for life.[11]

Tom Peters and Bob Waterman praised poker in their classic book *In Search of Excellence* as an apt metaphor for new product development in business.[12]

They wrote:

Experimentation […] resembles nothing so much as a game of stud poker. With each card, the stakes get higher and with each card, you know more, but you never really know enough until the last card has been played. The most important ability in the game is knowing when to fold.

When we share this analogy with managers, they agree that it is a good metaphor. After all, with most development projects, you never know for sure until after the fact whether it has been worthwhile. And, as the project gets rolling, each major

---

* Professor of Management, Cornell University.

step becomes much more expensive than the last—making it harder to quit psychologically. The crucial management decision is whether—and when—to fold and to cut your losses.

Knowing how to revise the odds in light of new information is crucial as well. Just as in poker, players possess both private and public information, with the latter increasing over time (as new cards are turned). Finally, you need the poker player's mental toughness to fold quickly and start over again whenever the current hand stops looking promising.

Here's Where the Problem Is

Managers have a much harder time, identifying what is not captured well by the poker metaphor (i.e., what's left in the shadows). And this is the main problem with metaphors; people rarely notice where they are incomplete. As our executive education students ponder what aspects of new product development are concealed by the stud poker metaphor, they usually point out that:

New product development is not necessarily a zero-sum game. Many companies might win or lose due to regulatory action (as in biotechnology) or wide market acceptance (as with personal computers and i-phones). Also, firms neither receive a new hand each round, nor ones that are entirely dictated by chance in cases where cards can be traded or bought.

Collaboration is encouraged in new product development (through strategic alliances and JVs), but this would be considered cheating in poker.

Unlike poker, the rules of the game are neither fixed in business nor predetermined due to lobbying and other changes to the regulatory and legal system.

To counter the seductive appeal of any single metaphor, we always challenge managers to consider others as well.[13]

Since is difficult to "see" what lies outside any single metaphor, we should ask, "What other metaphors could provide insight into the problems of new product development?" Typical answers include gardening, oil drilling, and biological evolution. In gardening, for example, you need to sow, irrigate and prune, and you might even consider cross-breeding or genetic engineering.

Seeing New Angles

These alternative metaphors usually trigger different imagery and suggest useful analogies for product development. For example, sowing naturally conjures up having a portfolio of development options; irrigation suggest adding money, patents or other resources; pruning legitimates pulling the plug early on losing projects, and genetic manipulation points to strategic alliances, bringing in new blood or even training. Oil drilling or biological evolution present similarly rich analogies that can help trigger new ideas about how to tackle tough business problems.

With multiple metaphors in mind, you will be better positioned to get to the crux of the problem you face and generate innovative solutions. So, whether poker is a good metaphor for product development, business or life in general depends much on the specific context you face and whether other good metaphors are available for the problem at hand.

The key lesson is to be careful not to become the prisoner of any single metaphor and always try to be a master of many.

9.4 WHY YOU NEED TO PLAY WAR GAMES

—With Toomas Truumees*

Before the SEALs raided Osama bin Laden's hideout in Pakistan, they worked for months on their strategy, studying satellite pictures of his compound, constructing a detailed model of the buildings and rehearsing exactly how the mission would unfold. A key part of the preparation was to have some participants play the role of the enemy—to simulate how the defenders would react—so that the SEALs could remain one step ahead.

In our consulting business, we often encouraged clients to make competitive simulations part of their business strategizing. Many called it war-gaming because metaphorically that's is the aim. It serves exactly the same purpose in business as for the SEALs, namely to win.

To illustrate, one client was a pediatric hospital grappling with how to respond to rapid consolidation in their metro area. Larger hospitals with adult patients were actively looking to merge or form strategic alliances. To prepare, the hospital CEO engaged his board in a simulation in which board members role-played their five major competitors. Each team was given wide latitude to explore possible alliances or mergers over the next two years. Thanks to the simulation, the executive team quickly realized that their most direct pediatric

---

* Senior Partner, Decisions Strategies International.

competitor would likely want to merge if certain adult hospital mergers were to occur. By chance, one such major consolidation was announced just a week after the simulation. The CEO and board were aligned and ready to act. They quickly approached the other pediatric hospital about teaming up and seized an opportunity that might otherwise have been lost.

Five Steps to a Good Simulation

The key to a productive simulation is that the players submerge themselves deeply into the business realities and mindsets of each competitor. If not, the game will fail to yield strategic insights. War-games are as much about the preparation for the simulation as about the performance of the simulation itself (remember garbage in = garbage out). To get this right, make sure you do the following well:

1. *Study each main competitor.* Examine their past actions, behavioral footprint, and mindsets. Try to involve people who used to work for the competition or know them well. All this homework should result in what we call a *briefing book.*
2. *Know your opponents.* Get into the mind of the top leaders by examining past decisions and quotes and commentary. Tap into your Board or leadership networks to gain inside feels for the CEO and other executive within each rival (strengths, weaknesses, ambitions, fears, hopes, etc.)
3. *Vary the simulations.* First, outline the most likely industry dynamics and run that as simulation 1. Then throw in some key shifts in the environment or competitive scene for simulation 2. This iteration should challenge the status quo and truly foster new thinking compared to the simulation 1. And then, repeat with even more unusual scenarios depending on the complexity of the market or industry.
4. *Keep decision logs.* Capture all team decisions, alternatives considered, presumed competitor reactions, triggering events, etc. Also, note the confidence level of each team in role-playing their assigned competitor. Teams need to move quickly and align on multiple decisions in short periods of time. This in turn tests confidence, comfort level with the data, and team dynamics.
5. *Hold dress rehearsals.* Each team should meet in character a few times before the simulation day itself to review recent relevant events and become comfortable with each other. If you have to look up information about your competitor, about products, channels, finances, etc., during the actual role-playing session, the game bogs down and the value of

the simulation is diminished. Wearing clothing characteristic of the simulated rival, assigning C-suite roles such as CEO, VP Marketing, and wearing name badges with titles are good ways to stimulate the teams. You can stop short of singing the company songs.

Old Scripts Can Kill You

Old ways of thinking in today's "new normal" can be truly dangerous. The same old scripts, with the same old players, will not suffice. You need to think about unexpected events, black swans and unfamiliar choices. Are you prepared for these? Most are not, and this is why war-games can pay off big in business. A little bit of play-acting before major market shifts can prevent a lot of unproductive drama afterward. So, get into your role, get other participants involved and let the war games begin.

What can also kill you however is forgetting to realize that *war gaming* is both a metaphor and a game but not the real world. The term war has strong zero-sum connotations and instills a mindset of not taking prisoners but killing them all. When your life is threatened in a knife fight, this may not be a bad metaphor. But when building long-term relationships and exploring options for joint gain, the war metaphor can be self-limiting. Try instead the drier but more accurate label of "coopetition" since business is about winning through both collaboration and rivalries, depending on the context and time frames adopted. In short, war gaming is a two-edged sword in many cases and can be a dangerous metaphor as such.

9.5 WAYS IN WHICH POKER AND BUSINESS SAVVY ALIGN

—With Viraj Narayanan*

After football and warfare, poker may be the single most overused metaphor for business, especially entrepreneurship. Both entrepreneurship and poker entail taking gambles, and both call for you to bluff and to hold your cards close to your chest, etc. But much of that misses the main points at the top levels of play in cards or business.

What makes a great poker player and a great business thinker is an unusually clear grasp of reality, and a better-than-average humility about one's ability to

---

* Principal, Decision Strategies International.

foresee the future. The rest of the lore of poker-as-business has little basis in reality outside of country music. So here are, more specifically, what great poker players and great business leaders both tend to get right:

Both Think in Probabilities

Poker aficionado Nate Silver, famous election forecaster, author of *The Signal and the Noise*, says that top players excel at probabilistic thinking.[14] Rather than bet on one hopeful outcome, they prepare for a wide range of hands and give each due weight based on the true odds of them occurring. The normal human tendency is to give excessive weight to rare but memorable "black swan" outcomes. But you won't last long in poker if you keep expecting to draw an inside straight, and you can't build a business by betting that your company will be the next Instagram or Google.

Good strategic leaders don't automatically attribute their success to smarts—they understand that they may just have been lucky. Tony Hsieh, CEO of Zappos, spent a summer playing poker and noticed how tempting it is to get mesmerized by good outcomes.[15] Smart business leaders and smart poker players realize that whenever chance plays a role, a good decision process can result in bad outcomes and vice versa. So, make sure that in your business you focus on what you and your team can control—namely, how you arrive at decisions, not the outcome of those decisions. As a leader, you need to reward good process and practice, not just lucky outcomes.

Both Keep Score Over the Long Run

All poker players lose hands; the best are comfortable with this and take a long-term perspective when scoring themselves. A loss does not mean they played poorly. What matters is whether they had an edge over other players and exploited it properly. Likewise, business leaders who take a long-term perspective are comfortable with some losses in the short run. When Amazon went public in 1997, Jeff Bezos emphasized it was *all about the long run*. Bezos stuck with that mantra, took losses in the short run and just focused on what customers wanted.

Great negotiators think more about the other side than themselves, and so do great poker players. Just as winning poker players study their rivals' expressions, twitches, and playing style so that they can exploit any patterns, strategic leaders use war gaming to anticipate what competitors might do. They simulate key rivals and walk in their shoes. Some go as far as to create psychological profiles of competitor CEOs, including behavioral footprints.

Both Refuse to Throw Good Money after Bad

Once you have been raised a few times in a poker game, research shows that your emotions push you toward irrational escalation and a desire to win at all costs. But if your hand is bad, the best tactic is just to fold. Great poker players move on from such no-win situations decisively, without any feelings of regret or ego dents. Strategic leaders in business likewise recognize that you don't have to play out every hand. You should treat doomed projects as sunk costs. Fail fast and move on. Or—to quote country singer Kenny Rogers lyrics—*know when to walk away, know when to run.*

Using poker as an analogy for business has its limits. In the business world, you never find out so quickly whether any given strategy is a winner or a loser, and you can't deal a new hand right away. Business is not a zero-sum game operating under iron clad rules, and in real life, you can pursue cooperative strategies without being called a cheater. But in both, the smartest players understand that they never know exactly what card they're going to be dealt next—and so they set their strategy cleverly based the odds they face.[16]

END NOTES

1 Morgan, Gareth. "Reflections on images of organization and its implications for organization and environment." *Organization & Environment* 24.4 (2011): 459–478.

2 Lakoff, George, and Mark Johnsen. *Metaphors We Live By.* London: The university of Chicago Press, 1980, p. 5.

3 Wyatt, Sally. "Danger! Metaphors at work in economics, geophysiology, and the Internet." *Science, Technology, & Human Values* 29.2 (2004): 242–261.

4 Sheth, Jagdish N., and Rajendra S. Sisodia. "Revisiting marketing's lawlike generalizations." *Journal of the Academy of Marketing Science* 27.1 (1999): 71–87.

5 Lucà, Franco. "Successful sustainability strategy: Procter & gamble case." *Award-Winning Case Studies* (2019).

6 Ghosh, Koushik, and Yurim Lee. "Reflections on the Volcker Rule: Innovations in the financial services industry and fixing too big to succeed." *Challenge* 65.1–2 (2022): 49–58.

7 Mangram, Myles E. "A simplified perspective of the Markowitz portfolio theory." *Global Journal of Business Research* 7.1 (2013): 59–70.

8 Rossi, Matteo. "The capital asset pricing model: A critical literature review." *Global Business and Economics Review* 18.5 (2016): 604–617.

9 Fletcher, Gina-Gail S. "Hazardous hedging: The (unacknowledged) risks of hedging with credit derivatives." *Review of Banking and Financial Law* 33 (2013): 813.

10 Congress, U. S. "JP Morgan Chase Whale Trades: A Case History of Derivatives Risks and Abuses." United States: Congress: Senate, 2013.

11 https://www.wsj.com/articles/SB117812153189389684.

12 Peters, Thomas J., and Robert H. Waterman Jr. "In Search of." *Of Excellence, New York: Harper and Row* (1982).

13 Schoemaker, Paul J. H., and Russo, J Edward. "Managing frames to make better decisions," Chapter 8 in S. Hoch and H. Kunreuther (eds.), *Wharton on Making Decisions*, Wiley, April 2001, 131–155.

14 Silver, Nate. *The Signal and The Noise: Why So Many Predictions Fail--But Some Don't.* Penguin Press. (2012).

15 'Delivering Happiness': What Poker Taught Me About Business. HuffPost Entertainment.

16 Duke, Annie. *Thinking in Bets: Making Smarter Decisions When You Don't Have All the Facts.* Penguin, 2018.

CHAPTER 10

VARIED LESSONS

"Kick your résumé through and you're hired."

FROM *HARVARD BUSINESS REVIEW*, MAY 2011. CARTOON BY RICO ROSSI.

© HBR.ORG

10.1 TWO BILLION DOLLARS IN TOBACCO UP IN SMOKE

—With Karen Stawarky*

CVS Health was America's second largest drug store chain in overall revenue in 2014.[1] The company announced late in 2014 that tobacco products would longer be sold in its more than 7,000 stores. The announcement delighted the socially conscious crowd as well as numerous advocates for public health and wellness. Skeptics wondered if this was just a clever public relations (PR) move and cynics doubted that it would reduce cigarette consumption across the country by much. But Forbes and other deemed it the right move six years later.[2]

The decision to ban a controversial product is by no means new in either the private or public sectors. Recall, for instance, former New York City Mayor Michael Bloomberg's attempted ban on sugary drinks, which wasn't successful, whereas his smoking ban spread worldwide.[3]

Each such decision, however, raises a host of thorny issues involving branding, ethics, profitability, consumer freedom, social responsibility, PR and fear of Big Brother. So, how should companies untangle these issues practically? We suggest the following five questions as a part of a business stress test when banning products for health or other social reasons.

1. *When does a product ban help?* For CVS, a strong health focus would help expand its Minute Clinics across all of its stores. The company also hoped to broadcast a more healthful message since it was making greater advances into being a healthcare provider rather than just a retailer. Making a strategy come alive is a path littered with tough choices—it's about what you say "no" to as much as "yes." If CVS was indeed serious about its strategic migration, it would need to review all of its current product offerings through a new lens, from high calorie snacks packed with additives to sugar-loaded energy drinks.

2. *How can a product ban be additive to the top and bottom line?* Relentless scrutiny from shareholders and a focus on quarterly earnings demands that a strong, credible business case is backing the move. CVS expected that dropping tobacco-related products would reduce revenue by $2 billion off a base of $123 billion in overall sales at the time. The company planned to launch an offsetting campaign by offering its customers new products and services to fill the void—including a smoking cessation program. The

---

* Senior Partner, Decision Strategies International.

food chain Subway announced around the time that it would eliminate a nasty chemical in the bread used for its "healthy" sandwiches. This specific chemical was also used to make yoga mats and shoe rubber. Subway claimed this move was already in works well before a food blogger launched a viral campaign asking Subway to remove the chemical.[4]

3. *How might a product ban affect your organizational identity?* Making tough choices has to start with a clear, grounded sense of who you are as a company. A striking example was Patagonia's move on Black Friday in 2013 to discourage customers from buying more. It advised customers to "Wear What You Own" by looking at their closets with a fresh set of eyes. This move was consistent with Patagonia's values around conservation and recycling, and thus was perceived as authentic. If CVS is serious about rebranding around health and wellness, then this must apply to all products and also its employees. After banning smoking among its employees at work and home, the Cleveland Clinic started to introduce bans on soft drinks and doughnuts on campus, as others have also done.

4. *Will a product ban resonate with your brand strategy?* A strong corporate brand strategy needs to reflect your organizational identity and so alignment between the two is very important. What beliefs and associations do you want your target customer to have about your brand? How will your strategic moves support (or hurt) those? The Whole Foods brand, for example, is about healthy eating and the company reinforces that via its non-genetically modified organism (GMO) Product Verification Program. This multipart process operates throughout its entire supply chain, so that customers can buy 5,000 non-GMO products with trust. In the same vein, CVS and others might consider offering a visual "map" (or virtual app) in each store to nudge customers toward making "good, better, and best" choices.

5. *Do your strategic move fit well with future scenarios?* Since various trends in the U.S. healthcare system put greater responsibility on the patient personally, aligning these market dynamics would be smart business. What will society expect from responsible companies ten years from now? Which companies will socially conscious Millennial and Gen X employees want to work for? Will the media or Wall Street treat a leading company like CVS better for having been ethical and consistent? Which new partners may want to team up with CVS if its commitment to health becomes even stronger? Thinking through future scenarios about how the business and social landscape might change will help formulate winning strategies as well solidify your own leadership position.

The advantages of ethical decisions can go far beyond dollars and cents as a form of "paying forward." While head of research and development at Merck, Roy Vagelos made an unusual request to the board to develop a cure for river blindness that everyone knew could never earn back its investment. River blindness was mostly found in poor isolated villages in Central and West Africa, afflicting millions of people who lacked the means to pay for new drugs. Merck nonetheless developed the drug at considerable cost and made it available for free in 1987 in many African countries. This moral fortitude helped to drastically reduce the harm from this dreaded disease and gained Merck much praise from NGOs and liberal media.[5]

Although a questionable financial decision short-term it seemed, the move paid off greatly in terms of pride among scientists, attracting top flight talent from academia and Merck's overall standing in the industry. In addition, when Japan decided years later to give just one Western pharmaceutical company access to its local market, it chose Merck. A key reason was its leading role in tackling river blindness, while presuming all along it would not make a profit on its drug. Merck garnered high yields in talent, relationship building, and market access over the long run, underscoring that do the right thing may bring unexpected rewards.

10.2 CHOOSING THE RIGHT POLITICAL CANDIDATE

As you prepare for upcoming political or organizational elections, locally or nationally, it pays to contemplate deeply what it takes to be a good leader in a democratic society.

Let's assume that the candidate field has narrowed to just two final individuals, as in the United States when finally voting for the country's President. Each candidate typically comes with different backgrounds, experiences, endorsements, and ideological positions. My aim here is not to recommend or critique any single candidate, but to offer a sensible framework for choosing between them for the greater good.[6]

Although we can easily list a host of problems the next U.S. President needs to tackle—from conflicts with China, Iran, Russia, and Middle East upheavals to threats from space research, viruses and AI —there will also be new challenges whose form and timing we can't grasp yet. They may come in the form of natural disasters, military conflicts, ethical dilemmas, or crucibles that test a President's values and global leadership at its core. So, we must choose a leader who has the requisite wisdom and judgment to tackle the unknown as well as the unknowable.

Although criteria such as experience and proper values are often central themes in political elections, most voters lack a sound framework through which they can judge a candidate's capacity to make sound decisions now and later. Past decisions are often a good guide to someone's values, thoughtfulness, and decision style. But judging past decisions is complicated by the hindsight bias. Decisions reaching the President's desk are almost always complex—otherwise other government officials would have handled them.

Presidential decisions are fraught with value conflict and uncertainty, whether they concern issues of war and peace or domestic tradeoffs among economic efficiency and social fairness. Because chance usually plays a large role in how these decisions actually play out over the longer run, it can be dangerous to equate bad outcomes with bad decisions or good outcomes with good judgment in any single past choice.

Those who have studied decision making judge decision quality more on the basis of process than outcomes. They would typically ask the following decision questions:

1. Is the decision framed well in terms of getting to the essence of the underlying issues?
2. Are creative as well as practical options being considered for resolving the problem?
3. Is the available information sound or does it need to be complemented in key areas?
4. Are the deeper values driving the policy objectives proper and in line with prevailing voter sentiments?
5. Are all the above elements integrated into a sound decision using a disciplined process that balances the heart and the mind appropriately?
6. Is there sufficient courage and commitment to implement the chosen course of action in a timely, effective, and responsible fashion for the long run?

I try to apply these kinds of criteria and others to my own political election deliberations. Also, we should ask how grounded our own decision frames are when it comes to judging political leaders? Are you a single-issue voter or a staunch party loyalist, or does your pocketbook drive your evaluations of candidates? How good are you at sorting out conflicting information and asking the right questions most of the time? Perhaps you are overconfident, disregard negative information about your favorite candidates, or seek confirming evidence from those sharing your political leanings. How well anchored are you in the core values that reflect your life experience, culture, ideology, sense of fairness, and hopes for the future? Is your reasoning sound, balancing the heart and the mind in the right proportions?

In our current era of facts, alternative facts, spin and conspiracy tales, being objective and balanced is hard and often we run with the social groups and friendship circles that are most like us. Do you have the courage and wisdom to challenge and depart from the dominant views in your professional and social environments if your own integrity demands this. Critical independent thinking is in short supply these days, so following a disciplined voting process is crucial. Finally, most important of all, how committed are you to following through on your political choice and actually making it to the polling booth to be counted. Otherwise, your political views will matter very little in the end.

10.3 HOW TO DO SWOT ANALYSIS THE RIGHT WAY

As discussed earlier, SWOT analysis is a widely used framework for strategic planning in which managers examine their company's internal *strengths* and *weaknesses* as well as external *opportunities* and *threats*. However, companies that use this classic model run the risk of naval staring and favoring status quo strategies.[7]

Below is some concrete advice on how to sidestep these pitfalls and make your strategy session more inspiring. Start by flipping the sequence of your SWOT agenda by placing the analysis of external threats and opportunities right up front. This avoids getting stuck in a rabbit hole where you heatedly debate your own strengths and weaknesses while paying lip service to the far more complex and important changes happening in your external environment. This is especially key if you are in search of innovative moves and more dynamic business models.

How to Examine Opportunities and Threats

Rather than labeling external changes—for instance, an aging population or new regulations—as being good or bad, examine them without prejudice. Just label them neutrally, as being important forces or undercurrents, and work hard to understand them and turn them to advantage.

1. Keep your focus on the outside world (not yourselves). How is it changing and why? Be sure to cover key forces, including social, technological, economic, environmental, and technological drivers.

2. Discourage fragmentary thinking (such as discussing just one force or one issue in isolation of others) Adopt a systems view.
3. Be honest about what you can't predict about the future: list the major external uncertainties and explore how they may play out.
4. Assess which external changes you missed in the past and why. Are you any better this time around at scanning the periphery for weak signals? And if so, why or how?

How to Examine Strengths and Weaknesses

The same caveat applies here: be careful with your labels since what is a strength or weaknesses depends greatly on your strategic adaptability as well as your benchmarks of comparisons.

5. Think in terms of core competencies rather than physical or intellectual assets, since the latter can be bought, traded, or imitated more easily than the former.
6. Depict your business model visually with arrows and feedback loops, to show how different capabilities interact and underpin your revenue and profit models.
7. Labeling something as a strength or weakness implies a reference point. Decide what yours is. Is it more past, present, or future oriented? And are you measuring against the best in your industry or the best in breed globally?
8. Include soft issues in your assessment, such as culture, organizational climate, leadership capacity, etc. These hidden assets are often your best weapons.

How to Set a Clear and Compelling Strategy

To the creative mind, there are no good or bad future scenarios per se, just good or bad strategies. You should be able to win in any new scenario if you think deeply about it and are willing to change your approach. Agree on an overall vision (what to become and how) that is not only robust across future scenarios but is also sufficiently adaptive when needed.

9. Clarify the balance between exploitation (strategically playing your current hand of cards) and exploration (creating new hands of cards through innovation).

10. Encourage leadership in all directions, not just top-down. Get buy-in through peer-to-peer initiatives and encourage bottom-up leadership where people educate their bosses.
11. Monitor key issues and scan for the unexpected. Try to see sooner how the external scene may alter and be fully ready to take advantage.

10.4 KEY DECISIONS THAT MADE MANDELA GREAT

—With Brian Isaacson[*]

Every entrepreneur, almost by definition, sets out to change *something*—an inefficient market, a previously unsolvable customer problem, an ossified internal culture, etc. Compared to what Nelson Mandela changed in his country's political arena all that seems rather minor. But what allowed him to succeed against utterly improbable odds were the same characteristics that you may need when trying to effect lasting change in your business arena. Leading through change takes earned authority, authenticity, commitment, mastery of communication, consistency of message and deep cultural understandings.

As researchers of strategy and organizational change, we were impressed by remarkable examples of transformational leadership in Mandela's life. He died on December 5, 2013 at age 95 and was the first President of South Africa after a fully representative democratic election. In his honor, we describe two favorite anecdotes that illustrate to us why he was so successful at giving people a reason to follow him—and to feel better about themselves for having done so.

He appreciated the Power of Symbols and the Moral Persuasiveness of Genuine Acts of Magnanimity

One of Mandela's greatest legacies was that he started the national healing process from the moment he was released from prison. An exceptional symbolic act was his visit to Betsie Verwoerd, the wife of the "architect of Apartheid" who was assassinated late in his life. Not only did Mandela visit his widow, but also

---

[*] Management Consultant, Johannesburg, South Africa.

he was willing to do so at her home in Orania. This was an Afrikaner homeland and a striking anachronistic symbol of racial separation. Mrs. Verwoerd chose to live there as a widow after apartheid had been abolished.

Mandela's recurring emphasis on mutual forgiveness was truly remarkable. In 1993, after his recent released from 27 years in prison, he said: "I am working now with the same people who threw me into jail, persecuted my wife, hounded my children from one school to the other [...] and I am one of those who are saying: *Let us forget the past, and think of the present.*" Later, in a 2000 interview with the *Christian Science Monitor*, Mandela reiterated the same message[8]: "*For all people who have found themselves in the position of being in jail and trying to transform society, forgiveness is natural because you have no time to be retaliative.*"

He Set an Example of Reconciliation and Vision for His Countrymen and Then Let Them Know He Expected Them to Live Up to It.

By the time Mandela became President in 1994, he already knew many high-profile business leaders and companies personally. It was not uncommon for him to summon some of them to support a project such as a health clinic for a rural area. One such leader received a call from Mandela's office requesting that he accompany the President to the Eastern Cape. This leader was less than enthusiastic and pleaded that he had an appointment around mid-day clashing with Mandela's request. But there was no denying Mandela, so the leader agreed to go—but first consulted with his financial director to set a reasonable limit on the size of the anticipated donation request. They settled on 500,000 Rand, or about $50,000 in those days.

When the Air Force plane landed, the President and he were whisked off in a military helicopter. The final destination was a large football stadium in an area that had been devastated by flooding. Mandela was visiting there to support and review the re-construction efforts. Upon landing, about 80,000 black school children—all adorned in crisp white shirts—simultaneously bowed to acknowledge the great man's arrival. As they were climbing down from the helicopter, Mandela planted his hand firmly in his guest's back and said, "Now, I hope you are not going to disappoint me?" The business leader decided in that instance to double the donation to one million Rand. After all, how could he tell a man who sacrificed as much as Mandela that he couldn't afford to be more generous?

10.5 HOW CULTURALLY AWARE AND SENSITIVE ARE YOU?

—With Sandra Martinez[*]

Suppose a Dane is leading a new product introduction for a global company. Your product manager is American, your tech team is mostly Indian while your marketing head is Brazilian. The issue is this: when work groups carry out complex tasks in an international corporation with multicultural settings, leaders must be especially aware that good project design and management are critical to its ultimate success. Cultural aspects may influence, in subtle but critical ways, what is effective in terms of team leadership, structure, process, and conflict resolution.[9]

When teamwork spans multiple countries, or brings diverse nationalities together in one local project, cultural dimensions will greatly impact how effective leaders as well as teams are. On this score, forget globalization since based on who the team members are and where they come from, they are likely to differ in how much they value leadership that is self-sacrificial, face-saving, bureaucratic, empathetic, or participative in style. To be an effective leader, you have to recognize cross-cultural differences and then adapt your approach to the team's expectations and demands of the project. Also, you may have to educate the team about cultural under currents.

To illustrate, suppose a company embarks on scenario planning, meaning that the team members will jointly have to envision diverse futures to plan for. The aim is to test how well the current strategy or plan will fare in each scenario, develop flexible strategies where uncertainty is high and track early indicators of external changes ahead. As with any complex management process, some crucial design decisions must be made upfront, such as:

WHAT: What is the time frame and scope of the scenario planning exercise?

WHO: Who participates within the organization (across levels and boundaries) and from the outside (like partners, suppliers, customers, regulators, media)?

HOW: How formal and detailed should the process be in studying the key external and internal issues?

WHY: Is the aim primarily to learn and change thinking, to test current strategic plans, or to build support and buy-in? And how much do other goals matter?

---

[*] President, Fénix Leadership & Development, Bethesda, Maryland.

WHEN: Is the process to be conducted over a period of many months or concentrated in a few weeks?

WHERE: Who owns the overall process and its output and how does it connect with other planning activities?

STYLE: What leadership style would be most effective to use during the scenario planning process and during the implementation stage?

SHARING: Which stakeholders should be kept apprised of the results of the scenario planning process as it unfolds and with whom should it finally be shared?

Cultural Dimensions	*Definition in Terms of Group Values*
Power Distance	The degree to which members of a group or collective expect power to be distributed equally.
Uncertainty Avoidance	The extent to which a society, organization, or group relies on social norms, rules, and procedures to mitigate unpredictability of future events.
Humane Orientation	The degree to which a collective encourages and rewards individuals for being fair, altruistic, generous, caring, and kind to others.
Institutional Collectivism	The degree to which organizational and societal institutional practices encourage and reward collective distribution of resources and collective action.
In-Group Collectivism	The degree to which individuals express pride, loyalty, and cohesiveness in their organizations or families.
Assertiveness	The degree to which individuals are assertive, confrontational, and aggressive in their relationships with others.
Gender Egalitarianism	The degree to which a collective minimizes gender inequality.
Future Orientation	The extent to which individuals engage in future-oriented behaviors such as delaying gratification, planning, and investing in the future.
Performance Orientation	The degree to which a collective encourages and rewards group members for performance improvement and excellence.

The answers to these questions depend on what leaders hope to accomplish as well as the organization's culture and customary management approach. We list above some well-researched cultural dimensions[10] that can help identify the best project approach.

The national culture of a country or a leader will indirectly influence how the project is managed and if the leader's style will be accepted by the team and others. Some leadership characteristics are nearly universally embraced across cultures, such as charisma, integrity, dynamism, team-support, clarity, administrative savvy, and being visionary, inspirational and concerned about team members. A few others traits are universally considered negative, such being dictatorial, non-explicit, a loner, non-cooperative, or egocentric. But many other leader behaviors are judged quite differently across cultures, such as being cunning, status conscious, ambitious, risk-taking, procedural, individualistic, or elitist. For example, in the West, it may be frowned upon if a leader is status conscious or assertive but not necessarily in Asian or Middle Eastern countries where privileged and strong leaders are often admired.

For a scenario planning project to succeed, it is critical to consider the acceptable levels of power distance between the leader and all those involved, the project's future orientation (how far to look ahead) and the organization's aversion to uncertainty (preferring to focus on the here and now). In our own experience, a scenario exercise conducted in the US, where the prevailing culture is future oriented and moderately egalitarian, the leader can safely stretch people beyond their comfort zones and normal planning horizons. But that same scenario project in Germany, Japan, or Russia may run into limited tolerance for ambiguity and cause frustration if the task, process, and expectations are not clearly defined. And even within one large company, that same project and methodology may be experienced quite differently due to differences in local cultures or leaders' national origins.[11]

Lastly, the leader's own management style, which can range from inclusive to distant or from hands-on to big picture, will matter in the ultimate quality of the project. The aim is to find a good fit between the demands of the project, the cultural expectations of the organization and the leader's own preferred style of management. Without sufficient congruency among these three components, the project is bound to encounter choppy waters and feeble team commitment.

END NOTES

1 https://www.cvshealth.com/news/community/tobacco-free-for-five-years.html.

2 https://www.forbes.com/sites/robertglazer/2020/04/21/cvs-lost-2-billion-with-1-decision-heres-why-they-were-right/?sh=c3987fd689cd.

3 Isett, Kimberley Roussin, Miriam J. Laugesen, and David H. Cloud. "Learning from New York City: A case study of public health policy practice in the Bloomberg administration." *Journal of Public Health Management and Practice* 21.4 (2015): 313–322.

4 http://www.lpbr.net/2014/03/the-politics-of-precaution-regulating.html.

5 Hernando, Yolanda, Kaela Colwell, and Brian D. Wright. "Doing well while fighting river blindness: the alignment of a corporate drug donation programme with responsibilities to shareholders." *Tropical Medicine & International Health* 21.10 (2016): 1304–1310.

6 Lau, Richard R., and David P. Redlawsk. *How voters decide: Information processing in election campaigns.* Cambridge University Press, 2006.

7 Helms, Marilyn M., and Judy Nixon. ' Exploring SWOT analysis–where are we now? A review of academic research from the last decade." *Journal of Strategy and Management* 3.3 (2010): 215–251.

8 https://www.csmonitor.com/2000/0210/p15s1.html.

9 Trompenaars, Fons, and Charles Hampden-Turner. *Riding the waves of culture: Understanding diversity in global business.* Nicholas Brealey International, 2011.

10 House, Robert J., Peter W. Dorfman, Mansour Javidan, Paul J. Hanges, and Mary F. Sully De Luque. *Strategic leadership across cultures: GLOBE study of CEO leadership behavior and effectiveness in 24 countries.* Sage Publications, 2013.

11 Carraher, Shawn M. "The father of cross-cultural research: An interview with Geert Hofstede." *Journal of Applied Management and Entrepreneurship* 8.2 (2003): 98.

PART III: LEADERSHIP, DECIDING, AND BIASES

CHAPTER 11

STRATEGIC LEADERSHIP

"These aren't our real numbers, but darn it, they're the numbers we deserve."

FROM HARVARD BUSINESS REVIEW, MARCH 2015. CARTOON BY PAULA PRATT.   © HBR.ORG

11.1 SIX HABITS OF TRULY STRATEGIC THINKERS[1]

If you find yourself resisting "being strategic," because it sounds like a fast track to irrelevance, or vaguely like an excuse to slack off, you're not alone. Every leader's temptation is to deal with what's directly in front, because it always seems more urgent and concrete. Unfortunately, if you do that, you put your company at risk. While you concentrate on steering around potholes, you'll miss windfall opportunities, not to mention any signals that the road you're on is leading off a cliff.

This is a tough job, make no mistake. "We need strategic leaders!" is a pretty constant refrain at every company, large and small. One reason the job is so tough: no one really understands what it entails. It's hard to be a strategic leader if you don't know what strategic leaders are supposed to do.

After two decades of advising organizations large and small, my colleagues and I have formed a clear idea of what's required of you in this role. Adaptive strategic leaders—the kind who thrive in today's uncertain environment—do six things well as explained in depth in my book *Winning the Long Game* with Steve Krupp.[2]

Anticipate

Much of the focus at most companies is on what lies directly ahead. Their leaders often lack "peripheral vision." This can leave your company vulnerable to rivals who detect and act on ambiguous signals faster. To anticipate well, you must:

- look for game-changing information at the periphery of your industry,
- search beyond the current boundaries of your business segments,
- build wide external networks to help you scan the horizon better.

Challenge

"Conventional wisdom" opens you to fewer raised eyebrows and second guessing. But if you swallow every management fad, herd-like belief, and safe opinion at face value, your company loses all competitive advantage. Critical thinkers question everything. To master this skill, you must force yourself to:

- reframe problems to get to the bottom of things, in terms of root causes,
- challenge current beliefs and mindsets, including your own above all,
- uncover hypocrisy, manipulation, and bias in organizational decisions.

Interpret

Ambiguity is unsettling. Faced with it, the temptation is to reach for a fast (and potentially wrongheaded) solution. A good strategic leader holds steady, synthesizing information from many sources before developing a definite viewpoint. To get good at this, you have to:

- seek patterns in multiple sources of data,
- encourage others to do the same,
- question prevailing assumptions and test multiple hypotheses simultaneously.

Decide

Many leaders fall prey to "analysis paralysis." You have to develop processes & enforce them, so that you arrive at a "good enough" position. To do that well:

- carefully frame the decision to get to the crux of the matter,
- balance speed, rigor, quality, and agility. Leave perfection to higher powers,
- take a stand even with incomplete information and amid diverse views.

Align

Total consensus is rare. A strategic leader must foster open dialogue, build trust and engage key stakeholders, especially when views diverge. To pull that off:

- understand what drives other people's agendas, including what remains hidden,
- bring tough issues to the surface, even when it is uncomfortable for the team,
- assess risk tolerance and follow through to build the necessary support.

Learn

As your company grows, honest feedback is harder and harder to come by. You have to do what you can to keep it coming. This is crucial because success and failure—especially failure—are valuable sources of organizational learning. To do this well:

- encourage and exemplify honest, rigorous debriefs to extract lessons,
- shift course quickly once you realize that you are getting off track,
- celebrate both success & (well-intentioned) failures that provide insight.

Do you have what it takes?

The above list may seem like a daunting task and no one is born a black belt in all these different skills. But they can be taught and honed; whatever gaps exist in your skill set can be filled in. For starters, you can test your own strategic aptitude (or your company's) with our survey and then compare yourself against the benchmark data we published in the *Harvard Business Review*.[3]

11.2 FOUR SECRETS OF CRITICAL THINKERS

—With John Austin*

In 2009, J.D. Wetherspoon, a chain of more than 800 pubs in the UK, was facing declining sales.[4] Demand for beer had been down for five years. In addition, pricing pressure from super market chains was intense, and higher alcohol taxes further squeezed its already tight margins.

What would you say is the company's real business problem?

Most people see it as a sales problem and recommend better marketing and promotion. But this reflex may be wrong. In Wetherspoon's case, the company examined the problem more deeply, looked at data, and framed the situation from multiple angles. In the end, they found the real problem: a subtle but profound shift in consumer preferences. As a result, the chain responded with much bolder actions, transforming all its pubs into family friendly cafes during day hours.

The strategy worked. Wetherspoon saw its earnings per share jump by 7.1% in the first year. Two years after this frame shift (in 2011), it has maintained its earnings per share and, with the investment in this new strategy, its free cash flow is up 12.9%. Exploring multiple problem framings, by zooming out rather than in, gets you to the root of issues and more creative solutions.

If you fail to do this, you risk solving the wrong problem.

---

* Consulting Partner, Decision Strategies International.

Ironically, the more experience you have, the harder it will to break from conventional mindsets. Leading companies often get stuck in old business models. Kodak engineers developed an early version of the digital camera, while the rest of the company remained focused on chemical film processing. Microsoft executives doubted the value of online search as a revenue model. Barnes and Noble seemed convinced that people would always want a physical book in their hand.

In his book *Thinking, Fast and Slow*, Nobel laureate Daniel Kahneman attributes shallow framing to people substituting easy questions for hard ones.[5] We often miss the crux of the issue by drawing imaginary connections between what we see and what we expect to see. As our own book *Winning Decisions* explains, the essence of critical thinking is to slow down this process, learn how to reframe problems, see beyond the familiar and focus on what is unique in any important decision situation.[6] Here are four ways to hone these critical thinking skills:

Slow down. Insist on multiple problem definitions before moving towards a choice. This does not have to be a time-consuming process—just ask yourself or the group, "How else might we or others define this problem—what's the core issue here?" This should become a standard part of every project scoping conversation you have, especially when the issue is new or complex.

Break from the pack. Actively work to buck conventional wisdom when facing new challenges or slowly deteriorating situations. Don't settle for incremental thinking. Design ways to test deep held assumptions about your market. Of course, different is not always better so seek to understand the wisdom inherent in conventional wisdom as well as its blind spots.

Encourage disagreement. Debate can foster insight, provided the conflict is among ideas and not among people. Increasingly, we live in a world where people can choose to interact only with those who agree with them, through social media, favorite news sources, or our friendship cliques. To escape from these cocoons and echo chambers, approach alternative views with an open mind. Don't become a prisoner of your own myopic mental model.

Engage with mavericks. Find credible mavericks, those lonely voices in the wilderness who many dismiss, and then engage with them. It is not enough to simply be comfortable with disagreement when it happens to occur. Critical thinkers seek out those who truly see the world differently and try hard to understand why. Often you will still disagree with these mavericks, but at times they will reframe your own thinking for the better.

In our polarized world, in terms of culture, politics and values, it is especially important for leaders and team members to learn ways to overcome toxic relationships. A good start, based on research in social psychology, is to approach deep conflict indirectly after having established some basic human rapport and having shown interest as well as respect for opposing views.[7]

11.3 STRATEGIC LEADERS ALWAYS THINK TWICE

—With Jacqueline Claudia*

Uncertainty can be scary—but what is even scarier is how insidious the human mind can be in the face of uncertainty. To make sense of the continuous stream of data being pelted at us from every direction, our mind creates filters so that we can survive and function.

These filters are so effective and dangerous that only about 5% of the stimuli trickle through. Your mind has become your worst enemy—it only lets through information that conforms to your current beliefs and expectations. When faced with new data and important decisions, that can lead to really bad outcomes including deadly ones.

Misinterpretation Can Lead to Disaster

Consider a classic example of misinterpretation at Pearl Harbor in 1941. The captain of the destroyer USS Ward had just dropped depth charges on an unidentified submarine moving into Pearl Harbor suspected of spying. En route to port shortly thereafter, the captain heard muffled explosions and remarked to his commander, "I guess they are blasting the new road from Pearl Harbor to Honolulu." Operating from a peacetime frame of mind, the captain mistook the muffled explosions of the first Japanese air raids for road construction. He failed to link his encounter with a suspect submarine that morning with the loud explosions he just heard. His mind was insufficiently prepared to interpret the signals for what they really were all about, the start of the Second World War for the U.S.[8]

Such misinterpretation, due to looking at new data through old lenses, is quite common in business as well. Instead of challenging our assumptions, we search for information that proves our old ideas right. Unfortunately, this

---

* Partner, Decision Strategies International.

confirmation bias further delays us coming to terms with a new reality. Instead, we should constantly test our assumptions and actively look for disconfirming information that would prove our old ideas wrong when they are in fact wrong.

Be a Better Interpreter

Vigilant leaders must always be on guard for their evil twin who wants to interpret the world in terms of past realities rather than new ones. For example, your competitor drops its prices—how do you view this and what would you do about it? Your first interpretation might be that this is a desperate act to hold market share, a futile race to the bottom that will hurt all. But have you interpreted this situation correctly? Perhaps you are basing this knee-jerk reaction on old knowledge. Here's how you can tell:

1. Make a list of all the important things that have to be true for your interpretation to be correct. Arrange the list from assumptions that are easiest to verify information to hardest. For example:

- Your competitor's market share has been dropping.
- Lowering price can buy market share in this business.
- The competitor cannot make money at this new price.

2. Look for disconfirming evidence starting from the top down. Finding market share data is relatively easy, but be sure to check trends within different customer segments and also consider lags or biases in the data. Next, can you find examples where price drops did not result in higher market share? Why did it not work? Finally, challenge the assumption that your rival could not make money. Did it innovate its offering in a way that reduced cost? Could it be using a lower price to generate volume for higher value parts of its business?

If you can prove any part of your interpretation wrong, you should rethink your view and response to the situation. A statue in Helsinki, honoring former Finland president J.K. Paasikivi (1870–1956), is engraved with his motto that "all wisdom starts by recognizing the facts."

Three is the Magic Number

When looking for evidence pros and cons, try to find at least three sources for data about any new issue. Leonardo Da Vinci believed that he would never understand a complex subject without looking at it from at least three angles (what we now call triangulation).

The Internet makes this rather easy, but don't overlook traditional sources of information such as customers, competitors, suppliers, regulators, partners, etc. If there are differences in what you find, spend some time thinking about why those discrepancies exist and if they matter. What other patterns can you see in the data?

Some organizations use scenario planning as a way to make some sense of uncertainty and conflicting data. The aim of this methodology is to generate competing views about the future and use a wide lens to capture new signals from the periphery. Insights gained from this type of exploration and interpretation will not just help you avoid devastating pitfalls, but also highlight opportunities before your competitors see them as explained in our book *Peripheral Vision*.[9]

11.4 THREE DECISIONS THAT SET NELSON MANDELA APART

Nelson Mandela's life story has long since become a legend, one that transcends borders, race, language, or culture. His leadership truly belongs to the world.

It would be absurd—let alone disrespectful to Mandela's achievements—to suggest that the issues you may face as a business leader are as grave as apartheid, or that the stresses you encounter compare with his decades of imprisonment on Robben Island near Cape Town. Still, Mandela's decisions at key points in his career do hold lessons for everyone who aspires to be a great leader. In my opinion, these three decisions especially stand out and set Mandela apart from many other leaders.

1985: Turning Down Botha's Offer of Conditional Amnesty

In a 1985 speech to the nation, pro-apartheid President F.W. Botha offered Mandela freedom if he would renounce violence and other illegal activity. The President tried to shift the blame for imprisonment to Mandela himself: after all, he was now free to go, provided he would be law abiding. Mandela did not fall for this transparent ploy. Yes, he very much desired freedom after decades of hard labor and confinement in a small cell. But he also felt it would betray his principles, his leadership and his outlawed party's (the ANC) long struggle. Here is how Mandela replied, in part, to President Botha's disingenuous offer[10]:

> What freedom am I being offered while the organization of the people remains banned? What freedom am I being offered if I must ask permission to live in an urban area? Only free men can negotiate. Prisoners cannot enter into contracts.

Mandela turned down Botha and opted to stay in his cold, dark prison cell—about 8 feet by 8 feet in size—and was prepared to serve out the remainder of his life sentence. This strategic decision was enormously powerful, since it greatly elevated his position as the face of the ANC's opposition, while also drawing attention to his enormous personal sacrifice.

1993: Finding a Way to Make Peace in the Wake of Chris Hani's Assassination

The second strategic decision occurred shortly after Mandela became a free man but before he was elected President in 1994. The trigger was the 1993 assassination of Chris Hani, a popular black leader fighting for equal rights. Hani was shot in cold blood by a right-wing white extremist when stepping out of his car. The killer was identified by a white woman, who turned him in. The assassination ignited widespread fury and triggered huge demonstrations.[11] Many blacks wanted revenge, and the atmosphere was ripe for looting, violence and mayhem. Recently out of prison, Mandela rose to the occasion and appealed for calm. Here is part of what he said:

> *Tonight, I am reaching out to every single South African, black and white, from the very depths of my being. A white man, full of prejudice and hate, came to our country and committed a deed so foul that our whole nation now teeters on the brink of disaster. A white woman, of Afrikaner origin, risked her life so that we may know and bring to justice, this assassin. The cold-blooded murder of Chris Hani has sent shock waves throughout the country and the world. Now is the time for all South Africans to stand together against those who, from any quarter, wish to destroy what Chris Hani gave his life for—the freedom of all of us.* [emphasis as in original]

1994: Refusing to Stand for a Second Term as President

His third strategic decision occurred after his election as president. Mandela decided early in his first term not to stand for a second election, although two were possible under the constitution. This was a remarkable gesture in a continent where leaders tend to seek maximum power (as Robert Mugabe, president of Zimbabwe did for life). Mandela knew that his speech would be watched by about a billion people on television around the world, and he wanted to signal clearly that he was deeply pledged to democracy and that he represented all the people of his country, regardless of color. The most famous lines of this landmark speech are inscribed in stone on Robben Island. Here is part of what he said:

> *We have, at last, achieved our political emancipation. We pledge ourselves to liberate all our people from the continuing bondage of poverty, deprivation, suffering, gender and other discriminations. Never, never and never again shall this beautiful land experience the oppression of one by another.* [emphasis as in original]

Mandela's extraordinary achievement was to encourage racial harmony, forgiveness without forgetting, power sharing, and a strong focus on the future, not the past. As a master of symbolism, Mandela supported his strategy by being magnanimous toward his former enemies. For example, in 1995, he visited the widow of the very man who was the main architect of the apartheid regime and in effect put him in prison (former Prime Minister Hendrik Verwoerd). He rejoiced when the national rugby team Springboks won the world championship even though this team had been a symbol of racism and Afrikaner power for decades. He proudly wore the team's shirt during the championship match, waved his hands in support and signaled to the world at large that he truly supported a rainbow nation. Such leadership is as precious as it is rare.

Mandela passed away on December 5, 2013 at the age of 95.

11.5 LEADERSHIP LESSONS FROM DR MARTIN LUTHER KING

—With Steven Krupp[*]

Black History Month happens annually in the U.S., and during February many of us are reminded of the epic leadership of Dr. Martin Luther King, Jr. and other great back leaders. Dr. King was that rare single man who changed the course of U.S. history and forced an ethical awakening across the country and indeed the world about morally corrupt social and political systems. So, what made King such an effective strategic leader?

While King is best remembered for his bold "I Have a Dream" speech, his journey demonstrates a profound mastery of several key disciplines of strategic leadership as listed below. They provide an inspiring and powerful roadmap

---

[*] Managing Partner & CEO, Decision Strategies International.

for leaders today interested in strengthening their own strategic effectiveness in volatile, uncertain, complex, or ambiguous environments.

Anticipate the Opposition

Dr. King anticipated what was needed to bring about change. He understood that a marginalized group of people, with limited education and economic means, could only become powerful by exercising their voting rights en masse. Like a grand master chess player, he thought several moves ahead, starting by leveraging local coalitions, organizing voter registration, and busing blacks to voting stations in large numbers. He outsmarted the opposition by staying within the law and practicing non-violence.

Challenge the Status Quo

King's strong vision for social justice compelled him to confront the most flagrant violations of civil rights in the South. He was fearless in confronting the arrogance of white supremacy, realizing full well that he was playing with fire, as the brutal murders of three idealistic freedom fighters in Mississippi so cruelly underscored. He employed powerful unconventional tactics, including the famous Alabama march from Selma to Montgomery, to shine a light on unjust racial prejudice that was deeply rooted in the South.

Interpret the Signs

King's careful selection of Selma as a focal point to escalate the struggle for voting rights was based on a keen analysis of the local political scene as well as the various scenarios that could ensue. His opposition movement had already encountered church bombings, lynching, imprisonment, water cannons, and brutal beatings. By recognizing and interpreting political undercurrents, moral awakenings in the North, and changing social mores—especially among younger Americans—King strategically set out to redirect political forces at local and national levels.

Weigh the Risks

Dr. King and his team considered multiple options when choosing targets and tactics, from non-violent civil disobedience to provocatively challenging segregation laws. Driven by an uncompromising vision of social justice, he always approached tactical decisions with a seasoned eye for risks, unintended consequences, and symbolic value. King and his powerful allies had the courage to make tough choices, such as moving forward with their campaign in the face of life-threatening attacks, including a bombing at King's home and an assassination attempt years later.

Make Strong Alliances

King was also very adroit, even as a young leader, at building mutually beneficial connections with local ministers and community organizers.[12] He also masterfully aligned himself with the powers that be, including President Lyndon Johnson, who slowly warmed to the idea of making history by enforcing voter rights protections. This protracted process, pushed through at the right time with reluctant and cautious politicians, required especially shrewd dialog with Johnson, who ranked among the toughest masters of hardball politics.

Learn and Adapt

Dr. King and his associates encountered numerous setbacks and surprises as they launched their historic uphill battle; King was jailed 29 times during the Birmingham campaign alone. He learned first-hand that no plan survives contact with the enemy and that many adjustments to the plan would be required. King and his team experimented with a wide arrange of tactics, including marches, protests, and even leveraging celebrities to create political pressure. Over time, they figured out a powerful tactical mix that worked wonders in the end.

King's impressive command of the above strategic leadership disciplines led to truly historic success but also his assassination in 1968 at age 39. They hold powerful lessons for all leaders, and underscore the courage and persistence needed to change the world. Leaders who want to change minds and overcome deeply entrenched prejudices, biases, and misguided values need to master the six disciplines profiled above, as illustrated through Dr King's words and deeds.[13]

END NOTES

1 This section about six habits of strategic leaders was among the first columns I published at Inc.com. It went viral quickly, reaching over 20,000 viewers; https://www.inc.com/paul-schoemaker/6-habits-of-strategic-thinkers.html.

2 Krupp, Steven, and Paul J. H. Schoemaker. *Winning the long game: How strategic leaders shape the future*. Hachette UK, 2014.

3 Schoemaker, P. J. H., Steve Krupp and Samantha Howland, "Strategic leadership: The essential skills" *Harvard Business Review,* Jan/Feb 2013, 131–134. This article was reprinted in HBR Press Series: *HBR Guide to Thinking Strategically,* 2019 as well in a special HBR Issue on *How to Think More Strategically,* Spring 2023.

4 https://en.wikipedia.org/wiki/Wetherspoons.

5 Kahneman, Daniel. *Thinking, fast and slow.* Macmillan, 2011.

6 Winning Decisions: Getting It Right the First Time: Russo, J. Edward, Schoemaker, Paul J.H.: 9780385502252: Amazon.com: Books.

7 Coleman, Peter T. *The way out: How to overcome toxic polarization.* Columbia University Press, 2021.

8 Wohlstetter, Roberta. *Pearl Harbor: Warning and decision.* Stanford University Press, 1962.

9 Day, George S. and Schoemaker, Paul J. H., *Peripheral Vision: Detecting the Weak Signals that Will Make or Break Your Company,* Harvard Business School Press, May 2006, 248 pp.

10 Schoemaker, Paul J.H, "Nelson Mandela as a Strategic Leader" *The European Business Review,* Jan-Feb 2014, pp. 48–52.

11 x201C;Thembisile Chris Hani," http://www.sahistory.org.za/people/thembisile-chris-hani.

12 Garrow, David J. *Bearing the cross: Martin Luther King, Jr., and the southern Christian leadership conference.* Open Road Media, 2015.

13 McGuire, David, and Kate Hutchings. "Portrait of a transformational leader: the legacy of Dr Martin Luther King Jr." *Leadership & Organization Development Journal* 28.2 (2007): 154–166.

CHAPTER 12

BOARD GOVERNANCE

'this is where the tenured faculty hang out'

12.1 GOVERNANCE—THE CRITICAL FACTOR MANY GET WRONG

—With Rob Arnold*

Success or failure, the creation of value or the lack of it, all come down to one thing: good decision-making. The make-or-break decisions at your company tend to fall into three inter-connected areas: strategy, leadership (finding the right people to make it happen), and governance (setting the framework for who decides what). In our experience, leaders pay far too little attention to governance. And too often, we have seen it tear their company apart.

The Crucial Role of Governance

Governance aims to make it clear who in your company can make which kind of choices, with what ends in mind, and on what basis. Who should get the right to irrevocably allocate scarce resources? How do you design the system to make sure the most qualified people are making smart decisions to create the most value for your company? Wrestling with these questions is not as glamorous, perhaps, as issuing mission statements and recruiting leaders. And true, good governance can't compensate for ineptitude in the other two areas. But if you don't get the governance part right, it could doom your company.

Governance problems come in many sizes and shapes.[1] A typical problem in many owner-led companies is the transition from the founder to the next generation. This issue is usually fraught with emotion, power struggles, hidden family agendas, and considerable anxiety among non-family employees. In one case we consulted on, the founder/CEO/chairman had three sons with very different abilities, but he was unable to distinguish among them in terms of roles and shareholdings. He could not separate running a family business, where he might take from the strong to give to the weak, from running a commercial enterprise, where the weak need to be let go at some point.

Why It's So Tempting to Ignore It

In many owner-driven companies, the owner serves as both CEO and chairman while being the majority shareholder. This is a problem if the primary role of the chairman is to fire the CEO when needed. As long as your company is

---

* Chairman of SLC, a strategy consulting firm based in Singapore.

completely private, you can pretty much govern yourself as you please (with some exceptions). But you shouldn't: Any company, at its root, is a voluntary collaboration in a spirit of cooperation, mutual fairness, and respect, and you should always consider the needs and wishes of other key players.

In one of our own companies, we took great care to lay out the decision rights of the CEO by specifying which choices that person could make alone, which need board notification and which required board approval. These understandings covered such key decisions as setting senior compensation, developing talent, making new investments, licensing IP, raising capital, and entering strategic partnerships.

This meant that the CEO had to give up some power and privilege, but the return—in efficiency and employee engagement—was well worth it. Without sound governance, decisions stall, cash drains away in redundancy and inefficiency, key employees lose commitment and leave, and internal conflicts lead to poor decisions. All these varied symptoms eventually metastasize and can cripple your company.

To assure that you get the governance model right, make sure it aligns with your leadership team as well as current strategy. This way, you will get high-quality decisions throughout your company, on a reliable, consistent basis, to the benefit of many.

12.2 DEFUSING ETHICAL TIME BOMBS IN YOUR COMPANY

—With Tom Donaldson[*]

Nothing keeps a business leader up at night like the nagging feeling that ethical time bombs are ticking somewhere in his or her company. Human nature being what it is, no company is immune from problems—from the deliberate frauds and rogue actions of traders gone wild to the gradual erosion of values and ethical standards because "everyone does it." As a company director, it is your responsibility to sniff out lingering problems before they explode. The good news, so to speak, is this: If there is a time bomb in your company, some people know about it. You just need to get them to tell you.

The roadmap to high integrity and vigilant leadership consists of three main avenues: (1) prevention, (2) detection, and (3) remedy.

---

[*] Professor of Ethics and Legal Studies, The Wharton School.

An Ounce of Prevention

Traditional ethical strategies focus on compliance programs, ethics training, and traditional operational risk assessment. But you should focus instead on:

- Emphasizing not only "tone at the top" but "tone at the middle."
- Creating a culture where people can discuss risk and dubious behavior.
- Popularizing the use of ethical "tests": for example, "How would we look if this business practice became public?"
- Encouraging story telling about respected company leaders who overcame moral dilemmas in the past.
- Ensuring that reward systems don't create conflicts between business objectives and integrity norms.[2]

How to Learn about Problems Faster

Traditional tools of detection include hot lines and analysis of compliance data. They're not nearly enough. Newer tools emphasize:

- Better peripheral vision to detect anomalies sooner and then share
- Improving how to make sense of weak signals by shifting your frame
- Scenario planning to amplify weak signals and connect the dots
- Spotting signs that risks have been normalized ("everyone does it")
- Encouraging whistle blowers instead of shunning or punishing them
- Creating a centrally accessible data base with risk-relevant information for each employee

For example, KPMG has created a central data base about individual employees that can be used for risk assessment when making new assignments or promotions.[3]

How to Fix Them When They Occur

Traditional approaches emphasize the role of HR, legal and compliance programs. Newer tools emphasize:

- Encouraging leaders to engage in MBWA (Management by Walking Around) and skip-level sessions with employees lower down.
- Studying and copying best practices in the industry and beyond.

- Measuring and rewarding enterprise integrity in systematic ways.
- Investing in crisis management, team building and leadership skills.
- Learning how to handle external media, PR and employees internally.
- Discussing relevant lessons from the past for tips and common pitfalls.
- Developing contingency plans and training to help contain damage.

But the best solution lies in your attitude. Don't treat ethics as something for your lawyer or just HR to worry about, and don't assume that you have done all you need to do by writing rules that comply with ethical guidelines. People break rules, and lawyers are most useful only after the problem has become public. After all, most companies with scandals surging all over the Web *did* have top lawyers and *did* maintain complex compliance programs. You yourself have to set the tone of integrity and keep open the lines of communication that prevent smarmy behavior from festering.[4] As founder, CEO, and Board chair, it is your company. Its reputation is yours, and preserving it is ultimately your responsibility.

12.3 MAKING THE MOST OF YOUR MANAGEMENT BOARD
—With Rob Adams*

Presidents have their cabinets and staffs. Queens have their courtiers and ministers. As an entrepreneur, you have, well, yourself and maybe a co-founder or two. That's why a board of directors—a panel of supportive seasoned pros with experience navigating the entrepreneurial world and the industry you're in—can be such a great help. They can give you deep experience, independent oversight, a connection to new talent and customers, and much needed reality checks—on your business plans and on yourself as a leader.[5] The only problem is that boards take some work on your part if they are to live up to their potential. Here are five things you need to do to make a board work for you.

Tell Them Everything; Ask Them Anything

In order to be effective, the directors need to understand your business: its strategy, target markets, value proposition, customers and leads, product roadmap, job openings, internal challenges […] in short, the works. Chances are that one of your directors has some connection or prior experience that can

---

* Managing Partner, Next Stage Capital Management.

help you. But they can't help unless you make sure they know what you're up to and the issues you're facing. The more frequently you give updates and ask for advice—even if by informal emails—the more likely your directors will be up to speed when a chance encounter occurs that can help your business.

Demand Objectivity, Even When It Hurts

Invite your board to give you objective and critical judgments, and then—and this is important—don't be defensive when they do. A board of yes men is of no value to you, so let the directors challenge you in board meetings and allow them to outvote you even if you happen to be the majority shareholder and company owner. Set guidelines requiring at least annual, if not semi-annual, assessment of your performance, then actively solicit these reviews.

Lift the Financial Kimono Frequently and Consistently

If your board does not receive timely financial information in a consistent format from period to period, you are essentially asking them to guide you in the dark. Ask your directors what they expect and agree up front on what will be in the monthly or quarterly reporting package. Too many CEOs report financial or sales pipeline information in different formats each month, which results in directors wasting time trying to connect the dots from the prior period. Make sure to give your CFO the independence to serve the board as well as yourself.

Let the Directors Meet Your Team

Being a good director requires a lot of information, beyond standard board meetings and certainly beyond what you can reasonably provide directors by yourself. Take, for example, the task of evaluating you, which obviously requires candid feedback from people who are not you. So, you have to let your directors establish relationships with managers and others outside the boardroom. If you really want to make the most of your board, you have to integrate your directors into the company, rather than insulate them from it. Face it: This is not easy, especially if you're the controlling type (and what entrepreneur isn't?) or if you're insecure about keeping your job (no comment).

Let the Directors Talk to Your Team

In addition to getting feedback *from* others, your directors should also provide feedback *to* others within the business. If one director is strong in sales or business development, use that network to generate leads for the sales team. If another excels in finance, hook that director up with your CFO. If some directors have technical backgrounds, engage them with the product team. You might have to pay the directors extra, but if you leverage your directors' unique expertise and connections for the company's benefit, everybody wins.

12.4 DO YOU KNOW THE ANIMALS IN THE EXECUTIVE ZOO?

If you want to have a place in the C-suite or Board Room of larger companies, you need to master the lingo. The following creatures have all earned a place in the pantheon of business speak and you may be considered a dodo if you are clueless about their meanings.

Dodo Bird: This extinct bird was last seen around 1662 but has retained a really bad image over the centuries. Indigenous to Mauritius, the dodo has been depicted in travel journals and paintings as a fat, hapless, and clumsy bird. Without native predators, the dodo feared nothing and could just nest on the ground, having lost its ability to fly somewhere along its evolution. All this made the dodo easy prey for hungry European explorers as well as an enduring symbol of creatures too fat and happy to make it in the Darwinian jungle.

Black Swan: Made famous by Nassim Taleb's book of the same name by reminding us all that we live with blinders on at times.[6] Prior to 1697, for example, people in Europe believed that every swan in the world was white. They had never seen any other kind. Then Dutch explorers delivered the surprising news that black swans existed in Australia. Mentioning this black variant is a quick and safe way to remind business colleagues that the impossible—that 10,000 year flood or a sustained market collapse— sometimes does happen, even when it is totally contrary to received wisdom.

Butterfly: According to chaos theory, the tiny wing flaps of a butterfly somewhere in Asia could evolve into a hurricane in the Caribbean. Remember that poor fruit vendor in Tunisia who burned himself in protest against police brutality? Well, that single, seemingly isolated incident set off the Arab Spring uprisings. Small changes can have large consequences in non-linear systems, such as weather or markets, due to feedback loops that create snowball effects. As with avalanches, all hell can break lose quickly, with surprising consequences, which is why the butterfly effect is a key concept.[7]

Hedgehog: The Greek poet Archilochus wrote that *"the fox knows many things, but the hedgehog knows one big thing."* This insight later became shorthand for contrasting intellectual viewpoints based on flexible theories versus those pushing one big idea. In business, a hedgehog strategy means being really good in one thing that really matters, such as perhaps an excellent patent position, a low cost advantage or a privileged relationship that give you a durable edge.

Fox: In contrast, the fox excels at being cunning since it is blessed with many weapons and flexibility. Wharton professor Philip Tetlock used the hedgehog-fox distinction to explain differences in experts' forecasting ability.[8] Hedgehog pundits hinged their political prognostications on one big thing, for example the wisdom of the crowd or a computer model. Fox-like pundits (not to be confused with the dubious Fox News network) analyzed the same political events with more nuance and mental flexibility. They outscored the hedgehogs.

Gorilla: Where does the gorilla sleep? Anywhere it wants. This old quip highlights the appeal of being really powerful—and also perhaps the need for some antitrust laws. A more subtle appearance of this primate into business speak is the now famous video of the invisible gorilla.[9] When people focus intently on counting how often a basketball is passed in this video, half fail to notice that a person dressed in a gorilla outfit walked through the scene. It illustrates the downside of focus, namely loss of peripheral vision and the associated risk of being blind-sided.

Ostrich: This creature is commonly maligned in business speak for burying its head in the sand to avoid seeing danger. But the ostrich does no such thing, nor does it need to. This biggest of birds can actually outrun a horse and is also a very astute escape artists—as I experienced when riding one! Being flightless doesn't imply being defenseless. Unlike the dodo, the ostrich evolved to be very adaptive. So, the next time someone calls you an ostrich in a meeting because you seem to ignore danger, take it as a compliment and explain the difference to this dodo.

The above small sampling of animals, from insects to primates, bestows a special meaning in business settings. I focused on less well-known creatures that provide some conceptual insights into business. I skipped more common ones like Wall Street's bull and bear, swimming with sharks, teaching elephants to dance or how not to become a dinosaur. My aim is to endow C-suite aspirants with sufficient familiarity, sophistication and practical insight to navigate the executive zoo. As in the animal kingdom, the business world is filled with predators. Learn these terms so you don't become prey.

12.5 BOARDS THAT TRULY LEAD

—With George Day*

Few firms were prepared for COVID-19. The ferocity of the attack of this virus surprised even the most vigilant of organizations. But some firms emerged stronger as the shock waves ebbed and the extreme uncertainty from lockdowns, economic slumps, and frozen markets abated. Successful firms avoid the pitfalls of wishful thinking, willful blindness, paralysis, or myopia when catastrophe surrounds them. Board members can manage future systemic chaos by following three navigation principles drawn from best practice, including COVID.

1. Fight the Current Fire and Probe for the Next One

Strategic leaders pay attention to multiple unfolding horizons of turbulence. While they are firefighting in the present by looking after their people, suppliers, customers, and cash, they are also looking ahead. This demands an organizational culture that is agile and curious. The digital transformation of industries continued to accelerate during the crisis. The pandemic gave a big boost to digital mitigation in health care, while nearly all organizations tried to operate virtually as much as possible. Here are some general questions that board members should ask to get beyond a new system crisis that derails their industry, country, or global region.

- What are the biggest uncertainties across the horizon? What scenarios should management develop to capture them in combination?
- What strategic moves can the firm make to emerge as an industry leader? How robust are these moves across the possible scenarios?
- Are there opportunistic moves we can make now—takeovers, market entries or exits? And which ones should we approach flexibly, as options?
- Should we shift the allocation of our innovation resources? Where should we scan for emerging opportunities, and how can we seize the best ones ahead of rivals?
- What new leadership talent and organizational capabilities will be needed to prepare the enterprise for the longer term?

2. Turbulence = Opportunity

Vigilant organizations will systematically nurture dynamic capabilities that foster agility and preparedness. Familiar environments can usually be navigated

---

* Emeritus Professor of Marketing, The Wharton School.

with ordinary capabilities focused on the proficient execution of current processes, such as supply chain management, routine transactions, and reliable performance. If you have to navigate deep uncertainty, however, firms will need a much more vigilant toolkit customized around three dynamic capabilities: *sensing change* sooner than rivals, *seizing* opportunities early on, and *transforming* the organization to stay ahead.[10]

With the right set of dynamic capabilities, an organization can remain agile when turbulence is high. Agility means being able to move quickly and shift resources to higher-value activities sooner than rivals. For example, Intuit formed a small team, a scrum, to explore why its new online payments system, Mint, attracted unexpected customers. The scrum quickly realized that workers in the gig economy, like Uber or Lyft drivers, found their product convenient, and so the company tailored a version specially for them.[11] Scrums function as self-managing teams, follow a transparent process, use design thinking methods to test prototype solutions, and learn quickly. These features are the antithesis of cumbersome, top-down processes with repetitive meetings, rigid command structures, and other impediments to action.

3. Speed Is Essential
Vigilant organizations develop a different perspective about speed than typical firms, namely, being ready when the time is right. Especially in the maelstrom of the coronavirus, speed will remain an especially useful creed, especially for supply chains. Delays tend to narrow the range of strategic options available because someone else may get to them earlier. Seeing sooner also gives vigilant firms more time to create flexible options to be exercised later.

But because the clock of business is whirring faster doesn't mean that leaders must operate in haste. Acting faster than rivals is about being ready for action when needed, and this starts with early detection and learning through probing questions by the C-suite, followed up with exploratory market forays. The aim of superior foresight is to have more degrees of freedom when quick or bold actions are called for, without being boxed in by rivals' moves.

Get Ready for the Long Game
Vigilant organizations employ many eyes and ears to scan the whole of the ecosystem, and are therefore better prepared to absorb mega shocks like the coronavirus. Companies such as Agilent, Intuit, Sysco, and Amazon cultivated the right leadership orientation, economic resources, managerial talent, and

organizational capabilities to seize emerging opportunities ahead of their more vulnerable rivals. Organizational vigilance is a collective capability characterized by curiosity, candor, and openness to diverse inputs. It is the antithesis of myopia, siloed thinking, and being held captive by outdated conventional wisdom. Our own research shows that the resilience of vigilant organizations in turbulent times derives from four strategic drivers[12]:

1. *Leadership's commitment to vigilance* is demonstrated by an openness to weak signals from diverse sources, encouraging everyone to explore issues outside their purview—thinking outside the box. The leadership team focuses externally and nurtures curiosity throughout the entire organization, which allows the company to reconfigure its internal systems and external partnerships on short notice.

2. *Investments in foresight* are made systematically, often through centralized foresight units, that scan the periphery while also collecting internal signals. For example, the supply chain function would have dashboards that flash early warnings when external events threaten timely deliveries. Rather than wait to see how key uncertainties might resolve over time, a vigilant organization proactively develops a flexible portfolio of options so it can probe and act fast when needed.

3. *Strategy making processes* are flexible and adaptive by adopting both an "outside-in" and a "future-back" approach. Outside-in thinking allows leaders to gain deeper insights into the changing circumstances of their strategic partners. By feeling their pain, they can make wiser choices for joint gain later. Future-back thinking is about envisioning what kind of organizational transformations will be needed once threats subside. Leaders can use future scenarios to decide what plants to seed now, while also relieving some of the near-term pain of their people, customers, and suppliers.

4. *Coordination and accountability* mechanisms in well-run enterprises are properly moored in place, such that information is shared readily with those who need it. By flagging and redressing uncoordinated activities and haphazard initiatives, the leadership team reduces decision-making ambiguity and creates the right conditions for continued vigilance. As soon as early warning signals about the COVID pandemic were detected, for example, truly vigilant firms created "plan ahead' teams to think about the future and evaluate promising initiatives from across the firm.

END NOTES

1 Weimer, Jeroen, and Joost Pape. "A taxonomy of systems of corporate governance." *Corporate Governance: An International Review* 7.2 (1999): 152–166.

2 Donaldson, Thomas. "Adding corporate ethics to the bottom line." *Financial Times* 13 (2000).

3 Bell, Timothy B., et al. "KRiskSM: A computerized decision aid for client acceptance and continuance risk assessments." *Auditing: A Journal of Practice & Theory* 21.2 (2002): 97–113.

4 Schwartz, Mark S., Thomas W. Dunfee, and Michael J. Kline. "Tone at the top: An ethics code for directors?." *Journal of Business Ethics* 58 (2005): 79–100.

5 Shen, Wei. "The dynamics of the CEO-board relationship: An evolutionary perspective." *Academy of Management Review* 28.3 (2003): 466–476.

6 Taleb, Nassim. "The black swan: Why don't we learn that we don't learn." *NY: Random House* 1145 (2005).

7 Vernon, Jamie L. "Understanding the butterfly effect." *American Scientist* 105.3 (2017): 130.

8 Mitchell, Gregory, and Philip E. Tetlock. "Cognitive style and judging." *The Psychology of Judicial Decision Making* (2010): 279–84.

9 Chabris, Christopher, and Daniel Simons. *The Invisible Gorilla: How Our Intuitions Deceive us.* Harmony, 2011.

10 Teece, David, and Gary Pisano. *The Dynamic Capabilities of Firms.* Springer Berlin Heidelberg, 2003.

11 Day, George S., and Paul J. H. Schoemaker. *See Sooner, Act Faster: How Vigilant Leaders Thrive in an Era of Digital Turbulence.* MIT Press, 2019.

12 Schoemaker, Paul J. H., and George Day. "Preparing organizations for greater turbulence." *California Management Review* 63.4 (2021): 66–88.

CHAPTER 13

TEAM PERFORMANCE

"All for one and one for..."

13.1 RALLYING YOUR TEAM AROUND A NEW STRATEGY

—With Steve Krupp*

When drafting the Declaration of Independence in 1776, Ben Franklin famously said, "Surely we must all hang together lest we all hang separately" (as traitor to the British Crown). When leaders bring new strategies to life, the biggest obstacle they face is aligning others along the desired path. The gap between strategy and execution remains devilishly hard to bridge.

Research suggests that only 30% of organizations execute their strategies effectively, meaning that 70% of projects are NOT executed well.[1]

Why?

- 95% of managers within an organization say they do not fully understand what the strategy is.
- 75% of managers do not have any stake in the success of the strategy.
- 85% of leaders spend less than one hour a month talking about strategy.

The inability to align stakeholders around strategy implementation takes a heavy toll on leader effectiveness.[2] Efficiency, productivity, and spirit are drained when needed most. The answer does not require divine powers, but rather a human touch that connects with people's interests and their natural desires to work effectively in teams.[3]

Communicate Your Intent Early, Often, and Simply

According to Chip and Dan Heath, authors of the best-selling book *Switch*, "What looks like resistance is often a lack of clarity."[4] Leaders can get so invested in their strategic agendas that they fail to realize that what is clear to them is fuzzy to others. Leaders at Royal/Dutch Shell often assumed that if it took the senior management team half a year to arrive at a shared strategic vision, then it might take the rest of the organization two years or so.

Without abundantly clear communication about where you are going and why, team members may default to behaviors that inadvertently undermine the strategic intent. In an uncertain world, transparency is not a luxury, but an indispensable necessity.

---

* Managing Partner & CEO, Decision Strategies International.

Reach Out to Those Who Have a Stake in Your Direction

The head of a client's R&D group shared a frustration we hear a lot: "The organization is stifling. I have to talk with 6 different people from different departments with different bosses who have different priorities to get everyone on the same page to move forward. It's impossible to get things done to support the strategy. The matrix is killing me."[5]

It was easier for leaders in "command and control organizations" to line up the troops and send them marching. Organizations have moved from hierarchical structures with clear lines of authority to horizontal networks where decision-making is more diffuse. Horizontally networked organizations should especially try to include all those with a significant stake in the outcome.

Such wider communication may slow things down at first, but you will easily make up that time by having better implementation and execution (as Japanese companies showed us with TQM). So, strategic leaders must learn how to navigate the maze and come out the other side with strong alignment, but few have the patience or the skills to pull this off.

Promote Open Dialogue and True Debate

One of the oldest axioms for change leaders is to *approach* resistance, not ignore it or fight it. Yet too often we fail to even surface, let alone fully understand, why people see things differently. This failure readily occurs when people have their heads down and are focused on immediate demands.

And yes, it is messy and often awkward to surface and deal with conflicting views. Yet, we pay a heavy price when we don't attend to differences up front. Strategic leaders must have the courage to face conflict, tease out diverse expectations, and manage differences to build win–win, sustainable solutions.

Reward Those Who Truly Take Ownership

Strategic change can only be achieved when people own the solutions in their guts and not just their heads. What we interpret as "buy-in" is often superficial agreement.

A client engaged us to help them translate their strategy into action. The first thing we did was a "lessons learned" debrief on why they failed to execute successfully before. It became apparent that many leaders did not share the same urgency or ownership of the prior initiatives, even those assigned to them. This is all too common when leaders fail to clarify their change agenda, connect key stakeholders, and promote debate of the issues. Make sure your colleagues have truly signed on to the same plan that you think all agreed to execute.

Rallying people around an execution strategy is hard work. Unless you rely on a proven approach to align stakeholders, you may have no more than an illusion of agreement and a failed project later on.

13.2 HOW TO CREATE A CONSTRUCTIVE LEARNING CULTURE

—With Franck Schuurmans[*]

Face it: you don't know everything. So, at the individual level, you should make a lifelong commitment to exploring new horizons. At the company level, establishing good learning practices turns out to be a much greater challenge. Here are three suggestions for creating a genuine learning culture at work.

Make Learning a Daily Habit

As with music or sports, unless you practice a lot you will not get better. True learning organizations reward new patterns of thinking and reinforce the underlying skill sets. Unfortunately, such learning organizations are not the norm. One problem is that many organizations make learning an optional activity, one from which the senior team is far too often (self)-exempt. Another is that they may not know how to learn best.

Since "learning from example" is contagious, the behavior of the boss becomes critical. Leaders should be the focal point as well as champions for learning. They are best positioned to shine a bright spotlight on success as well as failure, and see to it that mistakes become sources of new learning. To learn well, you must critically examine both the process and outcomes of the decision and ensure that others do so as well.

Don't Be Defensive—Confront Failings Honestly

A key imperative for learning from experience is the willingness to look squarely at one's own performance in a transparent and non-defensive manner. The U.S. Army institutionalized the practice of *After Action*[6] *Review* to immediately learn from what went well and what did not work in a mission. Avoid finger pointing when things go bad and instead try to diagnose the situation for new insights.

---

[*] Senior Consultant, Decision Strategies International.

After Action Review is a structured process for analyzing what happened, why it happened, and how it can be done better the next time. So, it should involve the main participants as well as those responsible for the overall mission. Frank discussions should take place without regard of rank or fear of retaliation. Today's asymmetric warfare entails high uncertainty and rapid change, with less room for traditional planning. What leaders know is less important than how well they can challenge, learn and adapt. In such environments, fast and furious learning trumps rigid protocol.

Allow Mistakes and Celebrate Them at Times

Mistakes are valuable sources of learning, and leaders should intentionally allow mistakes in some exploratory situations to challenge or valid deeply held assumptions. If your organization gives performance awards at key meetings, make sure to celebrate a few cases where the results were disappointing but the process followed was sound. A good decision process can still suffer from bad outcome (due to bad luck), just as a really lousy decision process will occasionally produce a good outcome as well (thanks to dumb luck).

Advertising genius David Ogilvy was especially keen on challenging key assumptions and thinking outside of the box. At times, he would run ads he did not believe would work, just to test his theories about advertising. He continually challenged conventional wisdom, including his own, recognizing the fast pace of change surrounding him. This mindset of learning and critical inquiry allowed Ogilvy to build a global media empire.

Create an Environment that Rewards Learning

1. Conduct pre-decision and after-action debriefs to extract insights.
2. Build the necessary discipline to look at failure as well as success.
3. Internalize mistakes and lessons learned, and then applying them broadly.
4. Stop initiatives that are not producing as expected; know when to pull the plug.
5. Conduct annual learning audits where cherished beliefs can be challenged.

13.3 WAYS TO BECOME A CREDIBLE LEADER AND TEAM

—With Hanke Lange*

You started modestly in your career and have made it to the management team—congrats. At long last, you are in control of your own destiny, or so it seems at least. But whether your team runs an entire company, a division, a business unit, or function, you are still subject to oversight and review.

At the most senior level, it will be a board of directors that evaluates the senior management team's overall performance. Having served on several boards and worked with many more in different parts of the world, we know that developing credibility is a key determinant of long-term success for management teams.

Why Credibility Matters

You might think that hitting your numbers and fostering good board relationships are the key factors, and yes, they do matter. But at a deeper level, much comes down to your board of supervisors' having confidence in your team's ability to deliver reliably on what is expected. It is all about *credibility*, because that will influence trust, resource allocation, strategy approval, empowerment, and risk taking.[7]

Based on our field research as well as decades of experience, credibility most depends on:

1. *Strong Results*
A supervisory board is usually most responsible for the long-term viability of the organization. A strong predictor of future performance is past performance, however that happens to be measured. If results are strong, confidence develops, conflicts reduce, reputations build, and mutual confidence grows. Once the risk of negative surprises declines, the team can start to aim higher and eventually shoot for the stars.

2. *Shared Vision*
It is not enough that the team leader has a clear vision. The vision must be supported by the entire team as well as the board. The broader the support plane for the vision or strategy, the more likely it will succeed. The vision needs

---

* Organizational Consultant, Bilthoven, The Netherlands.

to connect with other players' agendas and be viewed as a compelling story that excites them. If so, it will be shared further and start to energize the many others who can help achieve the vision.

3. Involvement

In many cases, credibility can be earned by engaging board members in key management decisions and discussing important dilemmas or tradeoffs. Those charged with oversight seldom want to be presented with a fait accompli. In most settings (but not all), they will expect to be consulted. If so, keeping them out of the loop will destroy trust and motivation.

4. Bench Strength

Credibility also hinges on how much confidence the board has in the *second echelon* in the organization (i.e., people reporting to the management team) and even lower. If they never see those folks, there is just more risk (especially in case key players leave). Bench strength impacts implementation success as well as succession. Also, it affects the quality of dialogue and challenge upward, because sometimes a counter-veiling force is needed to keep dominant leaders in check.

5. Being Part of the Solution

As long as the board views your team as part of the solution, you stand strong. This in turn hinges on the team's competence in solving critical issues as well as the team's motivation in getting the job done. Once individual managers or an entire team is viewed as part of the problem by their superiors, credibility goes out the window and they may be shown the door eventually. So make sure your team is viewed as being relevant, capable, constructive, practical, responsive, and above all highly motivated.

6. High Integrity

Integrity is directly tied to team members being true to themselves and others in terms of values and viewpoints. Authentic teams instill confidence, because they don't play political games and don't backstab others. Their word is their bond, and they can be counted on when things get tough or nasty. Integrity is closely tied to such time-tested ethical principles as honesty, fairness, and respect for others. It is important that team members do not abuse their privileges and power for personal gain, and that they are called on it when they do.

Business and commerce are at their root collaborative enterprises. We orchestrate competition to gain efficiency, stimulate innovation, and help people reach their fullest potential, but all within a broader context of voluntary participation. The six ways above are not listed in terms of importance, because much depends on the specific situation and the broader social as well as cultural context. But each of them matters in fostering team credibility.

13.4 DOES YOUR TEAM MATCH YOUR STRATEGY

—With Steve Krupp[*]

You just came out of your strategy review session with wind at your back. Your growth strategy was approved by the top bananas. They like your plan to move aggressively into emerging markets and to target small acquisitions to expand into new product areas.

"Go for it," they say—just make it happen! As you are celebrating with your team, you step back, look around the table and are hit by a jolt of cold reality. Can this team deliver on the promise? Is there anyone well suited to lead the emerging market strategy? Who can sniff out M&A targets, negotiate complex acquisitions, and manage the integration process?

Any team leader must periodically ask, "Does the current team match the strategy?" This means evaluating your current talent against the demands of a new business plan. You need to see if any serious gaps exist and if so, systematically address them. Even in highly competitive business markets, few leaders handle this well. It isn't always easy to align your talent and business strategy. Shaking up an existing team can be emotionally taxing and damaging to morale. The best you can do is to follow a disciplined approach when realigning your team:

Honestly Map Your Talent Needs to Fit the New Strategy or Plan

A pharmaceutical team leader created a simple chart to illustrate major areas of change needed to move team talents from the current state to the desire state in order to execute their new plans. One move was *from* focusing primarily on the physician customer *to focusing* more on the payer. For this particular shift, they listed the main implications for talent. It led them to include people who know how to work well with managed care payers like governments and insurance companies. Through this kind of systematic mapping, the leader identified experience and skills gaps plus the talent changes required for each element of their strategy.

---

[*] Managing Partner & CEO, Decision Strategies International.

Identify Those Few Critical Roles that Will Make or Break Success

A common mistake is to view all team roles as equally critical to executing the strategy. Another is to equate people's importance to project success with where they rank in the hierarchy. The team leader in the opening example embarked on an aggressive growth strategy in emerging markets with gusto. The GM role proved most critical to this goal, especially for business units in Asia and Latin America, so this got special attention. Top talent should always be allocated to the most critical roles for the strategy to succeed. The pharmaceutical company mentioned above put a laser focus on five key roles and heavily invested development resources in those critical areas.

Define the top capabilities needed for success in those roles

Be crystal clear about the capabilities for future success. If growth in emerging markets is the top priority, fostering a global mindset and acquiring local experience become essential. If the new strategy requires a matrix structure, then collaboration and managing across boundaries become paramount. So, take the roles from the previous step and design role profiles for each of them. Then spec out the experiences, skills, values and other attributes that matter most for each role.

Assess Skill Gaps and Find Talent Internally or Externally

Knowing which roles and skills are mission-critical is a good start, but the next step is even more crucial. Take an objective hard look at your current people and ask how well they fit the evolving criteria for each role. For the above example, are they sufficiently global, strategic, or collaborative? Use assessment tools that are specifically targeted at developing future capabilities needed. This will help surface gaps. Next, identify and invest in developing the needed talent across the organization to fill those gaps. Also, look outside since new strategies often require different mindsets and skills that are easier to buy than build.[3]

Having right talent is necessary, but may not be sufficient. Groom and support your talent. Create targeted training programs since they can be a powerful catalyst for transformation and development. Be mindful, however, that their degree of success is often proportionate to the level of senior management ownership, involvement, and support. Engage executives to mentor and coach new leaders in key roles. Periodically send strong messages and design incentives to support the behaviors tied to strategic success.

13.5 IMPROVING YOUR TEAM'S COMMUNICATIONS

Developing team alignment in our fast-moving, network-based organizations, with many virtual colleagues, takes special efforts by leaders and followers alike. The key is to create time for deep dialogues when needed while respecting cultural and professional differences.[9]

People from highly diverse backgrounds instinctively recognize the difference between deep dialogue and casual conversation. We all know that satisfying feeling of having really connected with someone. There are important cultural differences, however, in how this is achieved since it cannot just be ordered when needed. It takes investment in relationships.

When defining deep dialogue, people in the West focus more on having a "good exchange of views" or "a meeting of the minds," whereas Asians are more likely to emphasize "warm feelings "and a "conversation of the heart." Both groups agree, however, on several features that are essential for genuine deep dialogue: information exchange, mutual trust and respect, and shared interests.

My former colleague and friend Professor Howard Perlmutter conducted studies with global executives at Wharton and elsewhere that revealed five common types of dialogue deficits. They apply to relationships inside organizations as well as to those in one's personal life. Here is the assessment scale Perlmutter used to help assess where you currently stand with people you have to interact with or would like to.[10]

Types of Dialogue Deficit

Fallow: No recent conversation or positive encounters took place and there actually may be a degree of avoidance. Such moribund relationships suggest there is little knowledge or interest in the other and/or it may reflect underlying anxieties about establishing contact.

Failed: There were past interactions but at present there are no attempts at communicating. Bad memories, unhealed wounds, or unsettled scores conspire to resist efforts to renew attempts at dialogue and mutual understanding.

Failing: The levels of existing trust and respect are decreasing, and efforts to bridge differences are failing. There is also a marked reduction in bonding and a greater focus on differences than similarities, and the multiple gaps seem harder to bridge by each side.

Frozen: There is an emotional or cognitive stalemate in an ongoing but polarized debate, with participants being stuck in fixed positions or rigid viewpoints. No bridging appears possible. Intermediation has failed in what is seen by many as a chronic stalemate.

Feeble: There is minimal information exchange and people fail to share tacit or important information. Low openness, inattentive listening, defensive routines, and infrequent meetings mark these relationships. There is a narrowing domain of information sharing.

Developing Deep Dialogue[11]

Being a humanist at heart and an accomplished social architect, Howard Perlmutter was very interested in developing constructive approaches to improving the quality of dialogue at micro- and macro level.[12] Building on best organizational practices as well as social psychology and clinical counseling, he advocated the following seven strategies.

Bridging: Deal constructively with differences among people, which means respecting, celebrating, and transcending differences. It takes patience to bridge temporal, linguistic, cultural, and geographical differences but once achieved, information and new ideas will flow more freely. The greater the capacity to transcend differences, the greater the depth and quality of information that will be exchanged.

Bonding: Engage in activities that encourage mutual trust and respect. Good personal chemistry, feelings of friendship, and heart-to-heart conversations are key here. Bonding is closely associated with degrees of mutual trust and respect, as well as relating the other as a unique human, not as an abstract stereotype.

Banding: Emphasize "we" as part of a developing a collective mindset as opposed to "I" versus "you" thinking. A sense of harmony and unity is felt when engaged in dialog and collaborative interactions. There is a mutual desire to have fertile dialogues and to create interdependence or even a shared identity.

Blending: Combine ideas for innovations in a spirit of co-creation, building on distinctive strengths and constructive collaboration. Enhancing each other's ideas by saying "and" rather than "but" leads to new synergies with persons from different backgrounds and cultures.

Bounding: Focus collective energies on a meaningful task, a purposeful project, so as to find fertile domains for sharing. Also, set boundaries for collaboration such that valuable resources can be made available without fear of misuse or wasted effort.

Binding: Make a commitment to work on a shared project, with joint stakes in the outcomes, to foster mutual trust with an orientation toward the future. The key here is to make mutual commitments to carry out projects for joined shared gains.

Building: Take actions to help a joint project succeed, after having made a commitment to do so. Develop a clear architecture, with a shared vision and mutual governance. The key is to leverage diverse skills and cultures in the service of a joint objective.

The above strategies work better in combination than alone, and can be customized to achieve closer alignment among people when implementing a strategy or developing a strategic alliance. Especially in virtual teams, it is important to create face-to-face encounters so that bridges can be built and deep dialogue develops. Leaders must complement the task-oriented and often virtual nature of business with people-oriented activities aimed at creating a deeper sense of trust, belonging, and shared stakes in the future of the enterprise.

END NOTES

1 Why CEOs Fail It's rarely for lack of smarts or vision. Most unsuccessful CEOs stumble because of one simple, fatal shortcoming. June 21, 1999 (cnn.com).

2 Hrebiniak, Lawrence G. *Making Strategy Work: Leading Effective Execution and Change.* FT Press, 2013.

3 Sull, Donald, Rebecca Homkes, and Charles Sull. "Why strategy execution unravels—and what to do about it." *Harvard Business Review* 93.3 (2015): 57–66.

4 Heath, Chip, and Dan Heath. *Switch.* Vintage Espanol, 2011.

5 Krupp, Steven and Paul J.H. Schoemaker, *Winning the Long Game: How Strategic Leaders Shape the Future*, Public Affairs Imprint of Perseus, Dec 2014, p 169.

6 Morrison, John E. *Foundations of the After Action Review Process.* Vol. 42. United States Army Research Institute for the Behavioral and Social Sciences, 1999.

7 Williams Jr, Ralph, et al. "Building leader credibility: Guidance drawn from literature." *Journal of Management Development* 42.2 (2023): 106–124.

8 Cappelli, Peter, Anna Tavis, Lisa Burrell, Dominic Barton, Dennis Carey, and Ram Charan. "The new rules of talent management." *Harvard Business Review* (2018).

9 This essay draws on joint work I conducted with Howard Perlmutter (deceased) when he was Emeritus Professor at the Wharton School and Director of the Emerging Global Civilization project.

10 Based on https://knowledge.wharton.upenn.edu/article/dialog-or-death/.

11 Winters, Mary-Frances. *Inclusive Conversations: Fostering Equity, Empathy, and Belonging across Differences.* Berrett-Koehler Publishers, 2020.

12 Perlmutter, Howard V. "The race between the forces leading to a first or last global civilization." *International Business Scholarship: AIB Fellows on the First 50 Years and Beyond.* Vol. 14. Emerald Group Publishing Limited, 2008. 393–399.

CHAPTER 14

DECISION MAKING

"I was just looking for a simple yes or no."

FROM *HARVARD BUSINESS REVIEW*, NOVEMBER 2014. CARTOON BY BILL ABBOTT.

© HBR.ORG

14.1 MAKING BETTER DECISIONS—THREE EASY STEPS

—With Samantha Howland*

It's not often that a CEO sends a public note to key constituents taking responsibility for a bad decision. But Netflix CEO Reed Hastings did exactly that in his apology letter to customers. While some bloggers commented that the confession was like suicide, many others found his willingness to share the decision-making process refreshing.

Netflix created Qwikster in 2011 to spin-off the video streaming part of its business from its core DVD-by-Mail operation. To encourage online downloading, it unbundled its virtual and snail mail offerings, jacking up the combined price about 60%. Hundreds of thousands of enraged customers dropped their subscriptions in response. Netflix's profit was badly hurt as well as its image and trust: its stock price declined over 65% that year.[1]

One wonders how a successful entrepreneur seasoned by years of growing his company could make such a bad call. In his note, Hastings revealed the flawed assumptions about what customers really valued and he acknowledged that their priorities were not properly evaluated. He bared his thinking process, offered a mea culpa, and in the process invited derision as well.

The bigger the job, the loftier the title, the weightier most decisions get.

Employees and others usually help prepare the tough decisions that the chief face. Whether it's executing a big strategic move, evaluating resource tradeoffs, or addressing a minor issue, it is typically assumed that the more experience and seniority the leader has, the better their final decision making will be. This is a dangerous assumption. Most leaders need to find a middle ground between shooting from the hip and forever analyzing without pulling the trigger. Sometimes experience and personality get in the way, not to mention market changes.

In contrast to Netflix's rash decisions, quite a few leaders get wrapped around the axle due to "analysis paralysis." They are loath to make a call without conclusive proof to support their decisions. They seem unable to set an appropriate risk threshold that allows decisions to be made in a timely fashion. Their quest for the perfect decision causes them to miss windows of opportunity while frustrating their minions in the process. As Winston Churchill warned, the maxim "Nothing but perfection" often translates into costly paralysis.

In our survey with over 20,000 managers, the ability to decide scored lowest among six distinct skills crucial to strategic thinking.[2] Many leaders rated themselves poorest on the essential act of making a sound and timely choice. Formal feedback

---

* Principal at Decision Strategies International.

on the decision-making process is often non-existent in companies. Most people are evaluated on results—not on the quality of their decision process.

Improve Your Decision Process

Effective leaders combine experience and a strong decision process that forces them to evaluate, listen, adjust, and learn from each decision. Strategic leaders typically build in these three core steps when evaluating and arriving at *Winning Decisions*.[3]

1. *Carefully frame and then reframe your decisions.* Strategic thinkers consider what truly needs to be decided right now. They ask themselves: What is the crux of problem you need to solve or the opportunity you want to capture? Will the decision advance our overall goals?
2. *Balance speed, rigor, quality and agility.* Endless analysis loops do not make for a good decision; it takes courage to decide based on incomplete information and conflicting opinions, or when uncertain consequences lurk, and naysayers abound.
3. *Remain flexible.* Strategic leaders often break the decision down into smaller options or sub-steps. They reframe a binary yes/no decision as entailing more than two alternatives. They stage the decision over time and run pilot tests on key assumptions when possible.

If CEO Hastings at Netflix had applied the above three steps, he likely would have changed the timing of the decision, tested it with a pilot customer group, and reframed the decision toward things customers truly cared about. If so, he would have made a very different call. But his remarkable candor by admitting his mistake, and then publicly dissecting his decision process, is a welcome lesson for all of us. Other organizations likewise learn from their own mistakes by conducting post mortems periodically (like hospitals do) and then turn these into pre-mortems so that we—or others we care about—don't repeat the same mistakes.

14.2 WHY THINKING FROM THE OUTSIDE-IN IS KEY

—With Nadine Pearce*

Most of our problem solving is "inside-out," meaning that we start with an issue as we or others see it at first and then explore solutions within that initial

---

* Global Head Organizational Development, Oncology, Novartis Pharmaceuticals.

mental frame. Outside-in thinking, by contrast, means seeing the issue always from multiple external perspectives. For example, do you place yourself in the shoes of key stakeholders involved and do you look at complex issues more from a future perspective as well?

Intel CEO Andy Grove was a superb outside-in thinker and always on the lookout for "strategic inflection points" (a phrase he coined). Grove constantly prodded Intel's management to anticipate and react to game-changing shifts in their industry and the global economy. After he was appointed CEO, he asked his team: "suppose we had just acquired Intel, would we stay on the same path?" This key question changed Intel's strategy away from memory storage toward semi-conductors. Being confident enough to ask this kind of question is critical for any good leader.[4]

A Booz & Company's study found that *rather than breadth of experience, boards and recruiters should look for a proven track record of challenging conventional wisdom and experimenting with unconventional ideas.*[5] Doing this well entails at least three qualities: (1) humility in accepting that no person can see all angles, (2) courage in flinging the window open to whoever can offer new insights, and (3) developing a tolerance for well-intentioned failures. Tom Watson Sr., founder of IBM, counseled that *if you want to succeed faster, make more mistakes.* But this is hard in cultures that seldom praise or reward unsuccessful but worthwhile efforts.[6]

The French philosopher Voltaire argued that we should "not judge people by their answers but by their questions." A metal company faced the problem of a major discrepancy between its physical and book inventory. The management team tried to find explanations and someone suggested that it might be a case of theft—as had happened before. This juicy idea really got the group going, and various potential suspects were quickly floated in this whodunit. Then someone asked, suppose it is indeed theft: how much inventory would have to be stolen? The calculators came out and soon it dawned on everyone that about three truckloads of metal pieces would have to have been removed, through their security guard, with cameras all around. Highly unlikely.

This one crucial outside-in question killed the theft hypothesis and redirected the management team to more promising solutions. It turned out to be an accounting error occasioned by one data entry mistake and a freak combination of flawed estimates for work-in-progress inventory. The broader challenge in general is not to get sucked into just one hypothesis but to remain flexible as well as open-minded. Unfortunately, the confirmation bias[7]—in which we try to prove ourselves right—often blinds us to new information and perspectives, resulting in poor situational awareness and ineffective problem solving. Change versatility—defined as the ability to induce, manage, and learn from change—scores low in many company surveys and is often due to inside-out thinking with limited room for change. To grow as a business leader, you must know when to shift toward an outside perspective.

Why This Should Matter to You

Outside-in approaches matter especially for companies that have a strong focus on innovation, trend spotting, new ideas, team work, and relational skill building. These worthy goals can only be met if enough people engage in outside-in thinking. This skill has special salience when you must deal with organizational changes, such as the creation of a new division or the centralization of a critical function like R&D or sales. There is always the risk that functions or departments become worlds onto themselves (like silos), without interacting sufficiently with other parts of the organization and outside. One way to overcome silo behavior and distinguish yourself as a "boundary spanner" is to build social and relational capital with colleagues across organizational boundaries.[8] This will allow you to scan wider and develop better external peripheral vision, so you can see around the corner and act faster. Here are some other strategic benefits that will propel your career once you master thinking outside in.[9]

- People will notice in meetings that you have become more flexible in how you approach issues; your viewpoints will become less of the *same old, same old* kind.
- You will develop more empathy toward other people and their challenges; seeing and feeling issues through the eyes of another very much requires an outside-in approach.
- When managing complex negotiations in search of win–win solutions, you will spend more time thinking about other people's issues, goals and constraints than your own.
- Outside-in thinking will open you up to new experiences, different relationships, deeper insights and rekindle the joy of new discoveries (as shown in the movie *Yes Man*).

Apart from practicing all this yourself, try to notice in meetings who is good at outside-in thinking; are their careers progressing faster; do people gravitate toward them as leaders; and how might you emulate some of these special behaviors and values?

14.3 SIX WAYS TO SOLVE PROBLEMS FROM THE OUTSIDE-IN

It vital for business leaders not to get blindsided due to narrow frames or tunnel vision about the future. The key is to always see complex issues from multiple angles by insisting on more diverse perspectives. This means zooming in and out to obtain a more kaleidoscopic view of the issues of interest.

Six Proven Ways to Zoom Out

Encourage diverse views: To promote diverse thought, Hala Moddelmog, former president of Atlanta, Georgia-based Arby's Restaurant Group Inc., a fast-food chain with about 3,400 locations, surrounded herself with colleagues of different races, geographies, socioeconomic classes, and personality styles.[10] "You really don't need another you," she said. Staying open to different viewpoints helps ensure leaders are not unduly hindered by decision traps and can instead train their eyes on information or solutions that were not previously considered.[11]

Shift perspectives: Dennis the Menace is a classic cartoon character who is way too wise for his young age. One evening Dennis really botches his cooking adventure while his parents are out. The oven becomes caked in floury goo, dishes and baking supplies strewn across the kitchen floor; and the dog has his own baking mess. When his parents returned to see the war zone formerly known as their kitchen, they started to scold their young son. But then the precocious Dennis reframes the situation: "I know you are really upset right now, but in a few years we shall all look back on this and have a good laugh. Can we do that now?" Gary Larson's famous cartoons likewise contain great examples of changing our perspectives in humorous or enlightening ways.

Scan the periphery: Early in 2008, DuPont's CEO Charles O. Holliday Jr. noticed several weak signals in his environment that helped him detect the Great Recession sooner than most.[12] While visiting a major Japanese customer, Holliday learned that his customer's CEO had instructed the staff to conserve cash. Upon returning home to Wilmington, Delaware, Holliday learned that reservations at the prestigious Hotel Du Pont, near corporate headquarters, had dropped 30% in 10 days. Lastly, he learned that Detroit's automakers, who were big DuPont customers, were scaling back production schedules because orders for new cars were dropping. Triangulating these separate signals from the periphery convinced him that the company was about to hit a wall, as it did in 2018 when the Great Recession struck, for which DuPont was ready.

Bring in your personal life: The eccentric Scottish biologist Alexander Fleming returned to his lab after a summer holiday in 1928 and began gathering up various contaminated petri dishes for a good scrubbing. Suddenly, he noticed a small irregularity at the edge of one culture. Many biologists might have missed this anomaly, but Fleming knew bacterial growths as an artist knows the color spectrum. Fleming was an amateur artist, and his unusual "painting" hobby at the Chelsey art club consisted of shaping colonies of Staphylococcus into portraits of his coworkers. His keen peripheral perception about bacterial growth led eventually to the wonder drug penicillin, earning Fleming a Nobel Prize in medicine.[13]

Leverage nature: Gas pipelines in Canada, the U.S., and other countries can run more than 100 miles in length. One constant problem is detecting where leaks may be occurring, since gas is invisible and often odorless. Today, high-tech sensors can run up and down the pipeline—but nature can lend a helping hand more cheaply. Turkey vultures, for example, are attracted to odors that gas companies add to alert humans to gas leaks, such as ethyl mercaptan, which smells like rotten eggs. Once a gas has been augmented with the right odors, pipeline operators can use binoculars, or drones now, to see where the birds are hovering, inspect for significant leaks around there and repair them if necessary.

Remain hyper curious: Buckminster Fuller was the inventor of the Geodesic dome, a large, spherical structure modeled after bee hives and other sturdy architectures found in nature. He was honored for his many inventions and his face adorned a U.S. stamp. His success derived from his extreme curiosity about the world around him. Whenever he traveled, he randomly picked a magazine from a kiosk and forced himself to read the whole thing. The topics could be basket weaving, fly fishing, electronics, or politics. This kind of broad, unstructured learning stands in stark contrast to the ecochambers we create when pre-selecting the information channels we want and the social media networks to hang out in. Fuller tried hard to escape such bubbles by vigorously engaging in less filtered learning.

Practical Things You Can Do Each Day

Create "balcony moments" to take some distance, reframe, and de-escalate unproductive disputes; try to see things from a distance, as if on a balcony looking down.

Invest in broader personal and professional networks, to enhance your own radar system and stay more closely in touch with what is changing around you.

Reinvigorate your natural curiosity, the kind you had as a child; find joy (again) in exploration, chance discoveries, random walks and experimentation.

View failure as learning and always look for those silver linings of unexpected insights

Practice disconfirmation or reverse brainstorming; question commonly accepted knowledge and assumptions with new data or viewpoints.

In your own organization, try leading up; leadership doesn't only flow top down, but sideways and even up. Manage your boss and others higher up.

To understand customers better, imagine yourself stapled to a purchase order and visualize the hurdles, pains, and delays, they have to endure as part of your order fulfillment process.

Reflective Questions to Ask Yourself

How might this issue be framed from other people's perspectives? Do others consider me good at reframing issues? Am I considered an empathic person who can fully appreciate other people's concerns and problems? Can I easily place myself in the shoes of another emotionally?

How strong is my situational awareness—do I get blindsided very often? Do I commonly raise issues that others have overlooked? Think of specific recent examples.

How can I shift from automatically or prematurely judging and labeling problems, people and issues, to fostering a much more open and curious mind?

In strategy sessions, consider what might be possible now that was not possible before? Thinking from the outside-in should be liberating by casting off unproductive shackles from the past.

When dealing with someone whose opinions are very different from me— such as mavericks or contrarians—am I sufficiently curious and eager to understand them?

Do I welcome people who are different and do I explore situations that are novel and uncomfortable in order to challenge myself, learn and grow?

14.4 DO YOU KNOW WHAT YOU DON'T KNOW?

Knowledge is power but much depends on how asymmetric it is: what do you know that others don't and vice versa. Below are four strategically different levels of know-how plus some of the strategies you can use to leverage each to advantage.

The complex issue of handling asymmetric information is central to the field of game theory—a rigorous analytic discipline used widely in economics, business, strategy, political science, law, and more.[14] I'll address here the mind-twisting problem of how much you know about what others do and don't know, and conversely, what they know about what you do and don't know. This may seem esoteric but we encounter such issues daily. Let's start simple and then build up the layers of asymmetric know-how.

Level 1: Only You Know About a Misdeed. Suppose you find out that your main competitor has stolen some of your intellectual property (IP) or other assets, and is using this against you. It could be some proprietary software, a customer list, a supplier contract, wage scales, your pricing strategies, or other confidential know-how. Often the IP thieves will be within the organization, as happened to the National Security Agency and numerous companies in such fields as oil & gas, agricultural seeds, and all manner of technology. The U.S. Department of Commerce estimated that IP theft has accounted for trillions in lost value.[15] Much of this comes from industrial espionage by outsiders as well, especially China, although many countries and other rivals play this game.

Your first reaction when learning that your secrets were stolen may be to cry foul and call the lawyers. But there may be advantage in you knowing something about their misdeeds while they don't know that you know. First, you could infringe some of their IP as payment in kind, with a soft hint that two can play this game. This may lead to tacit collaboration, a formal licensing arrangement, or conflict resolution less costly than an ugly shoot out at high noon with legal gun slingers. Also, reconciliation can build understanding, trust, or even empathy. For example, when parents find out that their young child stole some of their cash, smoked pot or drank alcohol, they can jump all over the kid or gently signal awareness, in ways that allow for face saving self-correction and maturation of the child.

Level 2: The Other Party Knows You Know. Suppose, however, that your competitor finds out on its own—without you having informed them—that you know that they have violated your IP. What should you do in this symmetric knowledge situation about the violation? First, it may not be truly symmetric because the rival may not know that *you know* that they know. This is akin to a child knowing that his parents found out about the smoking or drinking, while still being unsure about whether they know that he knows that. For example, it could be that the maid told the child that the parents know. As before, it may be wise to keep such meta-knowledge (i.e., what each of you know about what the other knows) asymmetric since the situation may automatically correct itself. The child will either stop his misdeed or become even more devious perhaps—although he now realizes that his parents are not as clueless as he previously assumed.

Level 3: A Child Knows His Parents Know that He Knows. Suppose that the child discovers, perhaps from the maid, that his parents now know that he knows that they have uncovered his nefarious deeds. This would be embarrassing, even though some semblance of ignorance can still be feigned, since his parents have not directly confirmed this by confronting him. Perhaps the maid lied and is playing her own game to get the child to cease his infractions, concerned that the parents will blame her for not telling them. Without complicating this layer cake further, with the maid's varying degree of knowledge and hidden agendas, it should be clear that knowledge asymmetry can happen at multiple levels.

The first is knowledge about presumed acts of behavior (such as an IP infringement). The second level concerns the parties' awareness about what the other side knows and doesn't know. The game theory aspects of just the two-party conflict becomes more complex at this higher strategic level. It will seldom be optimal to put all cards on the table if tactical advantage is the aim, since judicious signaling, while avoiding loss of face, may lead to better outcomes. In international negotiations about violations of trade agreements, for example, a piecemeal approach may lead to better outcomes than fully escalating the conflict with hurt egos and further recriminations.

Level 4: Full Parity—Everybody Spills the Beans. Suppose, however, that parents tell their child that they know he knows that they know; the strategic situation now will reach a different level of meta-knowledge yet. If the indirect approach mentioned in level 3 does not work, then in anything from corporate disputes to child rearing to marital infidelity, it may pay to put all cards on the table. If restricted to one single issue, such as a stolen customer list or a child smoking pot, talking it all out may—perhaps with the help of a professional counselor—be cathartic. But when multiple issues are at stake, or if there are more than two aggrieved parties, the situation may call for seasoned negotiators who know when to separate or combine issues. One problem is that you will never know for sure that everyone has shared all they know, although legal clauses with punitive damage levels may get you close.

The general advice in complex cases of conflict is to pursue *principled* negotiations rather than *positional* bargaining, as explained in *Getting to Yes*.[16] Try to agree on the principles that should govern the issue to be negotiated, such as trade dispute or a salary raise, before haggling about dollars or concessions as though you are in a Turkish bazaar. For example, should the primary reference point when hiring new managers be their past salary, your own internal payment scale, or the amount an outside party is offering them? Once you agree on that in principle, the remaining negotiation will be much easier. Also remember that good negotiators spend more time understanding the other side's hopes, fears, and context than just their own agendas, plus any knowledge asymmetries that might exist.

14.5 TAKING CONFLICT OUT OF CONFLICTING ADVICE

—With Phil Tetlock[*]

What should you do when people you respect offer conflicting business or personal advice? First, realize that nearly all real-world advice contains a mixture. There are real facts, presumed facts, personal values and cognitive inferences, all of them intermingled, often in complex ways, perhaps invisible to the advisers themselves. Second, try to untangle this mess using a divide-and-conquer approach. Here are some examples to guide you:

The Denver Bullett Battle

Six decades ago, a highly charged controversy confronted Denver's mayor: should he allow the police to use deadlier, hollow-point bullets. The officers were being outgunned by criminals and felt vulnerable. But critics argued that the police should not become judge, jury, and executioner all at once. Hollow point bullets are meant to enhance "stopping power" —the ability to immobilize suspects—but cause far more bodily harm. Various citizens groups disliked hollow point bullets and street protests escalated, with each side marshaling its own ballistics experts.

To solve the brewing crisis, the mayor reached out to Professor Kenneth Hammond, a decision expert from the University of Colorado. Hammond interviewed each side and found that the opposing ballistics experts did not disagree much on the injury potential, stopping power or ricochet risk of the bullets. Their divergence stemmed from different implicit tradeoffs they made between safety, suspect rights, bullet costs, and the cops' desire not to be outgunned.

---

[*] Professor of Psychology, University of Pennsylvania.

Likewise, citizens demonstrating in the streets argued heatedly about ballistic kinetics, but without much expertise. The professor then built a simple decision model that clearly separated facts—based on the ballistics experts' judgments—from societal values, which a policy committee would rule on as part of standard democratic procedures already in place. This led to a weighted ranking of all bullets considered and solved the crisis to the satisfaction of most due to transparency and rigor. Also, there was an unanticipated solution: the bullet that came out on top was different from the old ones used and the hollow point ones desired by the police. The highest scoring bullet improved stopping power for the cops without increasing bodily harm.[17]

Attacking Osama bin Laden's Compound

But what to do you do if even the experts don't agree on the facts? President Obama faced this problem in the White House's legendary Situation Room when confronted by conflicting advice over mounting a commando raid to capture terrorist leader Osama bin Laden. As recounted in Mark Bowden's book *The Finish: The Killing of Osama bin Laden*,[18] the president listened intently as Central Intelligence Agency officers discussed the identity of a very tall man in a mysterious Pakistani compound in the city of Abbottabad. The CIA's team leader tells the president he is nearly certain the subject is bin Laden. "He put his confidence level at 95%," Bowden writes. Another CIA officer agreed. Others, however, were less sanguine. "Four senior officers at the Directorate of National Intelligence place their confidence level at about 80%; some were as low as 40 or even 30%." Yet another officer was 60% confident that bin Laden was in the compound.

"OK, this is a probability thing," the president sighed in response, according to one account. From a decision viewpoint, that is just 'so far, so good,' since Obama had decomposed the problem into facts versus values. He relied on experts for the best available judgments about the factual matter of tall man's identity without burdening them with bigger decisions about whether to attack the compound. Obama also knew that this critical, historic policy decision would clearly be his. So, after listening further to the wide-ranging probability estimates about the identity of the mystery man in the compound, Obama remarks with some frustration: "Look guys, this is a flip of the coin. I can't base this decision on the notion that we have don't have any greater certainty than that." That summary silenced everyone—and reveals how inadequately even the smartest leaders often handle uncertainty and probabilities. A simple wisdom-of-the-crowd average in that room would put the odds around 70%, even though Obama described it as a 50–50 situation. Was he revising down the group's probability estimate because he felt they might perhaps be overconfident? Was he just conservative himself in this case? Or was Obama just using a figure of speech to signal that much was unknown, akin to flipping a coin? And does it really matter if the true probability is 50% or 70% in deciding whether to launch an American attack in Abbottabad, Pakistan?

Takeaway for Leaders

There are some key leadership lessons to be learned from the bin Laden case about interpreting ambiguous advice. First, Obama views the disagreement among his trusted experts as problematic and frustrating; after all, they are supposed to be "best informed," so how can they differ so much? Second, instead of delving even more deeply into the reasons underlying their divergent views, Obama focuses on the average odds provided, rather than the considerable uncertainty surrounding them—where the real learning lies. Third, he does not quite know how to weigh the relative importance of each expert's view. Obama may privately hold some advisers in higher regard than others regarding their substantive expertise in this matter, but does he really know how well each person can express his or her opinion probabilistically?

Unfortunately, we don't really know the final determinants of why Obama ultimately decided to attack the compound. We do know that it was a nearly complete success. After debate and exchange of views has occurred, the question of how to combine expert opinions usually remains since consensus is rare. Synthesizing different views into a single, subjective probability judgment about a key event is not simple, as explained in the book *Superforecasting*,[19] which discusses this case and others. What is paramount, however, is not just how best to aggregate diverse opinions but to first delve deeply into *the root causes of divergent opinions*. Try to decompose them into differences about facts versus values, then discuss each source of conflict, and lastly, recombine the pieces into a better judgment overall.

The latter can be done by averaging final opinions, favoring some advisors over others, using statistical updating procedures, or forming an intuitive overall judgment. This is challenging perhaps but far from impossible. Importantly, much depends on the issues involved, the organizational context, the ultimate aims and the personal preferences of those responsible for the decision.

END NOTES

1 Gapper, John. "Innovators Don't Ignore Customers. Financial Times." *The Best Business Writing 2012*. Columbia University Press, 2012. 368–373.

2 Schoemaker, P.J.H., Steve Krupp and Samantha Howland, "Strategic Leadership: The Essential Skills." *Harvard Business Review*, Jan/Feb 2013, 131–134.

3 Winning Decisions: Getting It Right the First Time: Russo, J. Edward, Schoemaker, Paul J.H.: 9780385502252: Amazon.com: Books

4 Grove, Andrew S. *Only the Paranoid Survive: How to Exploit the Crisis Points that Challenge Every Company*. Crown Currency, 1999.

5 Skarzynski, Peter, and Rowan Gibson. *Innovation to the Core: A Blueprint for Transforming the Way your Company Innovates*. Harvard Business Press, 2008.

6 https://knowledge.wharton.upenn.edu/article/paul-j-h-schoemakers-brilliant-mistakes-finding-opportunity-in-failures/.

7 Klayman, Joshua. "Varieties of confirmation bias." *Psychology of Learning and Motivation* 32 (1995): 385–418.

8 Neal, Jennifer Watling, Zachary P. Neal, and Brian Brutzman. "Defining brokers, intermediaries, and boundary spanners: a systematic review." *Evidence & Policy* 18.1 (2022): 7–24.

9 Day, George S. and Schoemaker, Paul J. H., *Peripheral Vision: Detecting the Weak Signals that Will Make or Break Your Company*, Harvard Business School Press, May 2006, 248 pp.

10 https://www.forbes.com/sites/jennagoudreau/2013/03/21/eight-leadership-lessons-from-the-worlds-most-powerful-women/.

11 Day, George S., and Paul J. H. Schoemaker. "How vigilant companies gain an edge in turbulent times." *MIT Sloan Management Review* 61.2 (2020): 57–64.

12 Charan, Ram. "DuPont's Swift Response to the Financial Crisis." *Bloomberg BusinessWeek*. BLOOMBERG L.P., 7 Jan. 2009. Web. 11 Dec. 2013. http://www.businessweek.com/stories/2009-01-07/duponts-swift-response-to-the-financial-crisis#rshare=email_article.

13 Hughes, Willian Howard. *Alexander Fleming and Penicillin*. London: Priority, 1974.

14 Brandenburger, Adam M., and Barry J. Nalebuff. *The Right Game: Use Game Theory to Shape Strategy*. Vol. 76. Chicago: Harvard Business Review, 1995.

15 IP Report Industries.qxd (uspto.gov).

16 Fisher, Roger, William L. Ury, and Bruce Patton. *Getting to Yes: Negotiating Agreement without Giving in*. Penguin, 2011.

17 Kenneth R. Hammond, and Leonard Adelman, "Science, values, and human judgment," *Science* (1976): 389–96.

18 Bowden, Mark. *The Finish: The Killing of Osama bin Laden*. Atlantic Monthly Press, 2012.

19 Tetlock, Philip E., and Dan Gardner. *Superforecasting: The Art and Science of Prediction*. Random House, 2016.

CHAPTER 15

REDUCING BIAS

"I think we've all heard enough debate about the chair budget, Vickers. Now, are there any other areas where we can trim some fat?"

FROM HARVARD BUSINESS REVIEW, DECEMBER 2013. CARTOON BY PAUL GILLIGAN.

© HBR.ORG

15.1 HOW NUDGES CAN KEEP YOU CENTERED

—With Viraj Narayanan*

To make healthier choices, sometimes we need a gentle push in the right direction. Consider the seemingly innocuous habit of consuming one can of soft drink a day. In one year, that single can of soda snowballs into a cube of sugar weighing 50 pounds.[1] Think about that: that's the size of a small dog. It's not that we don't want to be strategic or long-term oriented. It's just not how we naturally frame things.

Your environment plays a big role in how you make choices—even for the simple decisions—like choosing to consume a soda. That's why we believe in creating "nudge" strategies to facilitate healthier choices. Take the decision of saving in a 401K account for a new employee. How that choice is presented has much influence on the outcome. If you are automatically "opted-in" as the default, you are much more likely to save than if the default is set as "opted out." As a result, many employers have adopted this nudge strategy to promote good saving habits. Similar nudge effects are seen in no-fault car insurance and organ donations, which some states in the U.S. have as their default and others do not. People mostly tend to stick with the default option.

The bestselling book *Nudge* by Thaler and Sunstein goes deeper into such strategies, including the underlying behavioral economics and decision psychology at work.[2] The challenge in designing nudge strategies is not to come off as manipulative, rather as helping people make choices more in line with their long-term objectives. So, nudge strategies must navigate a fine line between paternalism where the company dictates versus libertarianism which assumes that individuals know better what is best for them.

A group called People Analytics at Google has experimented with several nudge strategies in the context of consumption.[3] We eat in units. You have one carrot or one cupcake—not 1.5 cupcakes. At Google, they cut down the size of the "unit" for desserts so that you can finish them in a few bites. This means less calories and sugar. It also means that you have to think about getting another dessert if you are still hungry—forcing another decision. Their hope is to curb binge eating. Google runs other nudge experiments such as changing the physical placement of healthy food items (salads in the front and desserts in the back) or increasing awareness of caloric intake with small placards. The nudge parameters are designed to promote healthier habits but ultimately, the choice is still in the hands of the employee.

---

* Principal at Decision Strategies International.

Cleveland Clinic has implemented nudge strategies with a more paternalistic approach.[4] To promote healthier habits, they have eliminated soda machines, banned smoking on-campus, provided free gym classes to employees, and removed fried foods from the cafeteria. These changes were initially met with resistance but have slowly gained traction. The results are millions of dollars in healthcare savings and measurably healthier employees.

Nudging strategies can also be used at an individual level. By controlling your environment, you can create the right formula for better choices. For example, if you are on a diet—perhaps you need to remove junk foods from your kitchen completely. Taking sugary items out of the picture eliminates eating junk food as a choice. Another example could be using a gym partner as a nudge to make sure you exercise (since making the trip to the gym may be the hardest part).

15.2 DON'T LET NEW INFORMATION DISTORT YOUR JUDGMENT

—With J. Edward Russo*

The owners of a very successful Lexus dealership in Haverford Pennsylvania, an affluent suburb of Philadelphia, decided to open a second sales location to be closer to their many customers in Chester County who had to drive 30-to-40 minutes for service. In addition, this county was expanding, thereby offering many potential new customers.

The problem was that local townships within the county generally looked unfavorably on car dealerships. In Exton, where the dealer was looking, local zoning laws required a minimum of 25 acres and no such lots were available. After much searching, they found a promising property and pursued it. But hurdles mounted one at a time, such as strict zoning interpretation, slow application processing by township officials, and myriad other regulations. The deeper message was that the county really did not want another car dealership. But the owners strong desire to make this happen and the piece-meal nature of the obstacles they encountered—each seemingly manageable on its own—created something called information distortion.

The owners dithered away two years of effort and $1 million by continuing to believe they could obtain a location in a place that really didn't want them.

---

* Professor of Management, Cornell University.

Eventually, they decided to walk. As Dan Polett, the senior owner, reflecting on their headstrong effort noted that "If we were to go back and do it over, I think we would have responded more quickly to the negatives and not continue to pursue it."[5] This was a hard lesson learned about an insidious trap: people often interpret new information in biased, self-serving ways once some disposition has been developed.

Hidden Distortions

It is well-known from decision making research that after a decision has been made, people often escalate their commitment and thus become reluctant to pull the plug on a losing initiative. A number of reasons have been proposed for this misplaced persistence, such as overconfidence (hope springs eternal), rationalization of setbacks, searching for one-sided evidence to bolster a choice, and reluctance to publicly admit a mistake. This kind of sunk cost fallacy and its multiple remedies are quite well understood. One important implication is that project champions are the worst people to pull the plug on their own pet projects once underway and in trouble. The remedy is simple: let other people decide when to pull the plug or approve additional funding.

But how can you guard against information distorting your judgments *before* a final decision is made? A pernicious bias also happens here unconsciously whenever you develop some preliminary leaning toward one option over others. Research clearly shows that managers tend to evaluate new data in a way that supports their current leaning, if any.[6] Suppose you receive some preliminary information about two job applicants, such as their bios or some e-mail correspondence. If you happen to favor person A over B in your preliminary judgment, you will probably implicitly bias later information more in favor of A. You fool yourself unconsciously because of your deep desire to remain consistent with your current beliefs.

Changing your mind is more difficult than slanting new evidence to align with your prior views. There are several factors that can make this bias worse: (1) when you have a strong prior leaning; (2) when information arrives unevenly in chunks, with delay; (3) if the new information is inherently ambiguous; (4) if you tend to be judgmental by nature; or (5) if the organizational culture or your boss values consistency.

Some Remedies

Unfortunately, mere awareness of cognitive biases is not enough to cure them. Like optical illusions, they are quite persistent even after you have been told that your eyes or mind may be deceiving you However, several simple techniques can ameliorate the bias, although none will ffer full-proof protection all the time:

1. Try not to form interim opinions and keep an open mind until the end (as instructed in U.S. jury trials):
2. Focus on what the new information tells you, rather than whether it is consistent with your prior interim learning (some strategic amnesia can help here);
3. Ask others to interpret the new evidence as well, especially those whose views are known to differ from yours;
4. Reduce the use of subjective or piecemeal information processing where possible (e.g., don't look at every new data dribble that comes in).
5. Cultivate a tolerance for ambiguity through the discipline of keeping an open mind and forcing yourself to develop opposing hypotheses about the new data;
6. Whenever possible, try to get stronger evidence—for example, by asking probing questions so that there is less reliance on subjective interpretations;
7. Randomize the sequence of the information stream likely to arrive if possible, especially if adversaries seek to exploit this bias, for example in a negotiation;
8. If you can, organize the information into larger clusters, rather than wasting time evaluating each additional crumb of data that may arrive;
9. Raise the burden of proof for favoring option A over B, for example by listing all options in a spreadsheet and scoring them in terms of pros and cons using numerical scales.

So, if you want to truly hire the better of those job candidates A and B, try to postpone interim judgments and collect all information in one file or spreadsheet without any premature interim evaluations. And try to follow the courtroom instructions that judges always give jurors in U.S. court trials: wait until all the evidence is in before deciding the case (which is not easy).[7]

It is difficult for many people to suppress their natural tendency to form interim leanings, even if the information is incomplete, flimsy or even biased. Try to be less judgmental, more curious and systematic when evaluating data. That is your only hope to conquer our deep-seated bias toward prejudicial weighing of evidence, something to which we are all susceptible without realizing it.

15.3 NOBEL PRIZE RESEARCH ABOUT BIASES

Professor Richard Thaler from the University of Chicago won the 2017 Nobel Prize in economics for injecting much needed behavioral insights into a field of study that has long resisted them. He follows Herbert Simon (1978 Nobel) and Daniel Kahneman (2002 Nobel) in this great honor since all three emphasized that economists are overly enamored with the idea that humans make rational decisions and that unfettered economic markets are highly efficient.[8]

I got to know Dick Thaler and his work while I was doing research in this field at University of Chicago (where he was based later when receiving his Nobel prize) and the Wharton School; his award is much deserved. The field of behavioral economics that Thaler helped pioneer, inspired by Daniel and Amos Tversky, holds many implications for real-world entrepreneurs and business leaders.[9]

Keep in mind that markets may still be efficient even if we as humans are not always optimal in our decision making. What matters is whether margin traders, who disproportionately make the market, are rational. As a simple example, suppose you are driving on a four-lane highway and your lane is going much slower than the others. Unless you really like to go slow, it would be irrational for you to stay in that lane and not switch to a faster one. But since other drivers will be doing this as well, the differences in traffic speeds among the four lanes may not last long.

This example presents in a nutshell what needs to be examined in economic markets; how many rational traders does it take for the whole market to be efficient, so that no single participant is sub-optimal. Here are some of the research topics in behavioral economics also associated with Thaler's Nobel Prize:

Status quo bias

Richard Thaler himself did pioneering work early about the so-called endowment effect, meaning that people overvalue what they have and will not easily switch to something else. When students in a class were randomly given either a coffee mug or a nice pen of equal value, most wanted to keep what they were handed when given the opportunity to trade their gift for the other. Rationally, about 50% should switch, assuming the items are indeed equally desirable on average. This status quo effect makes us sticky.[10]

One thing entrepreneurs excel at is upsetting the apple cart since disruption often creates new opportunities. The message here is that you must also appreciate why you will encounter much, and not necessarily logical, opposition along the way.

Overbidding

Thaler also examined the so-called winner's curse. In auctions, all bidders try to be rational in their assessment of what is on offer and what they should pay at most but, being human, their bids will contain some random noise. This means that some people will bid too low relative to their true preference and some too high. Since the high bidder wins, it is likely that this person's bid contains an upward error—thus producing the winner's curse. Later on, they may regret their bid. To avoid this trap and the downside of over bidders cutting corners later, some government sales of oil or gas tracts use a sealed-bid Vickrey auction in which the winner pays the price of the second highest bid (which is not known to them), but not their own higher one.

So, when bidding aggressively for talent, patents, or office space in your business, don't fall victim to the winner's curse. Sleep on your aggressive move for a night and see if you still favor it.

Nudge strategies

Cass Sustein and Thaler wrote their best-selling book *Nudge* for teachers, parents, managers, and policy leaders to overcome some of the biases we are all prone to. Rather than adopt a strict disciplinarian approach, with hard and rigid rules, they favor a supportive strategy whereby the decision context is changed enough to bring about the desired behavior. So, no more candy displays at the school cafeteria's cash register—healthy snacks only. Or, making it a default on driver licenses that the organs of fatal accident victims can be donated for transplant, unless the license holder has explicitly opted out. Various governments, including the U.S. and U.K., introduced nudge strategies to avoid being overly paternalistic.[11]

The aim of a nudge is to guide people toward making better choices on their own with respect to eating, saving, education, parenting, exercising, and more. But sometimes nudges may not be enough, and we need stronger medicine. If so, then the following 'nudge plus' strategies can be pursued voluntarily with an eye toward improving future behaviors, at times with external support.[12]

Precommitment

Ulysses, the hero in Homer's epic Greek poem *The Odyssey*, realized he could not withstand the lure of the Sirens as he passed them on his ship. To resist their bewitching songs, he had himself tied to the mast in order to avoid steering his ship onto nearby rocks. Less beguilingly, Thaler examined how to tie ordinary people to long term savings plans, such as encouraging Christmas clubs in which you pre-commit to payments and pay a penalty if you skip one. Rational actors, which is what economic models typically assume us to be, would not wish to pre-commit to this choice since it is generally better to keep your options open. When structuring incentives in companies, it may pay, however, to pre-commit to certain plans or strategies to overcome sub-optimal temptations along the way.

You do need to know, however, who to tie to the mast and for how long, to contain their foolish impulsive behaviors. For example, how far should you commit your firm to key talent through severance and options contracts, or what guarantees might you offer customers re quality? After Captain Cortés landed in Veracruz in 1519 to conquer new lands, he told his soldiers to burn all the ships. This committed his troops to either victory or defeat, without any option of retreat. When a soldier ridiculed his move, Cortés promptly put a sword in his chest and killed him on the spot; point made.

Mental accounting

Thaler also researched the role of mental accounting, to uncover the roots of irrational behavior. If you have paid $30 to attend a football game and it starts to pour rain, will you leave early? Many people would say yes. But now imagine you paid $200 for that ticket. Will you stay longer "to get your money's worth." Some would, but that may not be rational; you should ask how much exposure to rain this game is worth to you. The money spent on the ticket is gone whether you leave or get wet, so it should cancel out of your cost-benefit equation. But likely it will not, just as people are more upset when missing their plane by 5 minutes than by 30 minutes. Should that 25 minutes difference really matter? You simply missed the plane and that is your loss.

Leaders need to understand how their customers and employees frame issues, especially in situations where their views are less than rational. For example, why do consumers focus on the percentage of a discount rather than the absolute dollar savings, or why do people prefer low deductibles in insurance policies when this is very expensive?

This is just a partial list of the many traps and biases that behavioral economists and psychologist study to better explain and predict human behavior in economic situations. Thaler also examined risk-taking biases, excess volatility in the stock market, the role of fairness, and even legal policy matters. Managers need to be aware of these before making their next big decision.[13]

There is some good news here as well, however, for business leaders since people's bounded rationality often creates opportunities for entrepreneurs. If markets were as well-informed and efficient as economists like to believe, there may be few ways to achieve above-average returns.

Entrepreneurial firms are valuable in that they try to fill unmet needs and develop new opportunities created by changes in society, technology, regulations, and politics. Those who excel at this type of innovation especially need to understand people's predictable irrationalities, in themselves, their colleagues, the market place and the world at large. This is why behavioral economics matters in business.

15.4 SEPARATING FACTS FROM VALUES IN DISPUTES

—With Philip Tetlock*

Let's define a fact as a statement that is true or false independent of what we think or want, and that is subject to empirical validation. It is also useful to distinguish between existing facts (which historians record, as well as scientists) and future facts, like tomorrow's temperature in location X or the price of oil a year from now.

Clearly there will be uncertainty about future facts but this can also happen with existing facts, such as the depth of the ocean in location Y yesterday, or all the facts that lawyers try to discover in lawsuits. Whenever the facts—past, present or future—are uncertain due to our limited knowledge, experts may differ in their estimates. That's when the question of how to integrate or weigh these varying expert opinions about facts becomes relevant.

After having broken Humpty Dumpty into facts versus values, the question remains: How do you recombine the components? First, this should be done only after you have thoroughly examined, tested, and reconciled the reasons why experts differ over either factual matters or value issues. Second, when decision time arrives, you may need to handle any remaining factual disputes differently from value differences that still persist. Debates about facts can, in principle, be settled empirically (even if time and cost may not allow that to be done easily) and as such they fall in the realm of science. Disputes about values, such as how important one objective or goal is over another, can be debated endlessly and may ultimately fall in the realm of moral philosophy.

---

* Professor of Psychology, University of Pennsylvania.

So, let's talk about the facts, or more precisely, about how to aggregate divergent expert opinions about factual matters, such as predictions about a future election or the price of oil next year. Ideally, one's political or moral views should not influence such estimates, just as the chance of rain—or your favorite sports team winning its next match—should rationally be independent of your own hopes, desires, and values.

Aggregating Estimates about Factual Matters

For factual disputes, a weighted-averaging process makes sense unless it can clearly be shown that one group member has a superior perspective and knowledge base. This person would presumably have influenced the views of others already in the group discussion, so taking a group average will already capture some of this, but with dilution.

Consider, for example, an exercise we did with senior executives from a large pharma company. We showed the 30 people a blind map of Europe with just the contours of the countries drawn, but without city and river markings, or any names listed. This map was then superimposed on a grid that showed, in the background, a 0–100 coordinate system so that each person could individually estimate the location of a country's capital. For example, the center of London might be guessed to be at point (23, 52), whereas Vienna would likely have a lower vertical score (X) but a larger horizontal (Y) value.

I used this very exercise once to demonstrate the wisdom-of-the-crowd effect with senior executives and when I averaged the individual estimates each person gave for each city's location, their mean scores were closer to the actual location of each capital than 90% of the group. But then here also was one person, named James, who actually beat the wisdom of the crowd by a big margin. Just before starting this exercise, several participants commented that James would probably do best at this quiz since he was renowned for his geographic acumen, having traveled the globe widely with gusto. But often, there isn't one clear expert.

The above example illustrates a conundrum of the averaging approach. We know that it often beats most individuals, whose judgments contributed to the average, but not necessarily all. Unfortunately, we may not know ahead of time who the hidden experts in our midst are and thus it becomes risky to bet on a single presumed genius unless the evidence is overwhelming. Also, the top expert must be able to express this superior knowledge in terms of precise numerical estimates, as in our geography quiz, before you can take that person's estimates to the bank. Several good books about this subject, such as the *Wisdom of the Crowd*[14] and *The Signal and the Noise*,[15] delve more deeply into conditions favoring group judgments versus betting on presumed experts.

Much hinges here on the distribution of knowledge in the group, as well as whether the random sources of noise in people's judgments are largely uncorrelated (in which case averaging really helps) versus being positively correlated (in which case the group average may be badly biased). It also matters, in case group members broadly agree on some key estimate, how much they relied on similar versus different sources. If they drew on different types of evidence and independently arrived at a similar conclusion, it may pay to "extremize" the group average. Furthermore, the averaging process need not be based on equal weighing but might from the start give more weight to some members, in essence handicapping people's predictive acumen, a priori.

15.5 WHEN WISDOM OF THE CROWD MISFIRED

—With Jim Austin[*]

The internet was supposed to make us all smarter, given its limitless access to information. This is still possible in theory if you know how to avoid the traps and pitfalls cleverly arranged at times by those seeking to obscure the truth. So, how do we know who to trust on what subjects and when?

Broadly speaking we have two strategies: (1) listen to genuine experts and, (2) if these disagree, assess the diversity of their viewpoints and add your own two cents with some grains of salt. We know that scientists are not perfect (who is?) but science remains the best game in town for truth finding by far. Science is a highly advanced, rational, and complex human endeavor conducted by well trained experts who are subject to peer reviews. But like all humans, all can be fallible at times or some even corrupt, and this can cause bias or blind spots as history has shown. Let's illustrate this with one notable medical case example: the odds of surviving a surgery around 1850 in Europe or the U.S. were about 50/50. Luckily, however, two breakthroughs emerged:

1. Ether treatment discovered by Drs. Morton and Collins at Boston's Massachusetts General Hospital,[16] and
2. Sterilization, based on radical new theories about germs published by Drs. Pasteur and Lister.

---

[*] Adjunct Senior Lecturer, Brown University.

So, how did the medical community and society react to these presumed advances?

How Experts Can Mislead

Within six months, all major hospitals in U.S. and Europe embraced the use of ether. It wasn't until early in the twentieth century that sterilization techniques became commonplace. But why? First, the anesthetic and euphoric effects of ether were immediately evident; not so with sterilization—since you can't see germs—even though post-surgical survival data had shown it statistically to be superior for healing. But doctors found the carbolic acids needed in sterilization cumbersome to apply, burning their hands at times (which eventually led to another innovation: rubber gloves).

In science, the better theories and techniques will eventually win out because the evidence becomes too compelling. Even so, experts remain subject to biases and myopic viewpoints as Thomas Kuhn examined in his famous book on scientific revolutions.[17] He found that it was senior established scientists who often retard progress; their retirements or deaths are what makes room for younger scholars to change the paradigm. As Jürgen Habermas noted, truth is very much about social consensus since other legitimation criteria may be weaker or less accessible.[18]

Typically, most people trust their own judgment far more than those of others but make exceptions when dealing with presumed experts like doctors, accountants, or scientists—if they stay in their lane. The politization of climate change research, for example, is partly due to some scientists staking out positions for personal or ideological reasons. Once subjectivity creeps in, credibility drops, turning a topic like climate change or the anti-vaccine movement into a free-for-all. However, as Senator Daniel Patrick Moynihan famously said "everyone is entitled to his own opinion, but not to his own facts."

What Can We Practically Do?

Unfortunately, we now live in a post-truth world where *alternative facts* are bandied about and traditional expertise has taken big hits. A deeper problem is that not everyone is interested in getting to the truth and that information distortion is common in politics and beyond. Many people may be more concerned—often subconsciously—with social validation or evidence that confirms their deeper beliefs than dealing with counter evidence.[19] This bias is compounded when one's livelihood and social standing depend on believing X rather than Y, independent of the evidence. If you're a coal miner, you're more likely to believe in "clean coal." The currency that matters most in many settings is that of influence, social fit, self-interest, and power rather than truth per se. As the saying goes, don't ask a barber whether you need a haircut.

Scientific truths alone are often cold or impersonal and so personal connections and context start to matter as well. An old consulting adage holds that clients will not really care about how much you know until they first know that you care about them. This partly explains the development of political parties, affinity groups, online chat rooms, identity relationship, and the appeal of cults. But independent thinking and wisdom also still matter and those require acknowledging the facts plus a willingness to change one's mind when warranted. If your primary interest is indeed to get closer to the truth, here's how to separate beliefs from facts, and truth from fiction. Keep in mind though that you still will have to deal with flawed human beings in a society where truth is too often negotiable or under-appreciated.

1. Have an open mind about the facts, arguments, and beliefs of another person,
2. Show respect to those holding different views and explore them deeper,
3. Establish common ground, or shared values, as part of a trust-building strategy,
4. Acknowledge the limits of your own views; where have you been wrong before?
5. Seek a range of possibilities when there is much uncertainty, rather than absolutes,
6. Try to simplify disagreements to their core; make your arguments short and clear,
7. Expect honest misunderstandings; do not overwhelm others with data or complexity,
8. Pick your battles selectively; only seriously engage those interested in genuine dialog,
9. Ask others and yourself also what new evidence would prompt a reversal of views,
10. Remember, you cannot fully convince others—deep down, they must do this themselves.

END NOTES

1 One Soda A Day Equals 50 Pounds of Sugar A Year, Says NYC Health Department. *CBS New York* (cbsnews.com).

2 Thaler, Richard H., and Cass R. Sunstein. *Nudge: The Final Edition*. Yale University Press, 2021.

3 In The Cafeteria, Google Gets Healthy (fastcompany.com).

4 https://hbr.org/2013/05/health-cares-service-fanatics.

5 *Philadelphia Business Journal*, September 15–21, 2006, p. 15.

6 Russo, J. Edward. "The predecisional distortion of information." *Neuroeconomics, Judgment, and Decision Making*. Psychology Press, 2014. 91–110.

7 Hastie, Reid, ed. *Inside the Juror: The Psychology of Juror Decision Making*. Cambridge University Press, 1993.

8 Benjamin Jr, Ludy T. "Behavioral science and the Nobel Prize: A history." *American Psychologist* 58.9 (2003): 731.

9 Kaushiva, Anamika. "Nobel laureate Richard Thaler's contribution to behavioral economics–a brief review." *International Journal of Research in Economics and Social Sciences (IJRESS)* 7.12 (2017).

10 Godefroid, Marie-E., Ralf Plattfaut, and Björn Niehaves. "How to measure the status quo bias? A review of current literature." *Management Review Quarterly* 73.4 (2023): 1667–1711.

11 Whitehead, Mark, Rhys Jones, and Jessica Pykett. "Nudging around the world: A critical geography of the behaviour change agenda." *Handbook of Behavioural Change and Public Policy*. Edward Elgar Publishing, 2019. 90–101.

12 Banerjee, Sanchayan, and Peter John. "Nudge plus: Incorporating reflection into behavioral public policy." *Behavioural Public Policy* 8.1 (2024): 69–84.

13 The Big Idea: Before You Make That Big Decision […] (hbr.org)

14 Surowiecki, James. *The Wisdom of Crowds*. Anchor, 2005.

15 Silver, Nate. *The Signal and the Noise: Why So Many Predictions Fail-But Some Don't*. Penguin, 2012.

16 https://www.ncbi.nlm.nih.gov/m/pubmed/22583009/).

17 Kuhn, Thomas S. *The Structure of Scientific Revolutions*. Vol. 962. Chicago: University of Chicago press, 1997.

18 Habermas, Jürgen. *Legitimation Crisis*. Vol. 519. Beacon Press, 1975.

19 Hotez, Peter J. *The deadly rise of anti-science: a scientist's warning*. JHU Press, 2023.

EPILOGUE

The 15 chapters of this book cover a broad range of topics which were examined at individual, group, and organizational levels depending on the issues involved. Each chapter presents five essays that relate to the overall chapter topic by focusing on a specific problem, issue, or relevant business case. When viewed in combination, this book covers fundamental themes that managers and leaders will frequently encounter in their own organizations. Four overarching ones are *improving problem framing, asking better questions, understanding organizational contexts, and rising to leadership challenges.* To take your team and company to the next level, as well as your own professional career, each of these broad themes matters in better strategic thinking and decision making. The remainder of this epilogue will examine these meta-challenges further, by delving deeper than any previous essays could alone due to limited scope and space.

PROBLEM FRAMING

One basic premise of this book is that new insights can come from asking better questions. So, let's start by understanding where questions come from. A useful metaphor is that of an iceberg since most of its content or mass is not visible from the surface. Likewise, much of what drives people's questions, interests, and mental frames operates below the surface (see Figure 1), making it hard to see for others or even yourself. The questions that come to mind when having group discussions or solving a business problem alone entail an amalgam of psychological processes that researchers are still unraveling. The thoughts that arise deeply from our mind, often spontaneously, reflect the goals we pursue, what solutions we contemplate, the consequences we envision, and the criteria we invoke to evaluate strategic options. These elements, collectively, shape our decision frames and problem definitions.

FIGURE 1   Pyramid of Thinking Levels

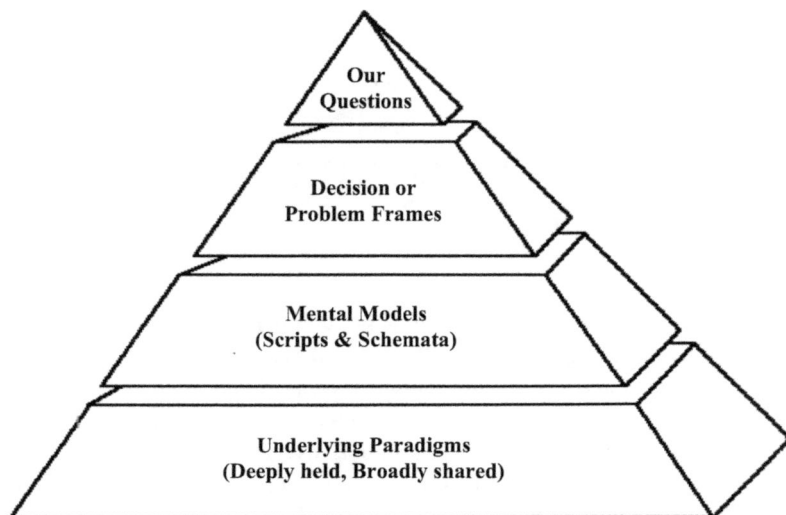

At a deeper level, however, these decision or problem frames emanate from our *mental models*, which are the ways in which we have organized the outside world in our own mind. Cognitive psychologists examine mental models by surfacing interrelated beliefs (including scripts and schemata) as well as deeply held assumptions. To illustrate this in simplified form, Figure 2 depicts the main components of the mental model of a R&D executive in a pharmaceutical company.[1] The inner circle lists items that this particular executive cared most about when interviewed. If others want to get her attention, they must push these buttons, or she will lose interest. The second circle contains items that still matter to this executive, but only secondarily in terms of mindshare, interest, and decision relevance. And the outer circle lists items that are truly tertiary or peripheral: yes, she knows they matter to other people and the company overall, but this is not what drives her own attention day-to-day.

In contrast to this R&D executive, a marketing executive or plant manager—even if working at the same company—will organize key elements differently in their minds, which is both the benefit and curse of specialization. To illustrate, Figure 3 compares just the inner cores of each person's mental map to highlight key framing differences in how they see their functional roles within this company. If these three leaders were to be in the same meeting, they would

FIGURE 2   Mental Model of R&D Executive

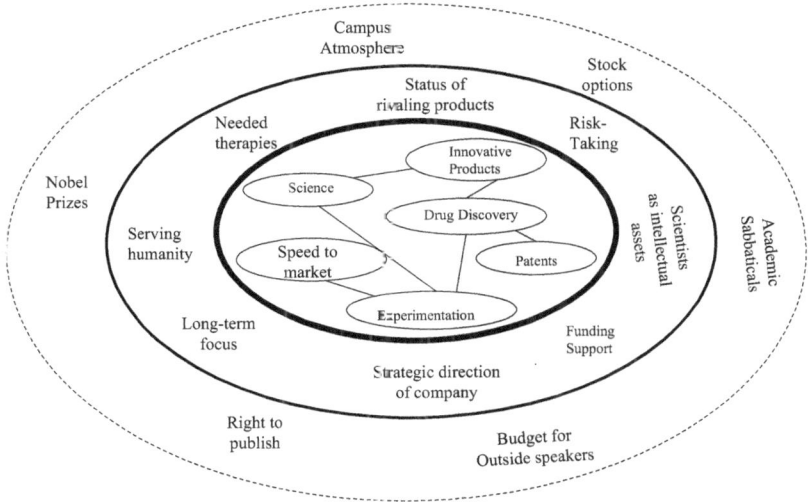

FIGURE 3   Three Mental Models in Pharma

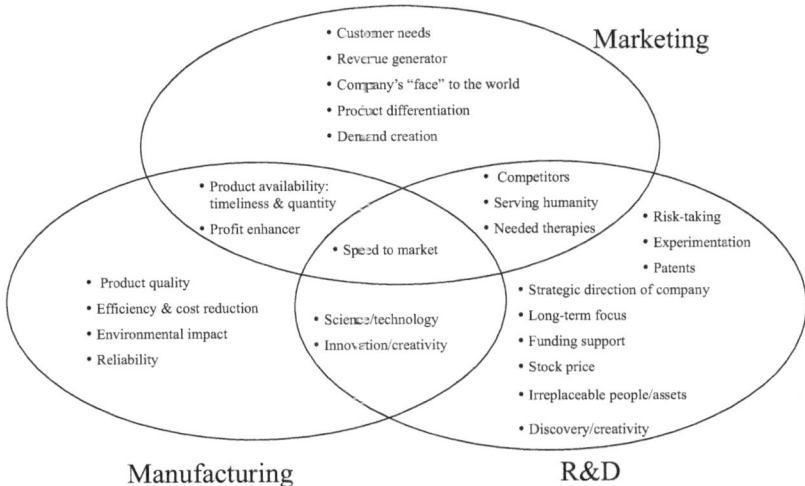

frame a given business problem or opportunity differently and thus would pose different questions and priorities. As the figure shows, there is only one item that all three care very much about: speed to market. The company's CEO was delighted to see this common overlapping attribute since he had worked hard to emphasize speed-to-market across the entire organization. But the absence of Profitability or ROI at the core of any these three mental models was a serious concern to him. My point is that the core of people's mental models—as depicted in simplified forms in Figures 1, 2, and 3—largely determine what questions they ask or solutions they recommend. If deep interest and knowledge of, say, innovation is lacking from a person's mental model, it is unlikely that questions or suggestions will be offered in support of that. However, once transformative thinking starts to take root in a company, thanks to training, incentives or culture change, a shift in the corporate mindset can happen. This should be evident, in time, via additional overlaps in the cores of people's mental models and the different questions being asked. But orchestrating such deep changes in an organization is seldom easy since teaching "old dogs new tricks" is an ongoing challenge. Indeed, it may require some new dogs.

Lastly, yet deeper down in our cognitive iceberg reside what scientists call paradigms. Thomas Kuhn defined this concept as deeply held and widely shared assumptions that underpin how most people see and experience reality in their lives.[2] Beliefs about capitalism, democracy, or human rights are examples of paradigms since they are often firmly rooted and impact a broad range of problems, from how to structure an employment contract to devising a business strategy. One problem is that paradigms are hard to change unless you are an intellectual giant like Isaac Newton, Charles Darwin, or Albert Einstein. Practical leaders are better off focusing closer to the surface in our metaphoric pyramid since the issues there will be easier to surface, challenge, and modify. The three circles in Figure 3, for example, depict powerful function frames that may need to be changed due to changing external challenges. Or they may need to be better re-aligned inside the organization so that teams can collaborate with each other more effectively. For strategic leaders, this also means transcending their own functional or intellectual frames perhaps since strategy formulation and making tough choices entail ongoing shifts in trade-offs and compromises.

ASKING BETTER QUESTIONS

Management guru Peter Drucker suggested that most innovations are driven by the kinds of questions leaders ask.[3] In too many companies, incremental innovation has driven out the kind of radical innovation that typically produce significant wealth.

The reasons include managers preferring to stay in their comfort zone, incentives that encourage risk-aversion, and mental blinders that prevent leaders from seeing new product or market opportunities. The cold reality is that the stock market places a high premium on top-line growth that exceeds the rate of normal market expansion. So, how should leaders achieve the goal of significantly increasing their growth rate? The answer lies in asking different questions that challenge conventional thinking and open new avenues for growth.

In many companies, however, growth is held back because managers and leaders are overly focused on operational questions. Such internal orientations divert attention away from strategic issues and will doom most organization to incremental growth. Leaders can use the questions below to assess to what extent their questions are strategic and innovative.

1. *Distinctiveness*: are you asking the same questions as everyone else, or do your questions bring a *different perspective* or approach to the problem? If the former, your results are going to be average, with incremental improvement at best.

2. *Discovery Potential*: do your questions lead you to potentially *new insights* about how the world is changing around you, due to consumer changes, competitive shifts, channel mix, regulations, new technology, etc.? Good questions should result in discoveries that are relevant to your business.

3. *Frame Challenge*: suppose that your team was solving the wrong problem or is still thinking about the issues in an old way. Will your questions potentially surface such misalignment by producing answers that make it clear to others that key assumptions are wrong or that serious blind spots exist?

4. *Big Ideas*: will your question help stimulate innovations that can lead to payoffs that can really move the needle? Many questions in business are incremental, focused on solving tactical problems in the here and now. Good questions for innovation stay clear of such mundane perspectives and focus instead on things that can really make a big difference in the future.

The French writer and philosopher Voltaire advised us to "judge a man by his questions rather than his answers." Too many managers ask questions that actually prevent them from seeing new opportunities. Consider the classic example of IBM's ill-fated decision in the 1960s to turn down the opportunity to acquire Xerox's new reprographic process on the cheap. The company hired the well regarded consulting firm Arthur D. Little (ADL) to answer one key question, "if we have a reliable, cheaper and faster process, how many more copies will people make in a given year?" Since copies in those days could only be made from an original specimen, with stencils or lithography, ADL set out to estimate the number of such copies made per year and then extrapolated forward in time. However, both IBM and ADL framed the question and the opportunity too narrowly as "copies from originals" and ignored a far larger new segment of the market that did not exist yet, namely copies of copies of copies ad infinitum. Today, this overlooked segment represents nearly all of the copying market around the world. But this huge opportunity could only have been foreseen if different questions had been posed, such as "how might the new Xerox process change how people make copies, and what will this amount to in total numbers of copies over several years?" In their defense, copies made from copies in those early days did not come close to the high-quality images we see now.

Few of us are blameless when it comes to asking the wrong questions or failing to see the big picture. This is especially hard to do in the heat of battle and when the fog of war is still thick. For example, consider the world of packaged goods which globally tops many billions a year. How should companies in this space think about the future of packaging? Rather than adopt a short-term and highly focused perspective, such as the cost of raw materials, changes in consumer expectations, or new regulations, a wide-angle view is far better. Truly strategic leaders would explore the following kind of questions: what will the world of packing look like in 10 years; what is the role of smart polymers, and what role might biosensors play; what kind of new materials might be available then: what will be the continued impact of conductive inks or 3D printing, of disintegrating plastics, of biomass materials? What new advances exist in keeping contents of packages at preset temperatures for hour or days if needed? Phase change technologies today can keep vaccines cold for days to be shipped overseas, or keep take-out orders from restaurants hot for hours. And finally, there is an overarching mega-question affecting many industries: how quickly will consumer sentiments move away from packaging materials based on fossil fuels?

Also, when exploring breakthrough innovations for the packaged food business, we should consider how the rules of the game might change. For example, are there analogies in another industry where relevant major changes are already occurring, such as in the fashion world? Nike comes to mind here since they brought numerous innovations to athletic shoes, several of which bear some similarities to the market dynamics of packaged goods. More specifically, ask how Nike or other disruptors were able to do this systematically? Also, outside-in searches for new ideas should not just focus on those that succeeded. Studying failures can be very instructive as well, either to avoid making the same mistakes or because failures at times produce brilliant new insights.[4]

UNDERSTANDING ORGANIZATIONAL CONTEXTS

Unlike humans, organizations can actually change their collective IQ or DNA by hiring new talent, changing their identity, merging with other entities, etc. The IQ of a human being may not change much over time—if they remain healthy—since it is deemed to be a fundamental trait relating to a person's built-in intellectual capability. Even though we can all learn how to take tests better, from the SAT to the IQ test, raising such test scores is not the same however as raising your true IQ.

Also, while humans share 99% of the same DNA, organizations may vary more widely and should perhaps be thought of in terms of multiple species as opposed to just one species. For example, some companies operate in developing countries vs. the developed world, others are very technology intensive, some are non-profits, etc. In addition, they may pursue different generic strategies, from cost leadership to differentiation to niche, or emphasize exploiting versus exploration quite differently.[5] With such a diversity of approaches, we face a problem akin to comparing IQs across species. How should we compare the IQ of say, a mouse with that of a frog and is this really a meaningful question beyond comparing survival odds? Such conceptual issues may explain why scholars have yet to develop a widely accepted measure of organizational IQ similar to human IQ measures. At a broad conceptual level, we could define the *intelligence* of living systems or machines in terms of their capacity to thrive in the type of environments they were designed for. But adapting to unknown new environments that may be quite different adds a whole new dimension. We know that if companies remain *inactive* or just *reactive* in the face of change, performance will start to decline. To survive and thrive, as Russell Ackoff emphasized, organizations need to *proactively* position themselves for change and perhaps even become *interactive* by altering their own ecosystem as well as reinventing themselves.[6] The following questions may help assess how adroit your organization is at this at present.

1. How well is your organization performing at present, relative to competitors or general yardsticks like ROI, after adjusting for luck and advantages of the past that are still at play today?

2. What kinds of different scenarios may happen in the future environment, based on a thorough study of external socio-economic, political and technological factors, that could make your industry different from today?

3. What is your organization's capacity to foresee change (via foresight and insight) and devise strategies that leverage your organization's core competencies, agility, and leadership savvy?

Question (1) above can be assessed most objectively, question (2) is quite subjective although there could be some historical calibration as well as forward looking scenario analysis to answer it, and question (3) is closely tied to what we discussed in Part I of the book about navigating uncertainty. For this last question, we would need to measure the following specifically for a given organization:

(a) the extent of strategic foresight or insight into the future,
(b) degree of flexibility embedded in current strategies,
(c) organizational agility to accommodate change and crises if needed,
(d) dynamic monitoring of the external and internal environments,
(e) information sharing across internal boundaries and external networks, and
(f) leaders' ability to manage the core of the business as well as the periphery.

The field of strategy has developed multiple viewpoints about competitive advantage and timely adjustment to changing circumstances, which can range from placid to highly turbulent. The dynamic capabilities framework of David Teece et al.[7] draws a key distinction between ordinary capabilities and the type of competencies firms need to sense change, seize opportunities, and transform themselves organizationally.[8] A different view of dynamic capabilities was proposed by Kathleen Eisenhardt, in which leadership and decision making in real time play central roles. In the same vein, the concept of organizational ambidexterity promulgated by Michael Tushman et al. is relevant here. It highlights inherent paradoxes in trying to excel in the current environment while also being able to change in time when new industry regimes take hold. These different approaches for strategic adaptation entail a host of sub-capabilities when implemented operationally and may differ across industries as examined by Day and Schoemaker.[9] At present, the strategy field falls short of having developed a broadly shared contingency framework for how to adapt to change, but its main components, which center on agility and adaptation, are becoming clearer. Eisenhardt and Martin recommend minimal structures and a few "simple rules" to stay on top of high-velocity environments. Simple routines keep managers focused on broadly important issues "without locking them into specific behaviors or using past experience that may be inappropriate given the actions required in a particular situation."[10] The basic advice in this view is that whenever "business becomes complicated, strategy should be simple."[11]

LEADERSHIP CHALLENGES

None of the various strategy or decision models referenced above, nor those discussed in this book's fifteen chapters, can fully capture the art and science of leadership in times of major change. Each model highlights relevant factors but their relative importance will much depend on the nature of the problems as well as the culture, history and objectives of the firm. Clearly, leaders play a crucial role in (i) framing current problems, (ii) assessing new opportunities, (iii) stress testing business models against future scenarios, (iv) architecting dynamic capabilities, and (v) implementing them at multiple levels in an organization. Doing this well requires balancing near-term goals with assuring long-term viability in the face of often deep uncertainty. Envisioning a new growth path and changing the organization's structure, internal processes, reward systems and culture cannot as of yet be relegated to AI or simply outsourced. It calls for full engagement of the senior leadership such that operational teams can function harmoniously, with sufficient diversity in viewpoints as needed. To illustrate, let's examine one problem in closing that many leadership teams still struggle with, namely how to get the most out of technical specialists.

Nearly all companies have staff people who provide functional expertise in such areas as accounting, legal matters, technology, finance, human resources, quality control, regulatory compliance, public relations and more. They face a dilemma, however, when asking these specialists to weigh in on broader managerial decisions since many may not be able to transcend their limited domain of expertise. Also, staff people often cannot put themselves easily in the role of a general manager or leader. So how can leaders turn one-trick ponies into show horses who can make bigger contributions to the business overall? A pressing problem today is how IT specialists should advise business leaders about the risks and benefits of GenAI in their own business. Few organizations were ready mid-2024, when I wrote this, to embrace AI fully due to its complex, expansive, and uncertain nature.[2] Since this is still unplowed terrain, consider how specialists in more traditional domains can become better team players.

How should a finance specialist, for example, give advice on tax accounting, financing, debt restructuring, and acquisitions in a large company? Suppose this person was just promoted to become the "finance point person" in a small management team of a growing new business line and is tasked with adding value to this unit and the company overall. How ready are such specialists to contribute beyond their traditional lanes and if not ready yet, how might leaders help them grow? Exploring these questions might surface a mix of issues to help diagnose the crux of challenges facing this specialist and the team being supported. Do the problems mostly concern the specialist's self-view and capabilities or is the deeper problem the dynamics of the management team itself? And if the latter, could these deeper team issues be related the organization's strategy, structure, procedures, internal expectations, compensation or the internal culture itself? Unless there is alignment among these different components, the situation will not improve easily on its own.

Comparing the answers to the above questions across multiple specialists may provide further insights about fashioning solutions that better align the roles, tasks, constraints, self-images, skill sets, and incentives at play. The most challenging part in many cases may be to find role models that already experienced the desired behaviors of specialists, either in this company or elsewhere. Since most successful executives in that firm probably served in specialist roles earlier in their own careers, and apparently did well enough to get promoted, why not use them as exemplars for others in the company. One caveat, however, is that what worked well in the past for these successful older leaders may no longer be the most effective way today since leadership models have evolved considerably over past decades.

In conclusion, the above example is just one of the many challenges leaders will encounter, especially when markets quake. In times of turmoil, collective curiosity becomes an important organizational attribute in order to fully benefit from many eyes and ears. To see external changes sooner, senior leaders need to foster a culture that is willing to challenge deeply held assumptions collectively. This means mastering the art of reframing problems from multiple angles, adopting a wide-angle view when facing multifaceted problems, learning how to approach problems from the outside in, and respecting that some decision uncertainties will remain unresolved for a long time. For those operating at senior management levels, while also serving perhaps as mentors for younger people, exemplifying how to see problems and opportunities in their full scope is especially important.

Just as a kaleidoscope highlights different aspects of an object, through light refraction, the key is to change the angle of view and see more facets, colors, or detail. In executive teams, where different leaders contribute their functional perspectives by design, a common challenge is to get everyone to see problems holistically as well; each team member should appreciate the total picture rather than just those aspects relevant to their own agenda. This requires managers to step away from their appointed roles, dominant frames of mind and primary constituents, in favor of an enterprise view that will surface solutions many stakeholders can support. Most executive teams still struggle with this kind of enlightened approach to strategic thinking and decision making, since it requires overcoming functional frames[3] and personal career goals. My hope is that readers will judiciously draw on the many aspects covered in the 75 varied selections of this book, in order to arrive at customized solutions that will fit their own situation well, for the short and long run.

END NOTES

1 Schoemaker, Paul J. H., and J. Edward Russo, "Managing frames to make better decisions," Chapter 8 in Stephen Hoch and Howard Kunreuther (eds), *Wharton on Making Decisions*, Wiley, April 2001, pages 138 and 143. Figures 2 and 3 came from this source.

2 Kuhn, Thomas S. *The Structure of Scientific Revolutions.* Vol. 962. Chicago: University of Chicago Press, 1997.

3 Swaim, Robert W. *The strategic Drucker: growth strategies and marketing insights from the works of Peter Drucker.* John Wiley & Sons, 2011.

4 Schoemaker, Paul J. H. *Brilliant Mistakes: Finding Success on the Far Side of Failure.* Wharton Digital Press, Fall 2011, 178 pp, Philadelpia PA.

5 March, James G. "Exploration and exploitation in organizational learning." *Organization Science* 2.1 (1991): 71–87.

6 Ackoff, Russell Lincoln. *Re-creating the Corporation: A Design of Organizations for the 21st Century.* Oxford University Press, 1999.

7 Teece, David J., Gary Pisano, and Amy Shuen, "Dynamic capabilities and strategic management." *Strategic Management Journal*, 18.7 (1997): 509–533; see also Teece, David J., Explicating dynamic capabilities: The nature and micro-foundations of (sustainable) enterprise performance. *Strategic Management Journal* 28.13 (2007): 1319–1350.

8 Teece, David J. "The foundations of enterprise performance: Dynamic and ordinary capabilities in an (economic) theory of firms." *Academy of management perspectives* 28.4 (2014): 328–352.

9 Day, George S., and Paul J. H. Schoemaker, "Adapting to Fast-changing Markets and Technologies." *California Management Review* 58.4 (2016): 59–77.

10 Eisenhardt, Kathleen M., and Jeffrey A. Martin. "Dynamic capabilities: what are they?." *Strategic Management Journal* 21.10–11 (2000): 1105–1121.

11 Eisenhardt, Kathleen M., and Donald N. Sull. *Strategy as simple rules.* Vol. 6. No. 4. Harvard Business Review 2001, pp 106–119, p. 116

12 Wilson, H. James, and Paul R. Daugherty, "Embracing gen AI at work." *Harvard Business Review*, September–October 2024, Vol 102, No 5pp. 151–155.

13 Reibstein, David J., George Day, and Jerry Wind. "Guest editorial: Is marketing academia losing its way?." *Journal of Marketing* 73.4 (2009): 1–3.

APPENDICES

APPENDIX A: DETAILED CHAPTER CONTENTS

Chapter 4 Managing Talent

4.1 Six Ways to Attract and Keep Top Talent (*with Thomas Johnston*)

4.2 To Hire Well, Throw Away the Job Description

4.3 Are You Sabotaging Your Own Hiring Process? (*with J. Edward Russo*)

4.4 Conducting a Good Performance Review (*with Josh Klayman*)

4.5 How Seasoned Leaders Redirect Attention

Chapter 5 Navigating Uncertainty

5.1 Seven Ways to Apply Scenario Planning (*with Arjen van den Berg*)

5.2 Why Deep Down We Don't Like Uncertainty

5.3 Know What Your Customers Want First (*with Steve Krupp*)

5.4 Think Your Thinking Sound? Take This Test

5.5 What You Don't Know Could Kill Your Company

PART II: INNOVATION, FAILURE, AND LEARNING

Chapter 6 Improving Innovation

6.1 Why Failure Is the Foundation of Innovation

6.2 How to Unleash Creativity—Poll the Crowd (*with George Day*)

6.3 Staying Ahead of Customers (*with Steve Krupp and Vivek Kumar*)

6.4 Want to Ace Your Startup? Master the Five Ms (*with Charles Robins*)

6.5 Vigilance: A Strategic Weapon for Entrepreneurs

Chapter 7 Managing Customers

7.1 The Ecstasy and Agony of Customer Service

7.2 Handling Customers You Rather Not Have (*with Nicole Adam Kraus*)

7.3 Bad Customer Service Happens, But Don't Accept It

7.4 Putting Risk Management on the Menu (*with Joyce Schoemaker*)

7.5 You Can't be Customer-Centric from a Distance

Chapter 8 Thriving on Failures

8.1 You Need to Make More Mistakes

8.2 How to Make a Brilliant Mistake

8.3 Managing Your Emotions After Failure

8.4 How to Make Hay When Things Go Hay-Wire

8.5 Make No Mistake: You Should Fail on Purpose

Chapter 9 Power of Metaphors

9.1 How Analogies Influence Your Thinking
9.2 A Hedge or Bet? A Matter of Perspective
9.3 Is Poker a Good Mindset for Business? (*with J. Edward Russo*)
9.4 Why You Need to Play War Games (*with Toomas Truumees*)
9.5 Ways in which Poker and Business Savvy Align

Chapter 10 Varied Lessons

10.1 Two Billion Dollars in Tobacco Up in Smoke (*with Karin Stawarky*)
10.2 Choosing the Right Political Candidate in Elections
10.3 How to Do SWOT Analysis the Right Way
10.4 Decisions That Made Nelson Mandela Great (*with Brian Isaacson*)
10.5 How Culturally Aware and Sensitive are You? (*with Sandra Martinez*)

PART III: LEADERSHIP, DECIDING, AND BIASES

Chapter 11 Strategic Leadership

11.1 Six Habits of Truly Strategic Thinkers
11.2 Four Secrets of Critical Thinkers (*with John Austin*)
11.3 Strategic Leaders Always Think Twice (*with Jacqueline Claudia*)
11.4 Three Decisions that Set Nelson Mandela Apart
11.5 Leadership Lessons from Dr Martin Luther King (*with Steve Krupp*)

Chapter 12 Board Governance

12.1 Governance—the Critical Factor Many Get Wrong (*with Rob Arnold*)
12.2 Defusing Ethical Time-Bombs in Your Company (*with Tom Donaldson*)
12.3 Making the Most of Your Management Board (*with Rob Adams*)
12.4 Do You Know the Animals in the Executive Zoo?
12.5 Boards that Truly Lead (*with George Day*)

Chapter 13 Team Performance

13.1 Rallying Your Team Around a New Strategy (*with Steve Krupp*)
13.2 How to Create a Positive Learning Culture (*with Franck Schuurmans*)
13.3 Ways to Become a Credible Leader and Team (*with Hanke Lange*)
13.4 Does Your Team Match Your Strategy (*with Steve Krupp*)
13.5 Improving Your Team's Internal Communications

Chapter 14 Decision Making

14.1 Make Better Decisions: Three Easy Steps (*with Samantha Howland*)
14.2 Why Thinking from the Outside-In is Key (*with Nadine Pearce*)
14.3 Six Ways to Solve Problems Outside-In
14.4 Do You Know What You Don't Know
14.5 Taking Conflict out of Conflicting Advice (*with Philip Tetlock*)

Chapter 15 Reducing Bias

15.1 How Nudges Can Keep You Centered (*with Viraj Narayanan*)
15.2 Don't Let New Information Distort Your Judgment (*with J. Edward Russo*)
15.3 Nobel Prize Research About Common Biases
15.4 Separating Facts from Values in Disputes (*with Philip Tetlock*)
15.5 When the Wisdom of the Crowd Misfired (*with Jim Austin*)

APPENDIX B: WHERE COAUTHORS CONTRIBUTED

Last Name	First	Chapter Sections	Position at the Time
Adam Kraus	Nicole	7.2	Principal, Decision Strategies International (DSI)
Adams	Rob	12.3	Managing Partner, Next Stage Capital Mgt
Arnold	Rob	12.1	Chairman of SLC, Singapore
Austin	Jim	15.5	President, JH Austin Associates Inc
Austin	John	11.2	Consulting partner, DSI
Claudia	Jacqueline	11.3	Partner, DSI
Day	George	3.2; 3.5; 6.2; 12.5	Professor of Marketing, The Wharton School
Donaldson	Tom	12.2	Professor of Ethics, Wharton
Howland	Samantha	14.1	Principal, DSI
Isaacson	Brian	10.4	Organizational Consultant, South Africa
Johnston	Thomas	4.1	CEO of SearchPath, an executive search firm

Last Name	First	Chapter Sections	Position at the Time
Klayman	Josh	4.4	Professor, University of Chicago
Krupp	Steve	5.3; 6.3; 11.5; 13.1; 13.4	CEO, Decision Strategies International
Kumar	Vivek	6.3	Senior consultant, Decision Strategies
Lange	Hanke	13.3	Organizational consultant, Netherlands
Martinez	Sandra	10.5	President, Fenix Leadership & Development
Narayanan	Viraj	9.5, 15.1	Principal, Decision Strategies International
Nuyts	Wijnand	1.4	Senior executive, Dutch Central Bank
Pearce	Nadine	14.2	Global Head of OD, Oncology, Novartis
Rao	Govi	3.4	CEO, Phase Change Solutions, NC
Robins	Charles	6.4	Managing Director, Fairmount Partners, PA
Russo	Edward	4.3; 9.3; 15.2	Professor of Management, Cornel University
Sandberg	Kirsten	3.5	Editor, writer and consultant, New York City
Schoemaker	Joyce	7.4	Microbiologist, author
Schuurmans	Franck	13.2	Senior Consultant, DSI
Stawarky	Karin	10.1	Senior Partner, Decision Strategies International
Tetlock	Phil	14.5; 15.4	Professor of Psychology, Univ of Pennsylvania
Truumees	Toomas	9.4	Senior Partner, DSI, USA
v/d Berg	Arjen	5.1	Managing Partner, DSI London

Note: The numbers listed refer to chapter sections; for example, 5.3 means Chapter 5, Section 3

APPENDIX C: CREDITS FOR CARTOON DESIGNERS

The *Harvard Business Review*, where I published five articles myself, kindly gave me permission to reproduce the different cartoons shown at the beginning of each of the fifteen chapters. This appendix acknowledges the creative artists involved and when their cartoon appeared in HBR.

Chapter 1: John Klossner, HBR Issue July–August 2015
Chapter 2: Elisabeth Westley & Steven Mach, HBR Issue December 2015
Chapter 3: Tom Toro, HBR Issue November 2016
Chapter 4: Randy Glasberger, HBR Issue May 2012
Chapter 5: Patrick Hardin, HBR Issue October 2014
Chapter 6: Teresa Burns Parkhurst, HBR Issue January–February 2016
Chapter 7: Crowden Satz, HBR Issue June 2015
Chapter 8: Teresa Burns Parkhurst, HBR Issue December 2010
Chapter 9: Paul Kales, HBR Issue May 2013
Chapter 10: Rod Rossi, HBR Issue May 2011
Chapter 11: Paula Pratt, HBR Issue March 2015
Chapter 12: Tom Toro, HBR Issue May 2016
Chapter 13: Bill Abbott, HBR Issue October 2014
Chapter 14: Bill Abbott, HBR Issue November 2014
Chapter 15: Paul Gilligan, HBR Issue December 2013

APPENDIX D: SCHOEMAKER'S ORIGINAL INC COLUMNS

Inc.com gave me permission to repurpose some of my own columns for this book. I list below the original Inc.com titles I drew upon for each section. As columnist, I did not repeat my own name each time below but do list all co-authors who joined me.

Book Section	Titles, Dates & Co-authors of Inc columns Used in Part
1.1	"Set Your Company's Business Strategy from the Outside In" *Inc.com*, Mar. 27, 2014.
1.2	"9 Ways to See Change Coming (Before it Kills Your Business)", *Inc.com*, Mar. 30, 2012
1.3	"How to Know If a New Strategy Will Work" *Inc.com*, Dec. 28, 2012

Book Section	Titles, Dates & Co-authors of Inc columns Used in Part
1.4	"How to Create Doubt & Manage It" *Inc.com*, July 27, 2016, with Wijnand Nuijts
1.5	"When Thinking Big Isn't Big Enough" *Inc.com*, Oct. 30, 2018
2.1	"How to Prepare for the Unexpected" *Inc.com*, Jul. 17, 2012
2.2	"Beware the Limits of SWOT Analysis" *Inc.com*, Sep. 8, 2014
2.3	"Can You Handle VUCA?" *Inc.com*, Sept. 27, 2018
2.4	"How to Predict the Future," *Inc.com*, Jul. 31, 2019
2.5	"You Can't Predict the Future, But You Can Get a Preview," *Inc.com*, Sept. 30, 2019
3.1	"Four Ways the Business World is Going to Change in 2020" *Inc.com*, April 1, 2015
3.2	"You Need to Get Better at Looking Ahead" *Inc.com*, May 18, 2018, with George Day
3.3	"Standing Still is For Losers: Six Ways to Stay Ahead of the Pack" *Inc.com*, Jun. 26, 2018
3.4	"Find the Future – Before It Finds You," *Inc.com*, Mar. 20, 2020, with Govi Rao
3.5	"Avoiding Surprises in 2015, *Inc.com*, Jan. 1, 2015, with George Day and Kirsten Sandberg
4.1	"6 Ways to Attract Top Talent" *Inc.com*, Mar. 26, 2013, with Thomas Johnston
4.2	"To Hire Well, Throw Away the Job Description", *Inc.com*, Feb. 10, 2012
4.3	"Are You Sabotaging Your Hiring Process" *Inc.com*, Jul. 22, 2014, with J. Edward Russo
4.4	"Constructive Performance Reviews" *Inc.com*, Aug 20, 2015, with Joshua Klayman
4.5	"Four Ways Smart Leaders Manage Their Employees' Focus, *Inc.com*, Apr. 11, 2018

Book Section	Titles, Dates & Co-authors of Inc columns Used in Part
5.1	"7 Ways to Apply Scenario Planning" *Inc.com*, Jul. 30, 2012, with Arjen van den Berg
5.2	"Rethinking Covid with Overcoming Biases," *Inc.com*, Aug. 26, 2021
5.3	"Knowing What Customers Want Before", *Inc.com*, Apr. 25, 2013, with Steve Krupp
5.4	"Think Your Thinking Is Sound? Take This Test to Find Out, *Inc.com*, Feb. 22, 2022
5.5	"What You Don't Know Could Kill Your Company, *Inc.com*, Jun. 13, 2022
6.1	"Why Failure Is the Foundation of Innovation" *Inc.com*, Aug. 13, 2012
6.2	"How to Unleash Creativity? Poll the Crowd" *Inc.com*, May 21, 2014, with George Day
6.3	"Staying Ahead of Customers", *Inc.com*, Aug. 25, 2014, with Steve Krupp & Vivek Kumar
6.4	"How to Ace Your New Startup?" *Inc.com*, Jul. 25, 2017 with Charles Robins
6.5	"Vigilance: The Next Strategic Weapon for Entrepreneurs" *Inc.com*, Nov. 27, 2019
7.1	"The Ecstasy with Agony of Customer Service" *Inc.com*, Jan. 27, 2014
7.2	"Dealing with Difficult Customers" *Inc.com*, Jan. 31, 2014 with Nicole Adams Kraus
7.3	"Bad Customer Service Happens, But You Don't Have to Accept It" *Inc.com*, Feb. 5, 2014
7.4	"Put Risk Management on the Menu" *Inc.com*, Aug. 12, 2020, with Joyce A. Schoemaker
7.5	"You Can't Be Customer-Centric from a Distance," *Inc.com*, May 31, 2021
8.1	"You Need to Make More Mistakes", *Inc.com*, Jan. 5, 2012
8.2	"How to Make a Brilliant Mistake", *Inc.com*, Jan. 23, 2012
8.3	"How to Control Your Emotions After You Fail" *Inc.com*, Aug. 14, 2012

Book Section	Titles, Dates & Co-authors of Inc columns Used in Part
8.4	"Learning by Error: How to Make Hay When Things Go Hay-Wire" *Inc.com*, Sep. 30 2013
8.5	"Make No Mistake – You Should Fail on Purpose," *Inc.com*, Mar. 27, 2018
9.1	"How Metaphors & Analogies Influence Your Thinking", *Inc.com*, Nov. 21, 2012
9.2	"A Hedge or Bet? A Matter of Perspective", *Inc.com*, May 14, 2012
9.3	"Is Poker a Good Metaphor for Business", *Inc.com*, Nov. 29, 2012, with J. Edward Russo
9.4	"Why You Need to Play War Games", *Inc.com*, Feb. 28, 2013, with Toomas Truumees
9.5	"What Poker Can Teach You About Business" *Inc.com*, Nov. 11, 2013, with Viraj Narayanan
10.1	"Was CVS crazy to Forgo $2 Billion" *Inc.com*, Feb. 6, 2014, with Karin Stawarky
10.2	"Election 2012: Undecided? Here's How to Choose", *Inc.com*, Oct. 28, 2012
10.3	The Right Way to do SWOT Analysis, *Inc.com*, Jan 28, 2015
10.4	"Nelson Mandela, Transformational Leader" *Inc.com*, Dec. 5, 2013. with Brian Isaacson
10.5	"How Culturally Aware Are You? *Inc.com*, Aug., 30, 2018, with Sandra Martinez
11.1	"6 Habits of True Strategic Thinkers", *Inc.com*, Mar. 20, 2012
11.2	"4 Secrets of Great Critical Thinkers", *Inc.com*, Apr. 16, 2012, with John Austin
11.3	"Great Strategic Leaders Think Twice", *Inc.com*, May 1, 2012 with Jacqueline Claudia
11.4	"The 3 Decisions That Made Mandela a Truly Great Leader" *Inc.com*, Jul. 28, 2013
11.5	"Leadership Lessons from Martin Luther King, Jr., *Inc.com*, Feb. 27, 2015, with Steven Krupp

Book Section	Titles, Dates & Co-authors of Inc columns Used in Part
12.1	"Governance: Most Owners Get Wrong", *Inc.com*, May 28, 2013. with Rob Arnold
12.2	"How to Defuse an Ethical Time-Bomb" *Inc.com*, Jun. 10, 2013. with Tom Donaldson
12.3	"Making the Most of Your Board" *Inc.com*, Aug. 28, 2013, with Rob Adams
12.4	"Do You Know All the Animals in the Executive Zoo? *Inc.com*, Feb. 23, 2018
12.5	"Are You Ready for the Next Big Shock," *Inc.com*, Jun. 26, 2020, with George S. Day
13.1	"How to Rally Your Team Around a New Strategy" *Inc.com*, Jun. 12, 2012, with Steve Krupp
13.2	"How to Create Learning Culture" *Inc.com*, Jun. 26, 2012 with Franck Schuurmans
13.3	"6 Ways to Become a Credible Leader with Team" *Inc.com*, Oct. 16, 2012, with Hanke Lange
13.4	"Does Your Team Match Your Strategy", *Inc.com*, Dec. 17, 2012, with Steve Krupp
13.5	"Seven Ways to Improve Your Team's Communication" *Inc.com*, Mar. 24, 2015
14.1	"Make Better Decisions: 3 Easy Steps", *Inc.com*, May 16, 2012 with Samantha Howland
14.2	"Why Thinking Outside-In is Key, *Inc.com*, Dec. 19, 2017 with Nadine Pearce
14.3	"Six Ways to Think Outside-In", *Inc.com*, Jan. 9, 2018
14.4	"It Pays to Know What You Don't Know," *Inc.com*, July 25 2018
14.5	"Taking Conflict out of Conflicting Advice," *Inc.com*, Nov. 29, 2018, with Philip Tetlock
15.1	"How a Simple Nudge Can Create Big Change" *Inc.com*, Sep. 10, 2012 with Viraj Narayanan
15.2	"How Information Distorts Your Decisions," *Inc.com*, June 22, 2017, with J. Edward Russo

Book Section	Titles, Dates & Co-authors of Inc columns Used in Part
15.3	"Key Insights from Nobel Prize Winner Richard Thaler, *Inc.com*, Oct. 12, 2017
15.4	"The Facts Are the Matter," *Inc.com*, Dec. 27, 2018, with Philip Tetlock
15.5	"The Art of Real: How to Get to The Truth," *Inc.com*, Feb. 28, 2019, with Jim Austin

APPENDIX E: BRIEF AUTHOR BIOGRAPHY

Paul J. H. Schoemaker was born and raised in the Netherlands until he was 21 and then transferred to the U.S as a student where he completed a B.S. in physics, followed by an MBA in finance and Ph.D. in decision sciences from the Wharton School. He started his academic career in the Graduate School of Business at University of Chicago School where he taught decision making and strategy for 12 years. During that period, he took a sabbatical with the planning group of Royal Dutch/Shell in London which became a leader in scenario thinking. Thereafter, he returned to Wharton where he taught strategy and decision making, while also serving for more than a decade as Research Director of Wharton's Mack Institute for Innovation Management. He published over 126 academic and applied papers which have appeared in journals ranging from *Management Science* and *the Journal of Mathematical Psychology* to the *Journal of Economic Literature* and the *Harvard Business Review*. His diverse articles received multiple awards including the prestigious Best Paper Prize of the Strategic Management Society in 2000. He also published 13 books, some coauthored, which in total were translated into 17 languages. His research, writing, and lectures address strategic planning, decision making, and the management of emerging technologies as well as innovation and strategic leadership.

Apart from his highly cited academic work, he also acquired much practical experience as a consultant, entrepreneur, private investor, and senior executive. He founded Decision Strategies International in 1990 as a consultancy offering strategic management, training, and executive development. This company has served hundreds of clients around the world in multiple industries and was sold in 2016 to Heidrick & Struggles. He also cofounded Strategic Radar in 2003 to develop software to scan weak signals and designed platforms for clients interested in tracking and interpreting external changes using multiple scenario lenses. In addition, he served as Chairman of the Board for two family companies both of which he helped prepare for sale. One was Public Salt, a wholesale distribution company in Canton, Ohio selling safety salt, water softeners and related products and equipment. The other was Vaessen-Schoemaker in the Netherlands, a food additives company with sales in Europe and beyond which was sold via a management buyout. He has also been a private investor in many technology ventures and served on the board of several of these. Finally, he has been active in philanthropy, starting with the Decision Education Foundation which he supported financially as well as a board member. Today, he mostly works through his own family foundation. Further information can be found at www.paulschoemaker.com.

INDEX

www.ingramcontent.com/pod-product-compliance
Lightning Source LLC
Chambersburg PA
CBHW031807190326
41518CB00006B/236